"Simply put, as manifested in this book by intelligent design, we can harness the extraordinary powers of business as a source of good, and make sure we are incentivised to keep on the trajectory of creating a regenerative society for all to thrive in, and to ultimately ensure a liveable and sustainable future for businesses, as well as the planet and humankind. I say let's choose light over darkness, wisdom over foolishness, and leave the winter of despair behind to enter the spring of hope. This book is a good place to start."

Jim Hagemann Snabe, *Chairman of Siemens, Boardmember of World Economic Forum and Adjunct Professor at Copenhagen Business School, Denmark*

"This thought-provoking book showcases how design can build a regenerative society, with practical examples from Danish design, questions on systems thinking and applications of circular economy principles. The author skilfully demonstrates the transformative power of design for a better future."

Catherine De Wolf, *Professor, Circular Engineering for Architecture, ETH Zurich, Switzerland*

DANISH DESIGN HERITAGE AND GLOBAL SUSTAINABILITY

With a bias for action, this book offers valuable insights into the origins of the much-celebrated Danish design tradition and how it can be employed to create design solutions to address today's environmental crisis using the planetary boundaries as positive creative constraints.

Danish design has long been revered for its high-quality aesthetics, materials and craftmanship, encouraging sustainability without compromise. This book explores the lessons to be learnt from Scandinavian design ideals, introduces the philosophy and principles of circular economy and showcases the potential power of combining circular economy and design in helping to mitigate the effects of climate change. It presents a range of case study examples across multiple sectors and includes interviews with Danish designers from architecture, furniture, fashion, digital and industrial design, providing unique insights by some of the world's leading contemporary designers.

Bridging theory and real-world insights and experiences, this book builds on the framework of the 4Rs – The Circular Way: Reduce, Reuse, Recycle and Replace to encourage innovation through the replacement of environmentally damaging materials and business models. A must-read for product designers, industrial designers, consultants, business developers, sustainability professionals and students interested in learning how to design and implement circular, sustainable models into practice.

Ditte Lysgaard Vind is a renowned circular economy and design expert and practitioner, based in Denmark. Ditte is known for pioneering new materials as well as business models while sharing the knowledge gained from practice through teaching and thought leadership. She is the founder of The Circular Way, the Chairwoman of the Danish Design Council and a member of the executive board of the Royal Danish Academy of Fine Arts Schools of Architecture, Design and Conservation as well as the global SDG innovation lab UNLEASH. Ditte previously co-founded Lendager The Circular Way, a subsidiary of the Lendager Group. She is also the co-author of *A Changemakers Guide to the Future* (2018).

DANISH DESIGN HERITAGE AND GLOBAL SUSTAINABILITY

Ditte Lysgaard Vind

Routledge
Taylor & Francis Group
LONDON AND NEW YORK

Designed cover image: Cover design by All the Way to Paris

First published 2024
by Routledge
4 Park Square, Milton Park, Abingdon, Oxon OX14 4RN

and by Routledge
605 Third Avenue, New York, NY 10158

Routledge is an imprint of the Taylor & Francis Group, an informa business

British Library Cataloguing-in-Publication Data
A catalogue record for this book is available from the British Library

Library of Congress Cataloging-in-Publication Data
Names: Vind, Ditte Lysgaard, author.
Title: Danish design heritage and global sustainability / Ditte Lysgaard Vind.
Description: Abingdon, Oxon: Routledge, 2024. |
Includes bibliographical references and index.
Identifiers: LCCN 2022034072 (print) | LCCN 2022034073 (ebook) |
ISBN 9781032198217 (hardback) | ISBN 9781032198200 (paperback) |
ISBN 9781003261018 (ebook)
Subjects: LCSH: Design—Denmark. | Sustainable design. | Circular economy.
Classification: LCC NK1458.A1 V56 2024 (print) |
LCC NK1458.A1 (ebook) | DDC 744.09489—dc23/eng/20221024
LC record available at https://lccn.loc.gov/2022034072
LC ebook record available at https://lccn.loc.gov/2022034073

ISBN: 978-1-032-19821-7 (hbk)
ISBN: 978-1-032-19820-0 (pbk)
ISBN: 978-1-003-26101-8 (ebk)

DOI: 10.4324/9781003261018

Typeset in Optima
by codeMantra

CONTENTS

FIGURES

CASES

Design in the Anthropocene has the capability to move us from Despair toward Repair and ultimately toward Re-imagine. That is shaping the unknown future by creating value for people while staying within our planetary boundaries.

Ditte Lysgaard Vind

FOREWORD

> It was the best of times,
> it was the worst of times,
> it was the age of wisdom,
> it was the age of foolishness,
> it was the epoch of belief,
> it was the epoch of incredulity,
> it was the season of Light,
> it was the season of Darkness,
> it was the spring of hope,
> it was the winter of despair
> we had everything before us, we had nothing before us...
>
> *Dickens (1859)*

Written by Charles Dickens in 1859, yet to me still so very relevant to the crossroads we are at today. While innovation, science and technology has brought great prosperity, it has done so with great consequences for our planet and our ability to thrive as a global community. With our entrance into the Anthropocene epoch, it is painfully obvious that we have the power to destroy – even if unintended. But with power comes opportunity so it is high time we seize that opportunity and use business as a source for good, benefitting both people and the planet because, as both the ancient Greeks and Spider-man says: With great power comes great responsibility.

We are indeed at a crossroad of both darkness and light and of hope and despair. The good news is that according to the United Nations Intergovernmental Panel on Climate Change (IPCC) 2022 status report, there are feasible and effective solutions that can reduce risks to people and nature. But they must be delivered now, as with every and any rise in temperature the opportunity space decreases. Therefore, NOW more than ever we must move from dialogue and protest to action and collaboration.

In order to get there, we must dare to dream of a better world in which people, planet and business thrive in synergy and work relentlessly to master the details and ACT. Here, design plays an important part. While the concept of design is easily seen as being about aesthetics, it is as much about functionality. About designing new types of processes, products and business models and more than anything about designing new ways of being. Design can help us do that. It helps us see a way forward both through design's ability to look beyond existing norms and systems and truly reimagine a better world. It is also because of the inherent tactility of design and its continuous prototyping enabling trial, error and ultimately improvement. Most importantly, as you will read throughout this book, design enables us to create a better future where our individual needs and societal desires are aligned with the planet. As highlighted through the Danish Design Heritage as well as current Danish design cases, sustainability does not have to be a compromise on aesthetics, convenience or price. Instead, it can be a positive creative constraint that heightens the level of ambition and ultimately ensures better solutions that are good for people, good for profit and good for the planet. Simply put, by design we can harness the extraordinary powers of business as a source of good and make sure we are incentivised to keep on the trajectory of creating a regenerative society for all to thrive in and ultimately ensure a liveable and sustainable future for your business, our planet and humankind.

So going back to Dickens' poetic description of the times we are once again in, I say let's choose light over darkness, wisdom over foolishness and leave the winter of despair behind to enter the spring of hope. This book is a good place to start.

Jim Hagemann Snabe, *Chairman of Siemens,*
Boardmember of World Economic Forum and
Adjunct Professor at Copenhagen Business School, Denmark

Reference

Dickens, C. (1859). *A Tale of Two Cities*. https://www.britannica.com/topic/A-Tale-of-Two-Cities-novel

ACKNOWLEDGEMENTS

Writing this book has been a great and meaningful experience largely due to the wonderful people who have agreed to be interviewed, to create cases and not least my friends, family and collaborators who have listened to and guided the project along the way. Thank you so very much! A very big thanks to Anders and team Lendager for always providing optimism and tangible action towards a better future – I could not ask to be surrounded by better people – a special thanks to Dani, Tim and Johan for the great work interviewing our collaborators featured in Chapter 13: Building The Circular Way. As this book is about design, the visual design of this book is of course important, and luckily, I have once again had the good fortune to work with Mahmud and Tanja from All The Way To Paris, who has created the cover art and guided the illustrative work. The biggest thanks, however, is to Kathrine Hagemann Snabe, who has been instrumental in creating illustrations as well as project managing the book and ensuring everything was in order. Last but not least, of course, thanks to Routledge and the Taylor & Francis Group and in particular, Matthew Shobbrook and Grace Harrison, for their support and willingness to bring this book to life.

A reading guide

The book is written to be read in full, but the chapters can also be read individually and used for a more specific purpose. A brief reading guide of what you can expect in the individual chapters is presented here. Each chapter concludes with a question to encourage reflection and applicability in the readers context.

Chapter 1: Design in the Anthropocene

This chapter sets the scene for the role of design as a solution maker in our global efforts to challenge the status quo and shape a regenerative society. Acknowledging that our actions have the power to do good as well as cause harm, I invite you to dare to visualise a better future that transcends what we leave behind. While we are aware of the problems, it is through design we will find the solutions. Design helps us cultivate the power of imagination and ACT for a world that is not yet ours. To achieve it, this chapter highlights design's ability to work intentionally within barriers and leverage the planetary boundaries as a positive creative force. It elevates our ambition and drives us to move from theoretical potentials to tangible actions that challenge the prevailing norms. To illustrate this, we examine the case of TAKT, a Danish furniture brand.

Chapter 2: Learning from Danish design

A brief history of the Danish design heritage with a particular focus on furniture design is presented in this chapter, giving insights into the founding of successful Danish architecture, industrial design and business models at large. This chapter zooms in on the essence of the book's raison d'ëtre, inspired by Kaare Klint's vision to see the power to shape the future by merging tradition, understood as the accumulated experience, with the opportunities of the present. An important lesson from the masters of Danish Design is the ability to embed a social purpose in their designs, thus elevating both functionality and form, thereby creating an inner cohesion between content and expression. By investing time in caring about materials, craftsmanship and aesthetics, the success of the design is valued based on its use rather than their monetary value. Many of these designs from that time have not become waste; on the contrary, they are still in use and highly valued today. This chapter includes a conversation with Danish architect Dan Stubbergaard, the founder of Cobe, and highlights a case example from Mater, a renowned Danish materials and furniture company.

Chapter 3: Systems design in the Anthropocene

Whether we examine human behaviour, new technologies or products, they are all part of a larger context, operating as part of one or more systems. This chapter is a deep dive on systems design and incorporates the insights of German sociologist Niklas Luhmann to understand the functions and logics of our systems. It also questions the ultimate logic: our scientific paradigm. Thus, emphasising the need for a fundamental shift towards understanding that our actions have consequences for the planet, which in return affect our abilities to thrive on the planet. Instead, a new logic is proposed, guided by the simple question of whether our actions are creating improvement for people while staying within our planetary boundaries? By doing so, we pave the way to reclaiming power.

Chapter 4: The troubles we are in

The chapter discusses the current state of the world and our imperative to act. It highlights the urgency to act fast based on the available climate data, emphasising that the window of opportunity is narrow. Key concepts such as absolute sustainability, the planetary boundaries, and the need for a roadmap towards a safe operating space, are introduced. This chapter concludes with a thought-provoking conversation with Danish architect Anders Lendager, who provides invaluable insights into the topic.

Chapter 5: Partnering with life: the essence of regeneration

In this chapter, regenerative leadership and design specialist Laura Storm shares her wisdom in the essay 'Partnering with life: the essence of regeneration'. She provides insights into what regeneration is all about, its importance and the key considerations we need to be mindful of to achieve it.

Chapter 6: Theory meets practice and magic happens

In this chapter I share some of the practical learnings on overcoming technical and commercial barriers and include a case on transforming Carlsberg's composite waste stream into valuable materials, such as chairs designed by Danish icon Nanna Ditzel. Drawing from my personal experience, this chapter reflects on the tangible steps taken to achieve this, acknowledging both the good and the bad as an entrepreneur moving from digital to physical realms. It emphasises the importance of progress over perfection and the need for collaboration among changemakers to create value for people while staying within the planetary boundaries and allowing the possibility of failure.

Chapter 7: Manifesto: design in the Anthropocene

Drawing insights from the Danish Design Heritage, as well as the contemporary discussions and case studies presented in this book, this chapter highlights ten important principles serving as an inspirational checklist for design in the Anthropocene, with the goal of creating value for people while staying within our planetary boundaries. The manifesto emphasises the role of a designer to be a world maker rather than a world breaker. It serves as a guide for designers to use and also a source for learning and inspiration for society and business to promote progress and improvement across various professions.

Chapter 8: The purpose of business is to solve problems

Business is an important driving force for change to achieve the necessary scale. This chapter focusses on the different types of businesses and implements the principles of the Danish tradition of business to address societal problems at the core of business. It thus questions our current short-term thinking and narrow understanding of value creation and growth. Instead, it proposes that we reclaim growth as a tool to deliver long-term prosperity for our global population. Based on practical experience, I present my methodology, Enlightened Action, which encourages greater ambition, embraces the potential for mistakes and most importantly ensures action. We illustrate this approach with the case example of Vestas, the Danish windmill giant.

Chapter 9: The Circular Way

This chapter gives an in-depth introduction to both the philosophy and principles of circular economy. Based on the planetary boundary framework, this chapter shows a new way: The Circular Way. This approach provides a map to a safe operating space for humanity and unlocking the opportunity brought by designing for circularity as a toolbox that enables us to act and find a way forward delivering value and global prosperity while staying within our planetary boundaries. This chapter includes the practical methodology the 4Rs – The Circular Way and takes the reader through the 4Rs being Reduce, Reuse, Recycle and Replace, while shedding light to the fact that Rethink is always part of the puzzle. It also includes an essay style format that draws on the fairytale of Klods Hans or Jack the Dullard from grand Danish storyteller Hans Christian Andersen to shed light on the vast opportunity of The Circular Way and the importance of doing and believing in one's own ability to create change and celebrate the out-of-the-box thinkers. Danish design icon Bang & Olufsen provides the case example.

Chapter 10: Nature's playbook

Nature serves as a valuable teacher and provider of materials for the future we must shape if we are to stay within our planetary boundaries. The chapter highlights innovation by remembrance that is relearning all of the opportunities nature provides us with, in terms of design and in particular materials. This chapter gives an overview of some of the most exciting current biobased materials as well as the next generation biobased materials being made available through bioengineering. It also features an essay titled A Fairytale of Complexity drawing inspiration from the fairytale of The Emperor's New Clothes by Danish storyteller Hans Christian Andersen. The essay reflects on the Danish design principle of simplicity and the role of complexity in society today. It explores the concept that less is truly more and highlights the talent and craft in keeping things simple.

Chapter 11: Technology: friend or foe?

Technology is a necessary tool for facilitating global transformation, and the chapter explores the potential and opportunities arising from various technological advancements, such as AI, bioengineering, 3D printing and quantum mechanics. It also reflects on both dangers and necessities. This chapter highlights the case of Stykka, a Danish newcomer making remarkable strides in competitive markets. Additionally, in an interview, Phillip Battin, a Danish designer gone global at Google, shares his perspective on the role of Danish design in a global perspective.

Chapter 12: Plastic not so fantastic

More than any other material in the world, plastics tell the story of how in our traditional linear mode of operation, even great innovations and improvements are unsustainable and problematic. From a global perspective, consumers are becoming increasingly concerned with the negative footprints their lifestyles leave behind and nowhere is it more present than in the demand for new plastic solutions. Thus, the chapter dives into the material and explores problems and opportunities for the future of plastics. Furthermore, the chapter reflects on the societal learnings we can gain from plastics and not least the importance of systems change.

Chapter 13: Building The Circular Way

This chapter explores built environment, which is currently responsible for almost 40% of our global CO_2 equivalent emissions. With rapid urbanisation, population growth and rise in the global middle, demand is increasing at rapid pace and so does the need to design better solutions for the built environment. Thus, the chapter is filled with practical experiences from pioneers on how to tangibly move from visionary idea to tangible result with the Lendager development Upcycle Studios as the case. It highlights interviews four pioneering developers on their hands-on experience building The Circular Way. The chapter also includes an in depth conversation with Mikkel Bulow Lehnsby, the co-founder of pioneering developer NREP, reflecting on both problems and opportunity within real estate as a tool to solve global problems and creating a regenerative society.

Chapter 14: Designing our cities the Danish way

This chapter delves into the rich legacy of the Danish Design Heritage particularly within architecture and urban planning. It explores the ideas and opportunities on how cities can help create regenerative and restorative societies, and how to design our buildings and cities in the future. This chapter presents factual information, interviews and practical cases for better understanding of the concepts. From a theoretical perspective, the chapter particularly draws on Geoffrey West's work A Science of Cities. Copenhagen and the Lendager development known as the Resource Rows serves as a compelling case example in this context. This chapter also features an interview with Helle Søholt, the co-founder and CEO of Gehl Architects.

Chapter 15: Copenhagenize: designing regenerative mobility

Copenhagen is known for its bicycling culture and enthusiasts and this is not without reason. The people of Copenhagen bike a great deal and that is no coincidence – in fact it is by design and both culture and the city's infrastructure incentivises citizens to choose the bicycle. This chapter explores the unique design elements that have made Copenhagen a global exemplar for bicycle-friendly cities. It features an essay by Jens Martin Skibsted, the founder of the renowned Danish design bicycle company Biomega. Additionally, the chapter explores a compelling case on The Bicycle Snake, a bridge designed by the esteemed Danish architectural firm Dissing+Weitling. Originally constructed to enhance the cycling infrastructure for Copenhagen, this bridge is now inspiring design of similar biking infrastructure globally.

Chapter 16: Trust the future – if we do the work to create it

This chapter underscores the importance of cultivating imagination and human ingenuity, emphasising that with dedicated effort and perseverance, there is hope for a better future. It highlights our opportunity and thus responsibility to ACT at global scale and acknowledges our collective effort to shape a story of prosperity. Rather than letting the dire situation numb us, this chapter emphasises that change has the best preconditions when we are optimistic. Acknowledging the immense potential that emerge from combining our global experiences across industries, this chapter advocates to harness the possibilities brought by tech and combine it with the intelligence of nature. Thus, balancing climate urgency with empowerment allows for optimism – rather than fear overpowering us.

1

DESIGN IN THE ANTHROPOCENE

The concept of design is often associated solely with aesthetics, but it encompasses far more. To me, design is consilience — an integration of arts, practicalities and craftmanship of the real world. As such, it is as much about functionality. Design has the potential of shaping an unknown future by bringing in innovative processes, solutions, systems, and, most importantly, new ways of existence. This need for change arises from the climate crisis and has been further elevated by the common experience of the COVID-19 pandemic and then the subsequent global events, e.g., the war in Ukraine, that led to material and energy scarcity. These events have made change become the new norm. It is, therefore, our responsibility to ensure that this change leads to a better future and improves the living conditions of our global population while respecting the boundaries of our planet. In short, it is time for improvement and design can help us do that. It enables us to perceive the world through new lenses and develop our ability to envision opportunities where previously we only saw obstacles. Ultimately, **design in the Anthropocene is about shaping a better world**.

Fortunately, with the advent of the Anthropocene epoch, we are gradually realising the importance of the role of design in our ability to thrive and prosper. However, we also need to be aware of the potential damage it can do if handled inappropriately. The concept of Anthropocene, first coined by biologist Eugene F. Stoermer and later popularised by the Nobel-winning chemist Paul Crutzen in 2000, may be challenging to understand and grasp its consequences. Fundamentally, it is defined by two factors. First, our climate will be more unstable, and second, human actions are the primary drivers of ecological changes on our planet. And while scientists are still exploring exactly

DOI: 10.4324/9781003261018-1

the defining moment that shifted us from the Holocene to the Anthropocene epoch, current investigations provide glimpses into its significance:

- the decline of once colourful coral reefs
- the presence of microplastic waste everywhere in our once pristine nature
- continuous detection of nuclear radiation in our air
- the rapid melting of the ice cap in both the Arctic and Greenland

These examples highlight the challenges and changes that define the Anthropocene. They are the result of our human actions and the systems we created. Our actions have shifted us away from the Holocene epoch, an era where nature provided ideal conditions for progress, and pushed us into the Anthropocene. This new era depicts less stable conditions, which will be described in further detail in Chapter 4: The troubles we are in.

Hence, we must accept the fact that a new reality has emerged on entering the Anthropocene: **Our actions have consequences for the planet, which in turn affect our ability to thrive on Earth**. Thus, a key part of the Anthropocene is to acknowledge that our actions and the choices we make can bring about positive and negative outcomes. And while we choose to focus on making good choices, it is essentially important to realise the choices or designs that fail to contribute positively and disregard our planetary boundaries. Discarding the unfavourable choices, we are accountable to alternative avenues for a better and more sustainable future.

This book serves as a blueprint for the necessary systems change taking us from our current state of climate despair to a future of repair and re-imagination. It is an effort to create value for our global population while working within the limits of our planet. Though easier said than done, the Danish design tradition is an inspiration that exemplifies that sustainability can be attained without compromising human well-being. By aligning the needs of people and the planet and addressing the societal issues, we can raise our ambition and witness remarkable outcomes, much like the Danish designers did after the Second World War.

It is of utmost importance and our responsibility and opportunity to make use of design to ensure that the global changes we are facing will result in transformative improvements, promising a better future. Design, in general, is brilliant in working within constraints, but unfortunately, the planetary boundaries are often considered as a negative constraint, diminishing the level of ambition and creativity in the final design. **We have collectively forgotten design's ability to thrive within barriers.** This perspective must change. We should cease to view our planetary boundaries as a burden or an excuse for compromising on quality and aesthetics; rather accept them as our driving force to go beyond to reach newer heights and enhance our designs. Therefore, this is the time for a paradigm shift, witnessing a design renaissance.

The inspiration behind writing this book *Danish Design Heritage and Global Sustainability* comes from my deep admiration and curiosity regarding the accomplishments of the Danish designers during the period after World War I and II. Danish designers such as Kaare Klint, Hans Wegner, Finn Juhl, Børge Mogensen, Bodil Kjær and many more not only achieved commercial success, but also left a positive impact on our planet.

They dedicated their time to solve societal problems and remained dedicated to producing quality products that stood the test of time, and to this day, they are deemed both aesthetically pleasing and functional. Thus, these products continue to be in circulation, benefitting the planet, the individual user and the businesses involved in their production and continued distribution.

However, it goes beyond the design of the individual product. A critical reason for their success is their innate care for societal wellbeing, and their belief in having a social purpose served as a positive, creative constraint that improved the final design. They cared about the usefulness, and the quality of the craftsmanship and materials used in their design. So, at the core of this book lies my perspective on design in the Anthropocene and the invaluable learnings offered by the Danish Design Heritage: It serves as a tangible example of the fact that sustainability does not necessitate compromise. On the

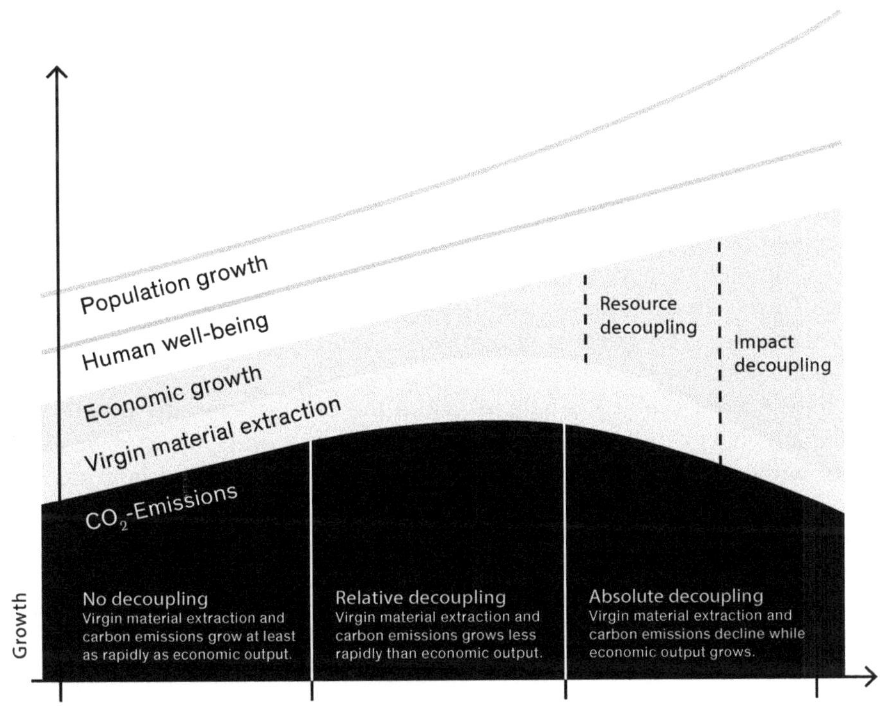

FIGURE 1.1 Decoupling graphic (All The Way To Paris).

contrary, it demonstrates that quality and care for both the user and the planet can be a positive, creative constraint. We need such examples to guide us because, for too long, sustainability has been associated with compromise on price, quality and aesthetics. Unfortunately, sustainability has become culturally associated with ugliness, costly and inconvenience. Whereas the Danish Design Heritage clearly contradicts this scenario. The Danish Design tradition particularly proves useful in achieving global sustainability as it embodies the balance that we need to achieve. It is a combination of both tangible products and skills and the philosophy and methodology to guide our reflections necessary to break free of our current societal structures and pave a better way forward. This concept will be elaborated further in Chapter 2: Learning from Danish design.

Furthermore, given this book focus on the transition from Denmark as a pilot case to global sustainability at scale, I also delve into organisational design and, in particular, the design of business models and systems. The strong tradition in Danish businesses to integrate societal purpose at the core of the business is truly remarkable. Rather than perceiving it as a barrier to commercial success, they consider it as a positive, creative constraint that help improve the overall solution. This successful Danish approach aided by purpose-driven businesses and design is testament to the country's achievements despite having a small population of not more than five million people. Danish companies have emerged as a global frontrunner in various industries such as renewable energy, life science, energy efficiency, water treatment, architecture, city planning and furniture production. For example, you may have seen their thermostats or heard about Danish energy efficiency giant Danfoss, but did you know that their founder, the engineer Mads Clausen early on, saw the importance of design and its ability to artistic shape-making? He collaborated with industrial designers and icons of the design heritage, Sigvard Bernadotte and Acton Bjørn, to create the iconic thermostat design. This serves as an exemplary case that proves how design-thinking has been pivotal in driving the success of purpose-driven Danish businesses and their sustainable outcome and impacts.

While natural science enlightens us on the problem and the progression of climate change and what we need to move away from, we have less idea about what might await us if we successfully transform. And how do you move away from something without having something to move towards? Without having something to dream of and to look forward to? We don't, as decades of inaction is the unfortunate testimony. To mitigate the challenges posed by the climate crisis is beyond physics, and to successfully overcome this crisis, we need cultural and behavioural change, and that is as much about creativity and social and human sciences. So what might a non-fossil fuel-based future look like? How might it smell? How might it make you feel? We need that presumption of possibility, a belief in that a better future might await us if we dare to create it. So, in Chapter 15: Copenhagenize: designing regenerative mobility, you will see an example of what a future without the same dependence on fossil fuels might look like. I was looking into how Copenhagen, the capital city of Denmark, reduced car traffic and carbon emissions through infrastructure design, making biking a desirable mode of transportation. This transformation not only improved public health but also enhanced Copenhagen's brand, positively improving the city's finances via tourism, talent attraction and business opportunities. Copenhagen has emerged a success story today after the redesign of the city, contrary to its state in the 1980s when it was on the verge of bankruptcy. This is a case for the potential benefit of implementing systematic changes through design, which is the need at global scale now to move from despair to repair and ultimately re-imagination.

By merging the arts with the practical real-world design elements, we envisage and thus shape a better future. Drawing from my own experience combining academia, entrepreneurship and turning discarded materials into resources, I aim to inspire and empower you to leverage design's ability to shape the future one prototype at a time. The goal is to make sustainable solutions relatable, non-intimidating and even desirable. I emphasise the importance of prototyping and real-world experimentation due to my experience having seen first hand the importance of trial and error to overcome both technical and commercial barriers and deliver the necessary solutions. I will elaborate on this in Chapter 6: Theory meets practice and magic happens, sharing my journey creating circular materials.

The concept of design-thinking has gained immense popularity recently, and for good reason, with the increased use, there is an excellent opportunity to expand the reach and use of design, but it also comes with a risk of dilution. Just because you use post-its in a workshop, it does not mean it is design, and even worse, it risks reducing design to mere thought exercise and too little about action. To address this concern, I introduce my methodology of Enlightened Action in Chapter 8: The purpose of business is to solve problems. It emphasises the purpose of business as a societal problem solver. In addition, Chapter 7: Manifesto: design in the Anthropocene serves as a guide on how to get going and start acting today.

The power of intentionality

So, does design matter? Yes, because design is deliberate. The design process holds an inherent value as it involves conscious decision-making. Whether it is selecting a colour, an object, a particular shape, our decisions are never random but always carefully thought through, driven by curiosity and a desire to challenge the status quo. Design embodies functionality as it enables intentionality and cultivates us to reflect upon choices otherwise culturally embedded. This is a trait of great importance today because we need the ability to ask questions and challenge our current system and culturally embedded norms. Therefore, i**t is the act of design that enables us to change the rules of the game**, which is essential for creating a regenerative society that fosters well-being for all.

If we fail to question the status quo, we run the risk of repeating our past failures. This becomes particularly important when we consider the dual nature of the opportunities before us, acting as both friend and foe in the necessary transition. Two key examples of this duality are the concepts of circular economy and technology.

On one hand, technology is an integral part for addressing the challenges and providing to our growing global population while staying within the planetary boundaries. It serves as a vital tool for generating value. However, the notion that technology can fix everything without behavioural changes is too convenient, and this favours especially the existing power structures. So rightfully, criticism citing that technology is nothing but a smokescreen for inaction cannot be refuted because, currently, that is partially true. But to fight those technologies that bring nothing but inaction, we need to embrace technology as part of the realm of solutions so that we can differentiate between technology that supports our goals and technology that obstructs them.

Similarly, the circular economy plays a crucial role in driving improvement. By adopting a circular approach, we can break or diminish the dependence of new resources and carbon equivalent emissions (CO_2e) for growth and improvement. This is achieved by extending the life cycle of existing resources, either by keeping them in their first use or by bringing them back into circulation in innovative ways. The circular economy recognises that business and a healthy planet are interdependent, and we can move beyond the traditional notion that growth and environmental protection are opposing forces. Instead, they are treated as natural prerequisites working toward the common goal of providing value for our global population while staying within the planetary boundaries. However, like technology in our current system, there is a risk that the circular economy can become an obstacle rather than an enabler for improvement. Currently, the more products we consume, the greater the demand for virgin materials and energy by companies. The consequences of this process that we witness is the depletion of Earth's resources and an alarming increase in CO_2 emissions and their equivalents. But again, it doesn't have to be this way. By adopting a design-based, circular approach to creating products, utilising materials, and implementing business models, we can create value and growth, which are disconnected from the use of virgin materials and CO_2 equivalent emissions. This perspective is described in detail in Chapter 9: The Circular Way and supported by the methodology the 4Rs – The Circular Way, guiding us to achieve a more sustainable and circular future.

As Christiana Figueres and Rivett-Carnac (2020) rightly say:

> We will not have a regenerative Anthropocene by default, but we can create it by design.

It is always recommended to listen attentively when Christiana Figueres addresses the audience. I greatly admire her remarkable achievements at COP21 with the implementation of Paris Agreement in 2015. This achievement was by no means an easy task, and while there is still a long way to go for our global political efforts to mitigate climate change, Figueres achieved what no one had deemed possible: An international agreement and consensus on the need for action to decrease temperature rise. As a result she has been successful in returning hope and a much-needed ray of sunlight to the global battle against climate change.

Building upon the groundwork laid out at United Nations COP21 and our collective global efforts to limit global warming within a maximum two degrees, the purpose with this book is to establish connection and foster collaboration between design and sustainability. My aim is to empower all of us to imagine and take action toward creating a regenerative future benefitting both people and the planet. While we know what we need to move away from, the real challenge lies in envisioning and shaping the path forward and devising the mechanisms to achieve it. Therefore, our task is to transition from a state of despair to one of repair and ultimately toward reimagining our global society as one where we exists in harmony with ourselves, each other and the natural world. Undoubtedly it is a daunting task, and design alone cannot accomplish it. To help guide us throughout the book, I will combine the learnings from the Danish Design Heritage with the practical experiences of pioneering Danish designers of today. Furthermore, I will integrate it with theoretical insights from notable figures like Kate Raworth, Donna Haraway and Johan Rockstrøm. By doing so, we can genuinely challenge the status quo, acknowledge that we have entered the Anthropocene and siege the opportunity to reimagine a new future within our planetary boundaries.

Designing our systems

In essence, design enables us to create the future we want. It opens our world and gives us the ability to question our choices, constraints, and previous beliefs and create a new world order. This new order connects economic value creation with respect and care for our planet and our climate. Economic growth is not a goal in itself but it holds relevance when it helps us achieve value for people while operating within the planetary boundaries. One key point is that it must take externalities into account.

In the past, as part of our progress, the mere fact that we became technologically able was reason enough to do something. However, things have changed now. Change itself is no longer a goal, nor is it a guarantee for progress. Instead, we must ensure that change, in fact, leads to a better future and that it brings long-term sustainability, while avoiding short-term disasters. This poses a significant philosophical and ethical challenge of our time: **When we can do it all, what do we choose to do?** We need to ask this question from different perspectives: The resources we use, the products we create, the way we design business models and the system in which we operate. In the Anthropocene, to create the necessary improvement, design is not just confined to individual products and business model designs. It involves designing and changing systems, which will be explored in Chapter 3: Systems design in the Anthropocene. We must ensuring that our systems empower us to make the choices that benefit both people and the planet, emphasising a holistic greater good in the long run, rather than prioritising short-term gains for individual systems such as the financial system. Economic growth and GDP no longer serve as our guiding star for value creation and progress. It's not that companies can't generate profit or experience growth; the key is that they must do so by addressing and solving problems. And most importantly, we must internalise the knowledge brought with the Anthropocene: Our actions have consequences for the planet, which in return have implications for our ability to thrive on Earth. Such consequences translate into cost in monetary terms. As such, a crucial part of accepting that we have entered the Anthropocene is that carbon equals cost, and it is rational to account for it.

As such, accounting for the externalities is the only way the market economy can function effectively. Most importantly, it is how we can restore the functionality of the system and work towards improvement, leading to the best possible outcome for humanity.

I talk of the best possible outcome for humanity because there is no predetermined universal solution to our climate crisis. Instead, we face a range of possible solutions as best described by the mathematical theory of quantum mechanics. In the 1920s, renowned scientists like Erwin Schrödinger and Niels Bohr made significant progress in the mathematical realm of quantum mechanics. They unveiled a remarkable discovery that the future is inherently unknown. This scientific revolution improved our understanding of our world and thus improved our ability to engage in scientific endeavours that improve our world for the better. With the advent of the Anthropocene, we are once again in a scientific revolution. During the era of discovery of quantum mechanics, there was a shift away from the believe in determinism and the idea that our future is already decided. The scientists started acknowledging the mathematical and philosophical understanding that the opportunity and outcome space in our physical world is not predetermined to a single answer. Instead, our physical world presents a multitude of different opportunities and possible outcomes where we cannot predetermine a singular outcome.

I draw attention to the transition from determinism to quantum theory because it not just signifies a scientific revolution, but it also reflects our situation in the midst of the climate crisis that we are facing today. Although we are aware of the severity of the crisis, we don't know the exact outcome for current and future generations. And while in some ways, it may seem comforting to embrace the mathematical philosophy of determinism to provide us with a sense of certainty even in the face of unfavourable results. The fact is that there is no singular possible outcome. Instead, we should find solace in having a range of possible outcomes. This gives us an opportunity — an opportunity to work incredibly hard and achieve the best possible scenario within the opportunity range for ours and future generations. By first taking decisive action to mitigate climate change and striving towards a better place of global prosperity.

The good thing is that nature shows us the way. Impressively nature takes care of 50% of our emissions (The Nature Conservatory, 2017) and stays beautiful and functional simultaneously. So let's innovate by embracing this knowledge and learn from nature. We should strive to do just as good as nature and learn to regenerate rather than exploit, as explored further in Chapter 10: Nature's playbook. Whether it is about mimicking nature's solutions or using natural materials to create new solutions, we are only just starting to see the immense potential through bioengineering. By combining the brilliance of nature with human ingenuity, we open the door to provide opportunities previously unimaginable.

But make no mistake, moving away from our exploitative reliance on fossil fuels while creating value and well-being for our global population poses the greatest challenge we have ever faced. So it is crucial to widen the scope of knowledge and ultimately our societal decision-making. Moreover, we must reevaluate how we define and measure progress (hint solely relying on GDP is not the answer). We must redefine our metrics, shifting away focus on quantity, instead, explore intelligent ways to measure and thus incentivise quality. We should collaborate across industries, professions, demographic and geographical boundaries to discover common ground and work together on solutions that work for the many rather than the few. **We need those capable of truly thinking not just outside the box but without a box in the picture.** We should encourage to experiment and innovate new and old in all kinds of more or less seemingly crazy ways, to try, to fail, fail again and hopefully ultimately succeed.

Drawing inspiration from Donna Haraway's notion of "Staying with the trouble" (2016), that is precisely what we need design to help us do. Design should help us feel at ease exploring problems, even when the solutions are yet unknow. It should help us evade the risk of the unknown paralyse us toward inaction. On the contrary, it should empower us to take enlightened action. I will explore this methodology in detail in Chapter 8: The purpose of business is to solve problems. Now what is important is reclaiming our future by not just getting comfortable exploring the problems within the system, but also exploring the problem that is inherent our current system in itself, as discussed in Chapter 3. Design and designers are not simply soldiers serving the current system sub-optimising to cover the problems and drive consumption for the sake of growth. They, instead, should break free to explore genuinely new radical innovation where people, planet and business thrive in synergy, rather than opposites as today. To accomplish this, we must get better at asking the fundamental question of why we design? The answer invariably should be for people rather than profit, and if not, it is our job to learn how to repair and reimagine to ensure that change is not for the mere sake of novelty but that it brings about improvement for the end user.

Why should you care?

So why should you care? The best way to answer that question is by sharing with you why I care. I consider myself a stubborn optimist, and firmly believe that we have the power to bring positive change. This conviction empowers me to act and bring change. The more I engage in the work, the more resilient my optimism becomes. It becomes a cycle, a circle of life that drives me forward. I was born in 1987, the same year the Brundtland report was released (The Brundtland Report, UN, 1987). The report introduced the concept of sustainable development and made it more than evident that we need to move toward sustainable practices. Throughout my life, we as a society have known that there was a problem. Unfortunately, however, way too little has happened. Frankly speaking, this is unacceptable. Action should have been taken much sooner, but dwelling on the past serves no one.

Instead, we must focus on taking necessary actions to move from the current short-term approach and work towards creating long-term answers that can take us toward a regenerative future for all of us. This is the task that lies before humanity today. Previous generations achieved significant technological progress, driving improvements for some of us, but it came at the expense of our climate. And at the same time, too many were left behind and many are yet to be included, e.g., basic facilities like providing a roof over their head, access to clean water, healthcare or even the opportunity to provide food for their children are lacking.

Therefore, it is now our turn to do our part responsibly and address the challenges. However, unfortunately, it seems that the progress of previous generations and the industrial revolutions have made us complacent or preoccupied with ourselves and turning our focus to trivial things around us. We need to break free from such mindset and strive for greatness. Currently, we are experiencing a new type of industrial revolution, driven by both despair and development. This requires a fresh perspective and a new narrative. It also provides an opportunity to do better, to increase the value of our innovations and find a collective purpose. So in a world where most of us are continuously looking for purpose, the opportunity of a lifetime lies right here in front of us. Ensuring not just the survival of our civilisation but a prosperous future for all of us to thrive in embodies a purposeful goal, truly creating the design renaissance and using the planetary boundaries as positive, creative constraints to heighten our ambition and get us there.

Therefore, my goal is not to point fingers, instead, to drive us collectively towards action and empowerment rather than helplessness and inaction. Regardless of how dire the situation is, it is our responsibility not to give up but to continue to try our best to change things for the better. In my experience, some people perceive me to be too radical in my efforts to mitigating climate change; while others see me as too commercial and compliant to the existing system. However, I feel that this duality strikes a good balance because it enables me to bridge between the two sides. In the grand scheme of things, we are all small parts of a larger ecosystem striving for change. Thus, each of us has a role to play, and different roles hold different values – but they all are significant in their own right.

Similarly, while we acknowledge the need for grand-scale change, we must not underestimate the power of individual action. While the ultimate goal is the systemic change necessary to deliver great absolute sustainability results, we must simultaneously encourage and appreciate small individual actions. Not that they single-handedly provide a solution to the problems but because they are part of the larger journey. So while they can be celebrated rightfully, we must not get complacent or feel that our job is done. Instead, individual actions are valuable because they can empower us towards collective action. We must ensure that individual actions are used responsibly, and not as a systemic tool for inaction, as we have unfortunately seen in countless examples. Instead, we must value individual actions for the continued empowerment that they generate.

You could say I am a theorist who actively engages in applying theories and ideas to real-world situations. You see, in my everyday life, I find myself wearing many different hats. But my preferred role is that of a stubborn optimist. With a strong bias towards action, I strive to secure the betterment and well-being of our society. This has always been my approach and it is precisely what this book is about. Drawing upon the philosophy and experience of the Danish Design Heritage, I aim to facilitate change on a global scale. Because **I believe change happens best when we are optimistic**. I have chosen to be an optimist and put in effort to nurture that mindset. This choice has shaped the life I lead, giving me the opportunity to meet and work with talented and ambitious people doing everything possible to make change happen daily. So in a world where an almost constant stream of facts alerts us to the challenges we face as a global population, remaining positive is a valuable trait. Why? Because it enables me to see things differently, to see opportunity and to act upon it. When combining our global experiences across industries, harnessing the possibilities brought by tech, and taking inspiration from the intelligence of nature, great opportunities arise.

Hope nurtures us; hope empowers us. Hope is the fuel and the driving force behind my determination to work towards developing solutions for the better. I cultivate my optimism by seeking new knowledge and surrounding myself with people who dare to act. So more than anything, I hope this book will enable you to stay optimistic and empower you to create change. For every day that passes, we need it more, so I highly recommend you, if you have the means and the opportunity, to embark on an adventure towards sustainability for all. Sooner rather than later. The world surely needs it, and perhaps you need it as well.

While the return on investment can be calculated in financial terms, there is no way to measure the intangible rewards. In particular, my journey as an entrepreneur, investor and environmentalist has instilled in me to remain an optimist. I am also increasingly optimistic about creating innovative products and materials and designing new business models in *The Circular Way* that makes it feasible to imagine that business and the environment can thrive in synergy, creating a better and harmonious world.

However, for the sake of argument, let's reverse and ask the counterargument: Why should we not care? Generally, I hear two opposing arguments as to why we should not take the responsibility to care. They are equally dangerous because both stand against action and improvement. The first suggests that things are not as bad as shown; nature will take its course to restore balance, and everything will fall back in place. Therefore, there is no reason to be alarmed and we can let business continue as usual. The second argument is put forward by people who believe that our actions hold no ground any longer as it is too late to rectify the adverse effects on our climate and secure a sustainable planet for people and nature.

As shown in the first section of this chapter, ample data demonstrates that the first argument is simply not true. But to be honest, there have been many times when the dire facts have been too distant for me to relate to and fully understand and connect with the problems. It is a survival mechanism. If you are looking for evidence of the existing problems, they are in abundance and it is unnerving to realise it. We are in a precarious situation, and scientific findings continuously confirming this grave situation. However, what is even more alarming is our continual reluctance to take meaningful action. As I once heard climate psychologist Per Espen Stoknes say, it is easier to justify current behaviour than to enforce the necessary behavioural change.

But I believe that **if we have the power to destroy, we must also have the power to rebuild**. This leads me to the second counterargument that it is too late to fix things and improve the situation. However, the truth is we are not certain of what the future holds. Therefore, how can we not do our absolute best and make every effort to try to bring the change? And take comfort in the many outstanding innovative achievements that humans have accomplished so far, as well as nature's remarkable ability for resilience and adaptability. I hope that if we release our human ingenuity in alignment with nature the best is yet to come.

World makers or world breakers?

Danish Design Heritage represents not only the quality of design, materials and craftsmanship, but also the principles of designing for utility and purpose. It combines functionalism and a philosophical approach and design methodology where societal values and ethics are interlinked with aesthetics to work in synergy to improve both societal value creation and use value. And last but certainly not least, it represents the ability to create and shape things that does not yet exist. In fact, the Danish word for design is "formgiving", which directly translated means shape-making. **To design is to shape** – an ability we are in dire need of, thus providing both opportunity and responsibility for designers in the Anthropocene. If we get it right, it will create a design renaissance combining beauty and functionality to solve our grand societal challenges and shape the future we do not yet know. As will be explored further in Chapter 16: Trust the future – if we do the work to create it, the focus will be on the transformative power of imagination, creativity and hope.

So, by highlighting the significance of Danish Design Heritage, my aim is to reposition design where it belongs: At the centre of the transformation necessary. My goal is to reactivate the potential of design. Despite coming from a business and sustainability background and not a designer by trade, I have had the privilege of working at the intersection of theory and practice, where design, green innovation and business merge. And this has given me the advantage of witnessing the great opportunities that arise when design is at the core of innovation. Design is positioned as a vital part of the innovation process from the start to the end and not to be treated in isolation nor discarded before the final product reaches the market nor included to simply improve aesthetics at the end. This will help bring forth the potential of design to build a better world. This perspective comes alive powerfully and brilliantly in the words and projects of the pioneering professor and architect Buckminster Fuller, who has inspired designers towards creating improvement for nearly a century:

> A designer is an emerging synthesis of artist, inventor, mechanic, objective economist, and evolutionary strategist.
>
> *Buckminster Fuller (1969)*

In essence, this is what a designer can and should be. However, when we look at the profession today, it is clear that design is at a crossroad: it must decide if design is required only for aesthetic factor or it is inherently needed for its transformational potential. So as much as society at large needs to look to design for solutions, **designers must take both opportunity and responsibility to future-proof the planet and the profession**.

How can this be achieved? By designing solutions that are future-proof, amalgaming science and arts and harnessing its ability to shape the unknown. That is precisely what design stands for, a mix of creativity, facts and technology. One of my climate heroes, Alexander Von Humbolt, who is a scientist, explorer, poet and author, among other things, describes it as *consilience* in his book *Views of Nature*, which is one of my favourite. Though written in 1808, it is still ever so relevant. A key point to capture is the significance of merging separate areas of science into one transformative whole. He advocated not just to combine different types of science but to connect science with the arts, which he refers to as Scientific Aesthetics, something he mastered perfectly, as exemplified in the following quote.

> But with the withering of each blossom of the spirit, whenever, in the storm of the times, the work of creative art is scattered, so forever will new life sprout forth from the womb of the Earth. Restlessly, procreative Nature opens her buds: unconcerned whether outrageous humanity (a forever distant race) should trample the ripening fruit.
>
> *von Humboldt (1808)*

As such, design is the ability to combine beauty with functionality by questioning the status quo and giving shape to our collective future. So, I propose that design in the Anthropocene means moving from Despair to Repair and ultimately to Re-imagination.

FIGURE 1.2 Words describing the "Ideal world" as shared in interviews (The Circular Way).

So, design is not just for those who are trained as designers, it is a toolbox, a mindset and a methodology that can be used and learned by all. It is just like most of us deal with economics in our work life despite not being educated as economists. It is about extracting what is useful and adapting it to our surroundings. I am not a designer, but I see the great value it creates and has thus imbibed a continued interest that blossomed into a career. Simply because I realised that design can transform problems into opportunities. It gives us the ability to question the status quo and break down current barriers and enable new solutions to sprout forward.

It also requires designers to collaborate with other professions. The value of a design cannot be measured solely on the innovative idea or beautiful sketches but on the final implementation in the given context.

While we indeed have the opportunity to design a regenerative world for people and the planet to thrive in, it is not guaranteed that it will happen. Instead it is our collective job to ensure that we achieve just that: Improve the world for the better and ensure **design is a tool for world makers rather than a service for world breakers**. Because with design comes the opportunity to design both solutions and problems. Let's ensure we do the former and make design friend rather than a foe.

Now it is time for design to make a choice. It must decide whether it will be a nice accessory to technology and the economic system, or a necessary world shaker and maker. As regenerative economist and creator of the Donut economic model Kate Raworth rightfully points out: "An economy that is regenerative by design is one in which people become full participants in regenerating Earth's life-giving cycles so that we thrive within planetary boundaries. This is our generational design challenge…" (Raworth, 2017).

We need to focus less on the theoretical potential and more on tangible actions and results to achieve our goals. We need to be biased toward action. What we need now are practitioners who can drive the transformation successfully. In other words, it is time for people and organisations with vision and courage to step forward and embark on a journey of experimentation, learning from failures and succeeding in the end. Whether it be in the private or the public sector, a truly sustainable future for all is only possible when we dare to go against the existing norm and move from despair to repair and ultimately to reimagining.

In the spirit of shaping the future, I encourage you to envision a world without resource scarcity, a world where our human actions do not harm our climate and where we can cater to global demand without compromising our mother Earth. Envision a world where waste no longer exists and where we are creating value for people while staying within our planetary boundaries. Unfortunately, that is not the world we live in today. However, I believe that we can achieve the world we envisage for us and future generation.

In this book, I celebrate and share the experience of some of the pioneers I have had the privilege of working with on our journey towards fostering harmony between people, the planet and business. These pioneers are

Case 1.1 TAKT – a modern take on the Danish furniture tradition

Building on the teaching of Danish mastermind Kaare Klint, TAKT truly embodies the philosophy of the Danish Design Heritage, that is, designing solutions in the nexus between tradition and the opportunities of the present, which is precisely what TAKT does. TAKT's approach is to combine the Danish Design Heritage with the possibilities of modern technology to questioning the current business model to deliver high-quality products at a democratic price point much like the masterminds of the Danish Modern's as explained further in Chapter 2.

Over the last 30–40 years, the Danish Design Heritage has broadly been managed as a luxury lifestyle topic. However, the great mid-century masters of Danish design were not occupied with luxury, but with how 'normal people' could live a better life. In the post-war era, it was a mission for many during the 1950s and 1960s. The Danish Design Heritage is about deep consideration for how people live their lives and supporting this with limited resources. The more recent focus in our industry on luxury lifestyles and maximising price points has deprived many people of enjoying good design and craftsmanship.

The uplifting opportunity we embraced at TAKT was the chance to contribute to a brighter environmental future, using modern distribution methods to make it accessible to a wider audience. You could say that while the designers of the mid-century period worked on the agenda of society to improve the living standards for many, our greater mission today is to find a way of living that preserves human life on Earth. In that sense, we believe that our work at TAKT is about updating and adding to the Danish Design Heritage. Our industry may have been without a deeper purpose for some years, but now we can gather around a common goal again and let that guide our actions.

What is true today is that our company's objectives must be woven into all aspects of our efforts. It goes beyond solely focusing on product, supply chain, or our dialogue with our users. Our endeavour is to align all aspects of our work with a common set of principles.

At TAKT we strive for clarity, delight and simplicity in all aspects of our business. These principles guide not only our product design, but also how we conduct our business. By selling directly to our users, so we have the privilege of engaging in direct dialogue with them without the intervention of any agents or retailers in between. This enables us to reduce costs and offer them products at better prices, while giving clearty on their needs and preferences.

Similarly as clarity in design allows users to decode the use and functionality of a piece, clarity in business means transparency with our users. They are provided with a detailed break-down of the pricing of the furniture, listing the cost of materials, salary to craftsmen, royalties to the designer, etc. Moreover, they can also see the detailed carbon footprint of their specific piece of furniture, along with our efforts to compensate for the remaining environmental impact.

The focus of TAKT is about creating delightfully crafted furniture with a natively sustainable approach. They go hand in hand because good sustainable furniture is inherently designed to last a lifetime, and nothing can secure a long aesthetic lifetime than good thoughtful design. For many people, the choice of objects to live with reflect their vision of 'the good life' – the values they hold dear. It is inevitable that the environmental footprint of the objects we surround ourselves with will have a huge impact on how we perceive them. It will be hard for most people to find pleasure in products that they know harm our environment. Sustainability must be an integral part rather than an afterthought.

FIGURE 1.3 T04 Soft Lounge Chair (Rasmus Dengsø, TAKT).

T04 Soft Lounge Chair is designed by Thomas Bentzen as a modern interpretation of a classic Danish armchair. The innovative application of veneer gives the chair a soft comfort while avoiding harmful padding, and the separation into components allows the user to repair the chair themselves if needed. All contributing to better circularity.

among the first to fearlessly embrace new business models, explored the use of reused and biogenic materials, among other things, in practice. They have demonstrated great courage by taking the initial risk so that others can learn from their experiences and see that while it is not necessarily always easy, it is, in fact, doable. I hope you will welcome these experiences and use them wherever they come in handy.

Question: How do you describe the world you would design?

References

Buckminster Fuller, R. (1969). *Operating Manual for Spaceship Earth*. Lars Muller Publishers.

Figueres, C., & Rivett-Carnac, T. (2020). *The Future We Choose: The Stubborn Optimist's Guide to the Climate Crisis*. Vintage Books.

Haraway, J. D. (2016). *Staying with the Trouble: Making Kin in the Chthulucene*. Duke University Press.

The Brundtland Report, UN, 1987. https://sustainabledevelopment.un.org/content/documents/5987our-common-future.pdf

Raworth, K. (2017). *Doughnut Economics: Seven Ways to Think Like a 21st-Century Economist*. Random House.

The Nature Conservatory (2017). Nature's Make or Break Potential for Climate Change, 15 October. https://www.nature.org/en-us/what-we-do/our-insights/perspectives/natures-make-or-break-potential-for-climate-change.

von Humboldt, A. (1808). *Views of Nature*. The University of Chicago Press.

2

LEARNING FROM DANISH DESIGN

Has mass production occupied our minds?

The famous Danish designer Poul Henningsen, known for his iconic lamps such as the PH lamp and the artichoke, finds a significant place in the Danish Design Heritage. They are still to this day some of the most revered and valued lamp designs globally. However, he did not only have a talent for design, but also an avid songwriter and passionate contributor to the societal discourse of Denmark and the Nordics. When Denmark was occupied by the Nazi Germans in World War II, he used his talent to write a song for the resistance movement, conveying with a clear message: Man binder os på mund og hånd, men man kan ikke binde os på ånd, which is translated freely from Danish to English as: One can control our movements and prevent us from speaking freely, but one can neither occupy nor control our minds and thoughts.

He eloquently proved his point by wrapping the message of resistance in a love song for a theatrical play in one of the Copenhagen theatres, thus managing to trick the German occupiers' censorship and obtaining approval for his performance. However, on the opening night, when the occupied Danes in the theatre heard the lyrics, they instantly understood the underlying sentiment. They knew exactly what it was about, unlike the German censorship committee. Spontaneously, the entire room stood up and sang along. Not long after, it was performed in theatres nationwide as a reminder of collective free will. In itself it is a beautiful and powerful story that highlights the crucial societal contribution made by one of Denmark's most excellent designers. It is important to acknowledge the great personal sacrifice made by Poul Henningsen, a successful designer, as publicly outsmarting Nazi occupying power during World War II was far from risk-free. Ultimately, Poul Henningsen and

DOI: 10.4324/9781003261018-2

his family had to flee the country. I have a reason to mention this here because it actually adds context to his subsequent statement to the song in the mid-1950s. He remarked that we have never been less free because mass production has now succeeded at occupying our minds. This was an early warning sign of the problems we face today. As such by questioning status quo he gave us an early warning sign of our systemic challenges of a shift from a focus on use value to exchange value.

Poul Henningsen (1894–1967) was a multifaceted Danish designer, architect, writer and societal thought leader. Well known for his critical insights and musical talents, Henningsen made significant contribution to Danish intellectual life. He edited and published the *Kritisk Revy*, a radical cultural journal, thereby significantly influencing Danish intellectual life through his writing. The journal was provocative in content and form, seeking to critically discuss emerging cultural, political and societal topics. Active from 1926 to 1028, the *Kritisk Revy* played an essential part in Danish cultural life and the history of the 1920s. Furthermore, in his debate book *What about Culture?* published in 1933, he criticised the cultural policy of Nazism and the passivity of the Danish government. As a result, he became a central part of the Association for the Liberal Cultural Struggle and its anti-fascist magazine *Kulturkampen*. However, his outspoken views led to divided opinions, and he was dismissed from the Danish newspaper *Politiken* in 1938. Additionally, the radical utterance about Nazism caused Poul Henningsen and his wife to flee to Sweden in 1943. After 1945 Henningsen became a regular writer for the Danish journals *Information*, *Politiken*, *Social-Demokraten* and *Forbrugerrådets Tænk* magazine. His social criticism and writing exemplify the significant roles that designers and architects have played in shaping public discourse (Danmarks Radio, 2010).

Tradition meets opportunity

In the late 1940s, when the world was focused on recovering from World War II and rebuilding our cities, businesses and society, a group of Danish designers emerged. Notable figures like Finn Juhl, Hans J. Wegner, Børge Mogensen, Bodil Kjær, Arne Jacobsen and more dedicated themselves to crafting their best and most treasured pieces of furniture and design. Their contribution led to the global recognition of Danish design, known for its high-quality materials, craftsmanship and aesthetics. But during the post-war years, the Danish design industry started to thrive, creating the iconic designs that continue to be revered.

As I write this, I find myself in the comfort of my apartment, which serves as a fitting reminder of the significant possibilities that arise when we combine the Danish Design Heritage with the technology and opportunities of the present era. The resourcefulness of Danish design legend Poul Henningsen comes to mind as he transformed an old attic into a practical living area, initially creating a home and an atelier for himself. Typically, attics are not compatible with good lighting, so how did it come to be that a world-class lighting and lamp designer could live and work in an attic that was converted into living space? Among other things, his use of design to repurpose the attic and installing new technology in the form of skylight windows resulted in this modern transformation. These innovative windows were provided by a newcomer in the market, now turned Danish industry giant the window company Velux. Indeed, combining tradition with the opportunity provided by the contemporary advancements showcase the power of combining the best of both worlds.

My desk by Ole Wancher is still in great shape, and so is the chair by Tove and Edward Kindt Lassen I am currently sitting on. These pieces serve as tangible reminders of the enduring relevance of the Danish Design Heritage where the emphasis on quality materials, craftsmanship and aesthetics ensures their functionality and desirability even after more than 50 years. Although the Danish designers may not have intentionally worked to stay within the planetary boundaries, their focus on the value of use rather than exchange, along with thoughtful attention and care, made perfect sense. It was a natural approach rooted in respecting materials and creating something that mattered and created value for the user. The norm was to be connected to the surroundings, society and craftsmanship and, in the process, achieve aesthetic resilience. My deep respect and insatiable curiosity for what that can teach us today is my *raison d'etre* for looking to the Danish Design Heritage for inspiration for future-proofing our global society and enable us to stay within our planetary boundaries. As I will explore in the coming sections and throughout this book, what I discovered has far exceeded my expectations. I found both philosophical connections and came across numerous companies putting these principles to practice continuously, thus highlighting the many valuable lessons we can apply today.

Every so often, I take a break from my writing and shift my gaze away from my computer screen to admire the chair positioned across my desk: The Faaborg Chair designed by Kaare Klint (1930). To me, it stands as one of the most beautiful objects I can imagine, with significant symbolic meaning. Kaare Klint was one of the founding fathers of the Danish design heritage and the first professor at the furniture school at the Danish Royal Academy and the Faaborg chair is considered the start of the Danish modern furniture era. It represents Kaare Klint's philosophy of **creating the solutions of the future by combining the traditions of the past with the possibilities of the present**. Seeing tradition as an accumulation of experience is not meant to hold us back but as something to build upon to create the future. This concept aligns with the case TAKT, the furniture company, discussed in Chapter 1: Design in the Anthropocene.

FIGURE 2.1 Words describing the "Danish Design Heritage" provided in interviews (The Circular Way).

Most of the designs from that era have never become waste but have instead thrived. Their enduring appeal, use of high-quality materials and their timeless look, has allowed the pieces to remain in use, passed down through generations, and even traded at prices higher than their original price. This illustrates how desirability and creativity can lead to a business that thrives in a post-crisis environment.

We recently bid farewell to one of the last traditional cabinet makers and a true craftsman of the post-war period, Ejner Pedersen. He played a pivotal role in introducing numerous designs of Hans J. Wegner and Poul Kjærholm to the world. He will be remembered for his profound remark (freely translated from Danish): "I usually say we make free furniture. If you give so much money for a chair today, you will be able to sell it for the same in many years—when you're done using it."

Again, for him, it was not a matter of designing for a circular economy or a green transition. Instead, it was a matter of quality—both material and design. It was about ensuring it would stand the test of time and still function and be aesthetically appealing many years later. Thus, good design is durable in terms of both functionality and durable desirability.

The interlink between social purpose and aesthetical ambition

After World War II, there was a great social purpose for design to help rebuild society and increase prosperity and well-being of the average Danish citizen. This created an ideal environment where design could thrive, interlinking between social purpose and aesthetic ambition. The focus was on creating visually appealing products having positive impact on the user's well-being.

These designs were accessible to a wide range of people in a democratic way, considering both price affordability and ensuring that design was relatable and understandable to the untrained eye. This ensures that design caters to an actual need with a greater purpose, and indeed proving a tangible example of how sustainability does not have to be a compromise. Instead, it can be a positive driving force for ambition and increased user value.

> While modernists in other countries believed furniture derived its value primarily from offering an interesting visual experience, to Kaare Klint, above all, it had to be a good tool.
>
> *Rasmussen (1960)*

As described in the above quote by Steen Eiler Rasmussen and reflected in Kaare Klints' inaugural teaching at the furniture school at The Royal Academy, the focus was about user comfort and ergonomics (1930), that is, the value experienced by user. This serves as a reminder for designers and all of us to pause and question if what we are creating has value and serves our purpose or if our actions are solely driven by exchange value. So, looking to the Danish Design Heritage enable us to reclaim the notion of value creation. We should ask ourselves what creates value and why we do what we do. As a designer, do you make products because they create value for the user, or do you make products to service a financial and economic system by generating recurring revenues? I would argue that, to a large degree, we have unfortunately stopped valuing the products beyond their sale and exchange value. And this is a fundament issue that we need to address and roll back. If we fail to do so, our discussion about sustainability will remain limited to minimising harm rather than achieving positive impact. It is essential that we bring back that connectedness and the user focus of the Danish Design Heritage. It is critical to design remarkable products serving both a societal purpose and aesthetic ambition and shifting the focus to their ultimate use rather than exchange value.

Initially, after the World Wars, Danish design served a critical societal purpose of rebuilding society and democratising design. With the climate and biodiversity crisis, there is a new purpose and opportunity for the Danish design methodology, which integrates societal purpose and aesthetics, gaining increased relevance. So design, in general, and Danish Design Heritage in particular, provides valuable lessons and tools to ensure improvement through critical areas such as functionalism and simplicity. By combining the learnings of the past with the opportunities of the present, we can bring a social and ethical purpose to the core of design without compromising on aesthetics and usability. These principles, instead, help in enhancing the ambition of the final result as elaborated in Chapter 7: Manifesto: design in the Anthropocene.

Reflecting on Poul Henningsen's insight about mass production overshadowing our consciousness, it becomes evident that designers, too, have gotten occupied with mass production, leading to a loss of social purpose and the ideal conditions for a thriving, innovative design culture. "Luckily", the climate emergency and dire situations we face as a global society have rekindled the need for a social purpose and the urgency for design solutions to accelerate progress and improve planetary well-being. Particularly in the younger design generations, we notice that innovative design culture is once again thriving. The need for responsible design solving society's problems is not considered as a barrier to good design but instead **seeing the planetary boundaries as a positive, creative constraint improving the overall design**.

Case 2.1 Mater – updating the classics

Mater, founded in Copenhagen in 2006, is a pioneering furniture of the future which is an expansion of Danish Design Classics and a medium for empowering new designers to create furniture design that moves us closer to staying within our planetary boundaries using both Recycling and Replace of the 4Rs – The Circular Way. This methodology will be explored further in Chapter 6: Theory meets practice and magic happens in which you will see a beautiful collection of outdoor furniture designed by Nanna Ditzel produced using Replastic. Thus, it is a great privilege to follow and collaborate with Mater, a brand with sustainability at its core. They share their story and yet another one of their beautiful designs, a Børge Mogensen design updated to be produced using coffee shell waste.

From the outset, Mater aspired to inspire a global design audience and to engage people in sustainable thinking. By blending waste material with timeless design, Mater achieves sustainability and circular production through collaboration with well-established new design talents.

After years of research and testing, Mater has invented a patented technology that allows to mix upcycled fibre-based waste materials with different kinds of plastic waste. In our journey we have teamed up with large corporations to understand how to upcycle their fibre and plastic waste.

The result is a unique mixture that can be applied to an existing technology within our industry: press moulding. The technique allows efficient upcycling of industrial waste and, simultaneously, reducing carbon emissions. By capturing carbon in our furniture instead of allowing the waste materials to be burned, we achieve in bringing a more sustainable approach to producing and enhancing environmental impact.

Conscious is a collection of chairs and tables designed in 1958 by the renowned Danish furniture designer and architect *Børge Mogensen*. For the first time, a collection from Børge Mogensen is relaunched using a different material than the original. The seat and backrest attribute a new sustainable and circular material, developed by Mater, made from waste.

The seat and the backrest of the new chair are made from upcycled coffee shell waste and industrial plastic waste mixed with sawdust from the FSC wooden base of the chair, in short, *Mater Circular Material*.

The new patented waste composite allows Mater to offer a circular take-back system. All elements made in the *Mater Circular Material* can be recycled and transformed into new furniture up to five times. This is an essential step towards Mater's vision of becoming 100% circular.

FIGURE 2.2 A photo of the Børge Mogensen Conscious Chair BM31622 (Mater).

An inner cohesion between content and expression

An old but ever-so-relevant principle of "form follows function" is deeply ingrained in the Danish Design Heritage, but not as a limitation. Instead, it is in synergy, allowing the function to improve the final form rather than restrict it.

As such, functionalism goes beyond an aesthetic style; it is also a philosophy ensuring that we have a purpose and places value creation at the centre of the design. Danish architect and professor at The Royal Academy Christoffer Harlang explains and exemplifies this principle through the works of Poul Henningsen:

> PH sought to put in scientific terms what he intuitively felt was correct and insisted that form had to emerge not from formal aesthetic principles but from thorough, rational studies of function. "Light's quality is not a question of psychology and taste and preference ... it is a physiological problem", thundered the master of light. And PH's lamps have become universal products that in the most beautiful way embody the view that one of Danish design's unique features is an inner cohesion between content and expression.
>
> *Harlang (2007)*

Another essential element of Danish creativity can be traced back to our architectural, furniture and film, TV and food tradition, where we excel at extracting maximum value from minimal resources. Practising the principle **less is more** is a crucial skill we all need to adopt if we are to meet the global demand while staying within our planetary boundaries. This is a skill imbibed out of scarcity of natural resources and the hard-working nature of Lutheran farming ancestors. This aspect came up in our recent conversation with Christoffer Harlang. This skill is important in today's scenario as we attempt to reduce our excessive use of fossil fuels and produce designs that serve a purpose and generate value while minimising adverse effects. The increased popularity of furniture from the 1940s, 1950s and 1960s that are still being utilised, valued and sold highlights the positive effect of aesthetic resilience, allowing the objects to stand the test of time. So, here are a few key learnings from the Danish Design Heritage before putting them to practical use as explained in Chapter 7: Manifesto: design in the Anthropocene.

First, just like the designers saw their social purpose as a tool to elevate the final design, we can also embrace our planetary boundaries as a positive and creative constraint. Rather than seeing them as a burden or an excuse that compromises qualities and values, we can see them as an opportunity to reach for the stars and improve our designs. Danish Design Heritage teaches us that design allows us to view the world through different perspectives, seeing opportunities where once we would have seen obstacles. Therefore, it should only be natural to start questioning our own choices. When doing so, we can be inspired by the craftsmanship of Danish design and take the time to care about the quality of materials, craftsmanship and aesthetics to ensure the designs stand the test of time.

Second, and this is where it gets even trickier, we must think of the end as the beginning. What do I mean here? We must consider the product lifecycle, what will happen to the design once it has been manufactured and used. We should think of ways to recycle the materials in order to never become waste. We must learn to use what is available and be confident that you have the capabilities to make it into good design. What is considered waste in one industry is often valuable in another. We must improve cross-industry collaboration to share and recirculate our resources at the highest possible value. In that sense, one man's trash is truly another woman's treasure.

And last but certainly not least, much like the designers of the Danish modern age, we must continuously seek new opportunities arising from technology and new materials. We must ensure that we can design a world with minimal waste and our resources are maximised at the highest value possible. Combining the traditions of the past with the possibilities of the present can we create sustainable solutions for the future.

Does the fact that the Danish Design Heritage inspire global sustainability today mean that we can avoid making changes or sacrifices? Certainly not. The transformation will undoubtedly require sacrifice, but the Danish Design Heritage serves as an example of the great value that awaits us if we embrace transformation. Therefore, it is a reminder that we need to be more thoughtful regarding what we define as value creation and increase our ambition. Design that does not consider society's needs is simply not befitting in the Anthropocene. The Danish Design Heritage is a compelling case highlighting that they achieved their goal of creating a better future by **embedding a social purpose in their design, thus elevating both functionality and form in synergy**.

Most importantly, by emphasising the Danish Design Heritage, I want to bring your attention to the fact that working within limitations combined with a higher purpose of value creation for both the user and society at large need not be at the expense of the quality of aesthetics, comfort or even price. Instead, working within our planetary boundaries and finding new ways to cater to growing global demand without compromising on neither people nor the planet can increase the value of the final product and solutions. A key part of that is thus valuing the success of the design based on its use rather than exchange value. To achieve this, it necessitates setting our ambitions high and seeing the planetary boundaries as positive and creative constraints.

Interview Dan Stubbergaard, Cobe

> There's no difference between a pessimist who says, "It's all over, don't bother trying to do anything, forget about voting, it won't make a difference," and an optimist who says, "Relax, everything is going to turn out fine." Either way, the results are the same. Nothing gets done.
>
> *Chouinard (2006)*

One of my favourite quotes from Yvon Chouinard's book *Let My People Go Surfing* depicts an excellent example of the work of Danish architect Dan Stubbergaard and his design studio Cobe. Dan Stubbergaard continuously devotes his work to develop ideas that are innovative and at the same time feasible. In my conversation with Dan, we touched upon the importance of balance in both specific solutions and for society at large, including how he and Cobe strive to balance the preconditions of a project site with the innovative opportunities of our time. An approach similiar to the grandmaster of the Danish Design Heritage, Kaare Klint's principle of working in the solution space between tradition and the opportunity of the current.

DLV: If you could design your ideal world, what three words would you use to describe it?

DS: The three words that I would use to describe an ideal world would be balance, nature and community.

DLV: What do you mean when you say balance?

DS: It is about creating cities, societies and a socially, ecologically and economically balanced planet and avoiding the polarisation that happens when things are not in balance.

I strongly believe in the importance of striking a balance between reality and our aspiration. In order to embrace transformation, we must balance the big vision of the future with tangible actions to create the necessary progress in a timely manner. Another reason for the need of balance is to bridge the growing lack of harmony among people and between people and nature. The imbalance is unacceptable, and we must act and restore balance. Therefore, balance is a fundamental design principle for us.

DLV: I remember reading that you would like a Cobe building to be recognisable from its compatibility with its surroundings. Is that also part of your principle of balance?

DS: Yes, exactly. We want our projects to grow from the surrounding design, structures and preconditions. Like nature, architecture must emerge from a particular area's conditions and resources. We know that when we plant in nature, we must take soil, weather conditions, etc., into account if we want the plant to thrive. The same can be said for architecture. So, at Cobe, we consider it vital to study the surrounding environment and context to create meaningful architecture. When successfully done, it links the building to the specific place, and the local environment and building nurture each other.

Designers and architects have the power to improve an area by understanding the existing values and advancing them even further. Recognising that a concept that functions well in one area rarely is ideal in a different setting is crucial. In that sense, it is a prerequisite for sustainability to start by exploring the local area, climate, social condition, cultural history and more.

DLV: So, a holistic point of view?

DS: Yes, which is also about balance. One must achieve a balance between acknowledging and treasuring existing qualities and, at the same time contributing with new designs that include sustainable and innovative approaches.

DLV: Your principle of balance and understanding the preconditions as a prerequisite for sustainability makes great sense. But I don't see a lot of industry players doing what you do. So why do you think that is, and how can we change that?

DS: The building industry tends to preserve business-as-usual procedures. From a short-term perspective, it is both time-consuming and expensive to invent new techniques, designs and materials, so it is often considered too costly to adopt new ways of doing.

However, it is essential that we keep challenging our approaches and encourage everyone to participate in demanding these changes. This type of change calls for both bottom-up and top-down action. First, it is essential to realise that the building industry is consumer-driven. Adopting the bottom-up approach, where consumers demand sustainable options, will effectively drive the industry to adapt. However, for the sustainable agenda to become profitable, demand must increase.

Second, the top-down method is equally important as political systems, powerful companies, etc., take the lead in demanding and creating change. A vital point to start is by being transparent and able to communicate what a building consists of. When you think about it, it is surprising that as consumers, we know more about the products we buy in the supermarket than we know about probably the most significant investment in our life: our home. Unfortunately, the top-down approach has proven to be slow, and I share the common impatience that the power of change is not happening rapidly enough even though there is growing demand from citizens.

On a societal level, communication is critical. We must first articulate and illustrate problems in tangible and understandable language. Knowledge is vital in altering people's perception. After creating this common understanding and addressing the "why" behind the demand for change, we can form clearer visions for the future. This process makes us understand the need and opportunity to drastically change our ways of doing. Although challenging, it also leaves us with a unique opportunity. As humans, we tend to stick to existing habits and routines, but now we have the chance to question and reflect on the motivations driving our actions. Hopefully, this self-reflection can lead to improved structures in our society.

Moreover, a book like this serves a critical role in making the abstract concepts of both problems and opportunities tangible with respect to their complexity.

DLV: When studying our Danish Design Heritage design, it seems that our goals and focus have shifted from the original intention of design, to create value for the users. Nowadays, with our increasing focus on growth and generating a profit, have we forgotten why we build and design?

DS: I think so. Because the long-term perspective has primarily disappeared in today's industry – and profits are too often more important than the use-value. Traditionally, the overarching purpose was to create housing and protection while leaving an impression and improving society for future generations. That is what is fascinating about architecture: If done right, it creates value and a better world for future generations. But at the same time, and as we see today, it is also the challenge of the built environment because if not done right, it affects our future generations negatively.

A massive problem we face in our industry today is thoughtlessness: The architecture of indifference. We all are aware of the outcome, buildings that have no value for the tenants or surroundings, nor is its quality. At a minimum, we need to make sure that our actions today lead to a better tomorrow, and if that is not possible, we should wait for the right opportunity. We need more decision-makers that are willing to say no to doing harm.

DLV: So, part of the solution must be that we start demanding better quality of both functionality and aesthetics?

DS: Yes, personally, I have Hans J. Wegner's Y chairs that I inherited from my grandfather. The chairs are over 40 years old, but due to the quality of craftsmanship, materials and aesthetics, they create value beyond generations.

DLV: Speaking of the Danish Design Heritage – what pops into your mind when thinking of Danish design?

DS: Holistic. From furniture to buildings and the creation of cities, the Danish approach sees design as holistically connected. Even connecting through time because Danish Design Heritage means knowing someone took their time to create something valuable that can be treasured for generations. Finally, to me, Danish design is tangible, accessible and inclusive. Meaning that when Danish design is at its best, it is honest and easy to understand and appreciate by the untrained eye.

DLV: That is a great point. Danish design is honest in that it does not need a lot of explanation or training to see whether it is good or not. So what do you think we can learn from that when creating the solutions necessary today?

DS: To create change, we must be able to explain problems and solutions in a tangible and relatable way – an honest way understandable to the untrained eye. We are responsible and can use design and architecture to make the necessary changes real and actionable. And show that this is not a trend that will pass, nor something that can be quickly fixed. It will take significant effort, but it is also a grand opportunity to change systems and habits that we unintentionally created and intentionally changed for the better and, as mentioned before, achieve a better balance.

DLV: Yes. I think one of design and architecture's most important tasks is to help us collectively imagine change for the better as a real alternative to today. I also started the interview by asking what the world would look like if you could design it.

DS: One tangible example of change for the better is the growing trend in the wildering of private gardens. Tactile and beautifully highlighting the importance of biodiversity. Similarly, the value of wooden rather than concrete buildings is a tangible example of how doing good for the planet can create value and well-being for people.

DLV: When looking toward the planetary boundaries, it's clear that climate and biodiversity are equally big challenges. However, globally we have tended to focus on climate and perhaps neglected biodiversity even though it might be easier to understand and act upon?

DS: The critical part is that we are mindful of both and find the proper balance in mitigating the crisis of both. Wood again proves to be a good example. We should build much more in wood but do it in harmony with nature and let nature take its time to do what it does best rather than plant more mono forests.

DLV: What actions are you most proud of? And what do you still want to do?

DS: I am proud that through our projects, such as the Silo, we have taken part in making transforming buildings cool again, and luckily there is an increasing awareness of the costs of tearing down a building regarding both CO_2, materials and monetary.

And I am proud to see how the norm has changed internally in our organisation and how mindful everyone is of the impact of our work, and how that affects both what we do and what we choose not to do. It gives me hope to see how many are transitioning to thinking The Circular Way and creating long-lasting designs by making buildings more adaptable for future functions and increasing transparency of materials and usage. And luckily, there is an increasing demand and a new generation of developers seeking to work with us. Right now, we are building a project in Berlin for a very innovative developer, essentially taking longevity and multifunction as a purpose seriously to the extent that our task is to draw a building that can be used for both residential and commercial use because we do not know what the first use will be. Seeing a new type of developer coming from other industries and demanding change, who are not afraid to be dogmatic about it, also gives me hope. It's not that money does not matter to them, but that money cannot stand alone as a parameter for success.

DLV: What inspires you?

DS: Ursula von der Leyen's New European Bauhaus project is inspiring. It is a prime example of the top-down approach needed within the building industry. She used culture and design to create a clear vision of how to change the industry that is both tangible and understandable. I hope companies and the national political system will embrace this approach and unite toward change. Especially in Denmark, with our heritage and current capabilities, we should be very well equipped to deliver on the vision of New European Bauhaus.

Dan Stubbergaard, Founder of Cobe, Architect MAA, Professor in Practice, Harvard University. He founded Cobe in 2006, and the company specialises in urban planning, architecture, landscape architecture and interior design. Its mission is to create long-term, sustainable solutions for cities, buildings and landscapes.

Bodil kjær, an icon of future, past and present design

As the chairwoman of the Danish Design Council, I had the great pleasure of awarding Danish design legend Bodil Kjær the Danish Design Council 2022 honorary award for extraordinary contribution to Danish Design. She was nominated by council members and elected by the council's election committee. Still, it was also a great pleasure and privilege for me to honour a personal icon and the beginning of a conversation and friendship with an extraordinary woman who is using her iconic status and experience to future-proof both design and society at large. Therefore, allow me the pleasure of also honouring her here by sharing my award show speech for Bodil.

Honorary award

As the chairwoman, I have the great honour of presenting the Danish Design Council honorary award given by the Council as part of our work as an independent council and collective voice for leading Danish Design professionals.

We aim to safeguard the continued value creation through design by pushing the profession forward – conceiving and exploring new perspectives on design. Therefore, in that spirit, the honorary award is chosen through nominations from the Council members and deliberations in the prize committee and given to celebrate a long and profound contribution to design, manifesting the value creation for users and society.

So without further ado, it is an absolute pleasure to present the Danish Design Council honorary Award to Bodil Kjær, an extraordinary designer who embodies the above sentiment and who brilliantly develops elements of architecture to solve problems of functional and aesthetic nature. Or, as she recently put it:

> I am not a furniture designer; I am a designer of environments. I am concerned about solving problems of the kind that can be defined. I am concerned about delight and beauty rather than opulence and vulgarity – the words of Bodil Kjær in Wallpaper Magazines' recent portrait interview to celebrate her 90th birthday.
>
> *Porter (2022)*

Never afraid to find and follow her path, on the contrary, as a woman in a male-dominated world, she swam against the current and found her way and with that great international success and acclaim among her peers – including her iconic The Office Desk featured in several James Bond Movies.

Not only is The Office Desk a great icon and part of defining the Danish modern (and mid-century modern in general). It is also a perfect blend of aesthetics, functionality, and what happens when you, like Bodil, combine anthropology, engineering and architecture and use a cross-professional approach to amplify the final design. An essential inspiration is Bodil's international exposure, her trained eye for new trends within society and, thus, the need to design new solutions. In this case, Bodil spotted the new era of management with less hierarchy and more collaboration – as embodied by the design of The Office Desk.

Similarly, when technology advanced, Bodil quickly explored new materials, such as plexiglass. Across her extensive portfolio of elements, she has consistently achieved a unique perspective driving the profession forward and bridging between the international and the Danish, the current and the heritage, furniture and industrial design – always with problem-solving at the core. Thus it is a great pleasure to award Bodil with the honorary award on behalf of The Danish Design Council and say thank you for all the great work you continue to do.

Question: What words pop into your mind when thinking of Danish design?

References

Carl Hansen & Søn (n.d.). Bodil Kjær. https://www.carlhansen.com/en/en/designers/bodil-kjar

Chouinard, Y. (2006). *Let My People Go Surfing: The Education of a Reluctant Businessman*. Penguin.

Danmarks Radio (2010). Poul Henningsen (1894–1967). https://www.dr.dk/skole/dansk/mellemtrin/poul-henningsen-1894-1967

Harlang, C. (2007). *Danish Architecture since 1754*. Arkitektens Forlag.

Klint, K. (1930). Undervisningen i møbeltegning ved Kunstakademiet [artikel om møbeltegning].

Mollerup, P. (2019). *Dansk Design ganske enkelt.* Gyldendal.

Porter, J. (2022). Bodil Kjær at 90: 'I am not a furniture designer; I am a designer of environments'. *Wallpaper Magazine*. https://www.wallpaper.com/design/bodil-kjaer-90-interview

Rasmussen, S. E. (1960). *Experiencing Architecture,* Second Edition. The MIT Press.

3

SYSTEMS DESIGN IN THE ANTHROPOCENE

We always believed that we could keep extracting from the Earth without facing any consequences. We thought that our planet's well-being was static or at least not impacted by the actions of humans. Science now makes a clear case: It is not true. Our actions have consequences for our planet's well-being which in turn impacts our ability as humans to thrive on the planet we call home.

That marks a scientific revolution and before before delving into the design of specific subsystems, let's first take a closer look at that scientific revolution. It is the battle for change in the scientific paradigm we are in the midst of. To understand the dire problems we are in and, most importantly, to find the necessary tools to enable the solutions, we need to scrutinise the scientific paradigm our systems are operating within or the rules implemented. We need to examine the lenses through which we perceive the world, including all of our systems and thus actions. Inspired by Thomas Kuhn and his analysis of the structure of historical shifts and revolutions in scientific paradigms (Kuhn, 1962), we must speed up the realisation that the current way of operating does not hold ground. It is about time we make way for the new scientific paradigm and truly realise and internalise that we have entered the Anthropocene.

If we look back, traditionally, scientific revolutions happened when new knowledge emerged. When despite continued efforts of the existing systems enabled by the prevailing scientific paradigm, the balance tipped at an inflexion point. The new paradigm had proved itself so effective that it could

DOI: 10.4324/9781003261018-3

no longer be denied and became the dominant paradigm. That struggle is precisely what Thomas Kuhn (1962) describes as:

> Why should a change of paradigm be called a revolution? In the face of the vast and essential differences between political and scientific development, what parallelism can justify the metaphor that finds revolutions in both? One aspect of the parallelism must already be apparent. A growing sense inaugurates political revolutions, often restricted to a segment of the political community, that existing institutions have ceased adequately to meet the problems posed by an environment that they have in part created. In much the same way, scientific revolutions are inaugurated by a growing sense, again often restricted to a narrow subdivision of the scientific community, that an existing paradigm has ceased to function adequately in the exploration of an aspect of nature to which that paradigm itself had previously led the way. In both political and scientific development, the sense of malfunction that can lead to crisis is prerequisite to revolution.

The fact that that the Earth is round rather than flat represented one of those historical tipping points when a scientific revolution led to a new scientific paradigm changing our systemic logic within science and society as a whole. And while it seems like an extreme comparison at first, if you look closer, you will discover sufficient similarities to make that scientific shift comparable to the scientific revolution we are currently experiencing.

First, both situations represent an advancement in human knowledge. We went from a state of not knowing to knowing something: **The Earth is round. Our actions have consequences for our planet and, thus, our ability to thrive on it.** And in both cases, we have successfully gathered and analysed the data to prove as much.

That we improved our knowledge is a great achievement. Therefore, our ability to detect, understand and acknowledge the crisis we are in and, not least, our role in the causes that have brought us so close to the planetary boundaries, serves as a testament to our scientific achievement. The knowledge of the fatal consequences if we go beyond the tipping points and cross the planetary edge is a scientific success story proving our continued ability to learn and explore our context.

I call it the planetary edge because, much like a car crossing the boundaries of the road, we find ourselves on the trajectory of crossing the limits of our planet's capabilities. This is similar to falling off the cliff, leading to the crash of our civilisation. To evade the situation, it is of utmost importance that we reach the inflection point of the new scientific revolution that acknowledges the impact, responsibility and opportunity we as humans have. We must use this understanding as a guiding star for our thoughts, actions and systems.

I am afraid that the window for timely action has already closed. However, hope is not lost. Now, more than ever, it is critical to create systemic change and adopt a new approach that incentivises the well-being of our people and our planet. This new approach not only prioritises short-term gains but also long-term value creation.

So how do we accomplish this? Well, much like previous scientific revolutions represented improvements, they thus also represented change. **And change, by definition, means leaving something behind.** Change means to do something different than what we were doing before, regardless if that change is in thoughts, actions or systems. Some will prefer the safe and convenient structures of the existing and see it as if their survival depends on avoiding the scientific revolution because unless agile, the new paradigm will make their thoughts, actions and systems a thing of the past and at worst obsolete.

As shared in the essay "A fairytale of complexity" in Chapter 10, Machiavelli's insights from *The Prince* prove valuable. They help us to understand the difficulties of introducing a new order before or during the inflection point, reflecting the thoughts of Thomas Kuhn (1962):

> In science, as in the playing card experiment, novelty emerges only with difficulty, manifested by resistance, against a background provided by expectation.

This is particularly true when the change is not just a new way of optimising within an existing paradigm but instead a fundamentally new overarching logic that affects our view of not just an individual system but the entire world. Similar to the historical the scientific revolutions, we have been engaged in the battle between scientific paradigms for quite some time. Let us consider the case of Exxon, dating back to 1977, hiding scientific evidence about climate change (Hall, 2015), exemplifying essential learning from Thomas Kuhn's perspective on the structures of scientific revolutions that there can only be one winner. One scientific paradigm guides our systems, and so far, we have yet to reach the inflection point of the new scientific paradigm and truly understand its meaning in our thoughts, actions and systems.

Let us reflect on the fact that since 2015 when The Paris Agreement (United Nations, 2015) was agreed upon and perceived as a global inflection point for mitigating climate change, with both nations and businesses widely communicating a commitment to it, the leading international banks continue to finance fossil fuels heavily and have made new investments in the amount of $4 trillion since the Paris Agreement was decided (Bloomberg, 2021). And even more alarming is, collectively, we are systemically encouraging it with the International Energy Agency IEA reporting all-time high public subsidies towards fossil fuels at USD$1 trillion in 2022.

Therefore, we still have a long way to go in supporting the new scientific paradigm and understanding the consequences and opportunities our past, present and future actions hold. Undeniably, we are headed for a catastrophic crash of our civilisation if we do not fundamentally redesign our systems based on the new scientific paradigm, making sure that our systems are designed to work for rather than against society. As such, a key point that has emerged with the advent of the Anthropocene and the new scientific paradigm, carbon emissions and their equivalents are a cost that should be accounted for. This approach aligns with the logical reasoning and embodies a critical step towards creating a sustainable future.

Yet while the new scientific paradigm is brought by improvement in our knowledge, our overall global improvement from the previous industrial revolutions does not seem to be doing us any favours in regards to reaching that inflection point and introducing the new paradigm benefitting people and the planet because while our industrial and technological advancements have brought us great things, it has also created a social structure so strong it has proved highly resilient and more difficult to change than in the case of any scientific revolutions we have seen before. Never before have global wealth and power been centralised to so few actors, which is also why economist and creator of the Donut economic model Kate Raworth highlights that decentralisation must be part of the solution.

While we usually consider resilience a good attribute, as highlighted here, its significance lies in how we have designed our systems. Systems are designed for resilience and to uphold themselves, which is why systems design holds so much importance. It is unfortunate that we have ended up designing our systems based on the old scientific paradigm as it influences the behaviour of our systems. However, as we explore based on Niklas Luhmann's systems theory later in this chapter, we discover that systems are not static. Instead, they are adaptive to their surroundings and able to change. So we need to ensure that the adoption aligns with the fundamental logic we want to control our way of being, a logic that benefits our global population and enables us to operate within our planetary boundaries.

Time is up for exploitation

As of now, we find ourselves fixed in the old scientific paradigm. Thus, we must systematically acknowledge the reality of Anthropocene and the irreversible consequences our actions will entail. In short, time is slipping away and we must waste no further. Thankfully glimpses of the new paradigm are starting to emerge, not least brought on by recent crises from COVID-19 and the energy and materials crisis accelerated by Russia's invasion of Ukraine in 2022. These crises have served as wake-up calls, highlighting that change is inevitable and the things we have taken for granted as natural ways of being could be very different. Thus, they have prompted reflection on how we live, our dependence on energy and our connection (or lack thereof) with each other and nature. So as horrendous as these crises have been, like an earthquake, they have helped crack open the ground and enabled the light of the new paradigm to shine through.

The new scientific paradigm acknowledges the connection between humans actions, consequences for our planet, and the subsequent impact on our ability to thrive on our planet. Therefore, the new logic for our societal system could simply be summarised as: **Is it creating improvement for people while staying within our planetary boundaries?** Yes or no. This simple question serves as the lens through which the new paradigm urges us to assess our thoughts, actions and systems.

Returning to the struggle between the existing and the necessary change, it become clear that it is indeed a fight in which there can only be one winner: Either the old way of exploitation or the new path of regeneration. We can't have it both ways, and that might be the most challenging reality to accept the new scientific paradigm's truth: Our actions have consequences for our planet and, thus, our ability to thrive within it. This realisation underscores the fact that we are into the Anthropocene era.

This is another reason why it is valuable to compare our "old" current scientific paradigm, which conflicts with our entry into the Anthropocene, to our historical scientific revolutions. We need to understand this as a fundamental change and how it affects the logic that governs our thoughts, actions and systems. It is neither an optimisation of the existing paradigm nor a convergence of various trends influencing our actions.

The fact that sustainability is becoming a mega trend and that more individuals and more organisations are actively working on creating solutions is encouraging. Not just from a scientific but from a business and innovation standpoint, it helps us reach that inflexion point quicker. Still, we need to be careful to avoid seeing sustainability as one way to optimise existing businesses by doing a little less harm. As such an approach will reinforce the existing paradigm rather than paving the way for the new. Unfortunately, we have already seen far too many misguided examples from both circular economy and technology. Instead it is a fundamental new logic that we must consider regardless of what we are pursuing to avoid crashing as a civilisation. The same goes when you hear well-meaning business leaders calling our dire situation a leadership crisis. Yes, leadership is essential when looking at the causes that have brought us here and how we will turn the necessary change into improvement. But we must never forget that the crisis is rooted in natural science; it is not "just" social science, and while social science and ideology might play a part in contributing to different solutions, we must always be able to see and analyse it from a perspective of natural science, recognising that our planetary boundaries are determined by its principles.

Therefore, as explored in Chapter 4: The troubles we are in, and Chapter 9: The Circular Way, my methodology is based on the planetary boundaries and our ability to operate within our natural science-based limits. However, we must seek to change within our social constructions and leverage the insights of social science to achieve this. While the problems are very real in our natural world, it does not change the fact that our social systems have been the primary driving force leading us towards our current predicament.

Hence, I will touch upon further in this chapter the importance of reclaiming growth as a tool rather than a goal. By doing so, it help us reach our purpose and deliver value, that is, improvement for our global citizens while staying within our planetary boundaries. It is crucial to acknowledge that improvement for our global citizens at large is a socially constructed goal intentionally chosen. However, our planetary boundaries, grounded in natural science, enable us to fulfil our social aspirations and that cannot be changed.

So, we need to make room and listen to the scientists, while encouraging them to move out of their comfort zone to increase the use of scientific methods to analyse not just the problems but also the opportunities. Scientists can also help society cope with the increased uncertainty as we move from a known past to the unknown future. This is where design comes in handy in its ability to cultivate the power to imagine. However, we must remember another essential learning from the historical, scientific revolutions; while they have all seemed daunting and unsafe initially, they have all improved prosperity for society and individual citizens in a way not even imaginable in the old paradigm. And there is every reason that a similar transformation will occur once we reach the inflection point and enter the new scientific paradigm. As we truly understand our interconnectedness with nature, we will realise that caring for our planet and taking responsibility for our actions is not just an agenda of doing less, of deduction and degrowth but of growing the things we value to create a regenerative society benefitting people within our planetary boundaries.

That is why I titled the coming section "Reclaiming growth". I believe that growth is neither good nor bad; what matters is what and how we grow it (hint: GDP as we know it today – should not be it), and that comes down to the logic or perspectives through which we see the world and design our systems with. But before we examine the tools, let's first remember the vital lesson from previous scientific revolutions: They have all brought unimaginable improvement within the previous paradigm. This offers an opportunity to reflect upon what we want to move towards. To aid you in this reflection, I invite you to engage in a small exercise.

What do you want?

We have created significant improvement and technological advancement, so much so that the great question today is: When we can do anything, what do you choose to do, and what do you choose not to do? Hopefully, in the future, that question will be guided by the principles of the new paradigm, based on whether or not it is contributing to the improvement for people while staying within our planetary boundaries.

The scientific revolution stands on its own, yet it emphasises the need for systemic change in the structures of society. The existing system's struggle for survival is why it has taken us so long to reach the inflection point for the new scientific paradigm and acknowledge the planetary impact of our actions. However, referencing previous scientific revolutions, such as learning that the Earth is round and not flat, it becomes apparent that such revelation did not stop us from leading our way of life. We continued to live in our homes, ate our food and carried on with our routine activities. However, such discoveries changed our perspective, mindset and the fundamentals on which we build our thoughts, ultimately leading to innovation and improvement in a way better than what was possible in the old paradigm.

So where does that leave us? It leaves us in dire need of the new paradigm planting its roots within our society, our systems, our thoughts and our actions. However, it is not just a matter about saving us from the crash of our civilisation; It should be a vision that fills us with anticipation and excitement. Rather than just leaving aspects behind, we should actively choose what we want to achieve – a better world. This is indeed the opportunity we have at hand.

Therefore, here I urge you to learn from design and take the time to care and create a space of intentionality. Start by asking yourself what a better world might look like. Consider what we would like to leave behind, what values we aspire to incorporate and the direction in which we want to progress.

To provide some insight, I have provided my answers below. However, I encourage everyone to answer the questions themselves, making the transition more tangible and hopefully less daunting. But, most importantly, it is an initial step in moving from despair towards repair and ultimately toward reimagining.

I had the opportunity to employ the exercise while teaching a combined master's degree in Design Engineering at Imperial College and Royal College of Arts. It sparked a fruitful conversation of purpose and desirability, providing both inspiration and guidance to the world we aspire to inhabit. Therefore, I encourage you first to create your own vision and then engage in sharing and discussing it with others.

What do I want to leave behind?

Most importantly, it is crucial to abandon the idea that our actions do not have consequences for our planet and, thus, our ability to thrive. I also want to leave behind the current success and growth narrative of more is better and that value is best measured in quantitative monetary terms. Lastly, I want to leave behind our current waste-producing system fuelled by exploitation, thoughtlessness, lack of purpose, and connectedness to each other and our planet. And I would happily do away with our air pollution and traffic congestion as well.

What do I want to take with me?

Our improvement, our ability to create and our extraordinary force of innovation are all things that I want to embrace. I want to bring our knowledge, technology, and ability to reflect and design as well as our values and love for each other, life and surroundings. On a more practical note, I want to ensure that we keep the tangible assets, be it buildings, infrastructure, etc., and reuse all of the embodied carbon by transformation rather than demolition.

What do I want to move towards?

I want to move towards increased connectedness with ourselves, each other and our planet. I want to move towards a higher purpose, guiding and infusing us with value and a sense of belonging: What we do matters and creates value.

I want to move towards thoughtfulness to improve mental and material hygiene and well-being because we have left behind all those quick fixes that were clogging up our minds as well as our physical spaces. Instead, we must make room for those things that matter, make us happy and create value in our life. But of course, just like in all the other scientific revolutions, the future beyond the inflexion point will surely be even more incredible than I can imagine yet.

Understanding our systems

Technology or behavioural change: A common debate revolves around rather technology or behavioural change holds the key to keeping us within the planetary boundaries. But we must remember that regardless of whether we are looking at human behaviour, new technology or a product – they are all part of a larger context – that is part of one or more systems. This context significantly influences our effectiveness of our actions and solutions, regardless of our good attentions. Therefore, to succeed at creating prosperity rather than despair, we must look at the broader context and the systems driving our thoughts, actions and organisations and reclaim power and use our systems as they were intended. The systems must be employed as a way of organising our resources efficiently to solve our problems and ensure societal improvement.

Systemic design and analysis are thus necessary to achieve long-term improvement rather than short-term quick fixes that merely address the problems at the surface. To broaden the understanding of systems theory, I will draw the insights of the German sociologist Niklas Luhmann, who propounded this concept in his book *Social Systems*. In it, he described our modern society, how we reduce complexity and obtain the ability to operate as a society through systems. Whilst a sociologist, his theory of systems was inspired by nature, particularly the notion of autopoiesis, originally developed by Chilean biologists Humberto Maturana and Francisco Varela (Cull, 2000). So inspired by nature's systems, their ability to reproduce and adapt, and their resilience, Luhmann viewed modern society as a living system with society as the encompassing system consisting of several subsystems such as the political, educational, arts, media and not least the financial system.

With society organised much like nature, each subsystem specialises in its unique function, contributing to the improvement of the society. Each system reduces complexity to operate according to its logic, such as the political system operating through the power dynamics, media news or non-news and the financial system based on profit and non-profit. Therefore, a key element in Luhmann's systems theory emerges. Each subsystem works by having a unique logic, and perceiving and interacting everything through that narrow logic. **By design, the individual subsystems are not balanced** but meant to be part of a larger "ecosystem" of subsystems that together embody society as the encompassing system embedding them all, thus creating balance.

To understand our problems and turn them into opportunities, we need to introspect the logic guiding our point of view. If we are unaware of the logic our systems are based on and thus instil in our culture and societal thinking, we risk operating blindfolded in new territory. I think we can all, by relating to the metaphor of the blindfold, agree that trying to find our way blindfolded is not the quickest way to move forward, and even worse, we risk getting lost and taking wrong turns. French Sociologist Pierre Bourdieu refers to such setbacks as symbolic violence (Bourdieu & Wacquant, 1992). This suggests trying to beat the system at its own game without knowing the rules thus ending up doing the exact opposite, instead reinforcing the existing structures we were trying to change. Without being mindful of the current logic or, as Bourdieu would call it, rules of the game, we end up inadvertently acknowledging them as the natural and only possible rules without realising they are social constructions currently ensuring that we are playing a game with rules rigged against us and thus against global human improvement.

An unfortunate example of accepting an unlevel playing field, through unnatural and rigged rules, is the emissions of carbon equivalents. For too long, we have accepted that the benefits of pollution and emitting carbon equivalents are privatised whilst the costs are socialised and for society to hold, benefitting one subsystem (the financial system) but not society at large. This has nothing to do with a free market; on the contrary, fossil fuels are still heavily subsidised. As such, a structural imbalance has been created, and our system no longer works for the benefit of society but for the interest of one subsystem. This happens when a subsystem prevails; its logic becomes so dominant that we forget to question it. This is also why design's inherent ability to ask questions and go outside the norm is essential; that is referencing Donna Haraway and this book's manifest for Design in The Anthropocene: To stay with the trouble.

Reclaiming growth as a tool

> We introduced the European Green Deal as Europe's new growth strategy – one that aims to transform the EU into a fair and prosperous society, with a modern, resource-efficient and competitive economy that emits zero net emissions of greenhouse gases in 2050 and achieves economic growth decoupled from resource use. Recent extreme weather events and the coronavirus pandemic have exposed the greatest challenges of our time: to keep ourselves and our planet, but also our economy, healthy.
>
> *European Commission (2019)*

Debunking the green growth myth has become increasingly popular, especially among climate activists. However, I am afraid that it will not be possible to cater to our global population whilst staying within the planetary boundaries in a timely manner if we do not use growth as a tool to drive human ingenuity. So instead, I believe that, as President of the European Commission Ursula Von Leyden highlighted in the above quote, we must embrace growth as a driving force for improvement rather than exclude growth entirely. But first, we have to reclaim and redefine our use and understanding of growth. We need to start seeing growth as a tool for problem-solving and improvement for our global society rather than a means to drive profits in the financial sector. We must intentionally steer growth towards being the tool for improvement it should be and ensure that we prioritise the right objectives and adopt appropriate methods. As such, taking inspiration from nature and mimicking nature's principles implies that growth is a part of the solution – through a different kind of growth than we are used to. This entails embracing a real, tangible growth that allows us to meet the needs of our global population and, most importantly, ensure that prosperity is equitably distributed. It embodies a growth that is different from what is currently defined as GDP (gross domestic product). Instead, we can use growth as a positive influence on climate change, becoming a mitigating factor rather than an accelerating factor to climate change. The Danish Design Heritage imparts valuable lessons, notably the intentionality and ability to use a social purpose to design. Moreover, it prioritises measuring success based on the use value of a design rather than its short-term exchange value.

Just imagine what we could do if we successfully decouple future economic growth from the excessive use of virgin materials, land use and CO_2 equivalents, currently an inevitable precondition for development. If successful, we can kickstart the development of new, regenerative societies – a goal brilliantly described in regeneration expert Laura Storm's essay in Chapter 5: Partnering with life – the essence of regeneration. It takes the combination of new ideas and a change of mind (hence the need for the new scientific paradigm) to redesign the system and start designing for regeneration rather than exploitation.

First, it is about using growth as a tool rather than a goal. Second, it involves recognising the need for differentiation when it comes to growth on a macro level; where the degrowth movement proves correct regarding redistribution. It is inevitable that certain sectors and businesses that were part of the old regime of exploitation, will become stranded. However, the growth in other industries and regions means we can include the people and the tangible assets of the stranded businesses there. What might a coal plant become in its next life? Where can the skills of the workers come to use in another industry? To be clear, a reduction is very much part of the answer. But, to find innovative solution, we need to strike a balance between reducing negative aspects and promoting positive growth while staying within the planetary boundaries.

While degrowth might not be the answer, it is correct to challenge the current measurement of GDP, which is seen as the overarching goal rather than a tool to create improvement for people. It is crucial to reclaim the notion of growth as part of the new paradigm. We need human ingenuity to make better solutions breaking down the barriers of our existing system and allowing the lights of the new paradigm to shine through so that we as a collective can start seeing and believing the new and improved world. Thus, we must begin fighting for something better than today. If we channel our collective efforts forward with nature's intelligence, we can anticipate greater accomplishments. In that sense, and what might seem a bit provocative, is that to me, degrowth comes to represent repair or doing a little less bad, not reimagining and regeneration, as explored in Chapter 8: The purpose of business is to solve problems. We cannot limit ourselves to the necessary solution space of regeneration if we are to cater to our global population within the planetary boundaries. Instead, we must fight consumerism, exchange value and the imbalance of the financial system being the guiding force. We must also transcend the old scientific paradigm that fails to accept the direct relation between our actions and our well-being on Earth. Fight it by redoing that balance and using our creativity to create a better world. Human-centred design and growth are tools to achieve our goal of creating value for people while staying within the planetary boundaries.

Of course, our current situation falls short of where we ought to be. The urgency to address the pressing issues is evident and we need to act at an accelerated pace. And so far, our progress is inadequate. Instead creating incremental change at a slow pace, and we have lagged behind in terms of innovation height and truly changing things around. This became painfully obvious with the 2022 update from the IPCC: Climate Change 2022: Impacts, Adaptation and Vulnerability (IPCC, 2022). The report highlights that whilst the window of opportunity is not yet closed, it is getting narrower. We have only three years to bend the curve and truly improve things. And so far, we have not been doing well; in 2021, we have released more greenhouse gases than any year before. It also clarifies that we cannot continue to grow things based on the metrics and logic we are used to. Again, that raises the question if we should give up on growth as a tool to ensure improvement altogether. I don't believe so. First, growth has been a powerful means of achieving progress. If we are to deliver the necessary improvement promptly, I believe growth and capitalism can be powerful tools. However it is important to correctly positioned as a subsystem working as part of a larger group of subsystems for society at large and not the other way around. How can you not believe in growth and the opportunity to do more good rather than just reducing harm when you come from Denmark, a small country of not much more than five million citizens but with a positive global footprint within renewable energy, energy efficiency and water treatment, among other things?

Because growth is a natural process that occurs in trees, children, and living organisms like fungi, it is inherent in our existence. One might even say that growing up is a beautiful part of who we are. However, it is necessary to understand that there is such a thing as too much growth, and nothing grows forever. Our challenge lies in keeping things artificially alive beyond their natural limits. In that sense, plastics are both a tangible and metaphorical example of how we as humans have become successful – going back to the critical ethical challenge of our time: **How do we differentiate between what we can (everything) and what we should?** To answer that question, we need to adopt the new guiding principle of the new paradigm: Does it benefit humanity while staying within the planetary boundaries? And only when growth helps us achieve that, is it of value. So, it is a systematic failure that the financial system rather than society is the encompassing system. The consequence is a lack of balance instead leading systems and, in particular, the financial system to suboptimal outcomes, prioritising profit or no profit rather than fulfilling its purpose of solving our societal problems in synergy with other subsystems.

Calibrating our systems

The financial system as the encompassing system and the focus on profit or no profit was never the intention of the critical capitalistic thought leader Adam Smith. His influential book *The Wealth of Nations* and his notion of the rational Economic Man played a crucial part in creating the role capitalism and the financial system have in society today, and thus, a symbol of the necessary change. But it was never his aim that it should be the only guiding system but one of several. However, Smith played a crucial part in contributing to the problems we are in today. Driven by his desire for recognition, he went ahead to prove himself within the scientific community and establish economics as a "real" science similar to the natural sciences like physics and mathematics. The problem is that while both are sciences, there are fundamental differences between natural and social sciences. Still, when it comes to economics, thanks to Adam Smith, we treat the economy more like a natural science than the social science it is, and thus for a very long time, we forgot to reflect and ask questions if it was creating value not just for the financial system but society at large, exactly as it was intended to do. In effect, we have treated our financial markets as forces of nature, while treating the planetary boundaries as social constructions. In reality, it should be the other way around.

It means that things could be different. Our economy is built primarily on social constructions, not on inherent natural states. The concept of rational economic man is the prime example. Unfortunately, this has led us to forgot that we have the power to change the system and correct our priorities. Another critical problem with the rational economic man is that it assumes he has no dependencies and he can solely focus on his own needs without consequences and that his surroundings did not affect his well-being. When that is not true from a natural science perspective. Instead, we have created a social construction that is not aligned with our biological systems. The fact is that we are interconnected with our environment and our actions have consequences for our planet and that, in return, affects our ability to thrive on the Earth.

The result is that the system has lost its intended purpose. Instead of creating the best solutions for societal problems, we currently have a system out of balance and thus, on the contrary, limits and, at worst, prohibits necessary problem-solving. Hence, we are in the midst of the dire planetary crisis and long neglected to act. So our climate crisis is a testament to the systemic failure of our social system. The system no longer prioritises societal improvement, but focusses on profit maximisation only. So far, we have been failing on a massive scale. One example is the huge amount of waste continuously generated by design. Another example is the failure of our food systems. They contribute to significant CO_2 emissions and produce excessive wastes, while a large part of our population remains hungry. Every day, millions of children go to bed hungry and malnourished. According to The United Nations World Food Programme, every 10th second, a child dies from malnutrition, and more than three million children die of hunger annually. To make matters worse, it is not because we globally do not have enough food or produce enough. It is due to local food shortages resulting from how our food systems are structured, leaving children to die in one part of the system while globally throwing away 17% of all food produced (World Food Programme, n.d.).

So, how do we reinstate that balance to reclaim growth as the tool that creates value for people within our planetary boundaries, rather than driven by short-term financial gains only? While I am not against capitalism, two changes must take place before it can once again play the societal role of creating improvement for people at large. First, we must reach the inflection point for the new scientific paradigm and truly realise the effects of our actions and the realm of the planetary boundaries. Second, the financial system should be considered as one of many systems that operate and help sustain our overall societal system rather than being the dominant system guided by its own interest. And until we achieve this shift, no amount of technology nor circular economy solutions will truly address the problem. What matters is what and how we grow if we are to survive in the Anthropocene era. It requires a systemic change and shift in our approach, ensuring our thoughts, actions and organisations create value for people within the planetary boundaries. As Irish author Oscar Wilde (1892) rightly puts it:

> The cynic knows the price of everything and the value of nothing.

Interview Nicolaj Reffstrup//GANNI

> The test of first-rate intelligence is the ability to hold two opposite ideas in mind at the same time and still retain the ability to function. One should, for example, be able to see that things are hopeless yet be determined to make them otherwise.
>
> *Fitzgerald (1936)*

A treasured quote that has always resonated with me is from F. Scott Fitzgerald's essay collection *The Crack-Up*, written in 1937. Although it may not directly address climate change, it nonetheless clearly represents the situation that we are in today and what we must strive to do. It reminds us to be aware of the significant challenges that we face and our continuing endeavours to overcome them. Nicolaj and Ditte Reffstrup, with their fashion company GANNI, represent that sentiment. Being incredibly aware of the severeness of our problems and the role that the fashion industry plays in that – yet continuing to insist on making it otherwise by minimising GANNI'S negative environmental footprint and maximising the positive impact. They do this by embracing both new technologies and solutions, by experimenting and collaborating with customers and followers on making climate change more tangible and empowering them to act. This makes GANNI a modern-day story of Danish Design Heritage combining sustainability with desirability as Copenhagen's most successful fashion brand. Nicolaj graciously agreed to share his thoughts on the vast problems we face and the urgency to act while working relentlessly to lead by example through GANNI.

D: Describe the world you would design?

N: The dream scenario is that we design a society that tweaks people to bring out the best in us. This would create a situation where opportunistic motivation could benefit everyone.

I believe that humankind is fundamentally built opportunistically. And I act just as opportunistically. Unfortunately, many of our actions have shown that we counteract not only each other but ourselves. Unfortunately, this has resulted in our society becoming egotistical. We need to rethink our society's structure, model and norms. We must structure our society in a new way based on the principles of circularity rather than expansion, extraction and materialistic items that give us a volatile feeling of happiness.

My interest in sustainability and circularity grew when I studied philosophy and economy and learned about game theory: Prisoner's Dilemma. At a certain point, I had an epiphany that we will never be able to solve our complex problems. It can feel overwhelming, and when genuinely diving into facts about our current situation, it often feels impossible to solve, but that is precisely why we must act.

However, it is challenging to determine the best course of action. As humankind, we are our most beautiful when evolving, inventing, and expanding our world. In recent years, we have experienced extreme exponential growth. With that comes a significant amount of accumulated knowledge and technology that enables us to do great things for the planet and people. However, we often degenerate when we reach the top and prioritise short-term gains over long-term regeneration.

D: I wonder quite a bit about how much of our problems relating to our behaviour are natural and how much is due to social constructions that could potentially be changed. Do you believe we could reclaim the notion of growth as being not a goal but a tool to drive sustainable development, perhaps inspired by Kate Raworth's doughnut economy?

N: Yeah, the challenge is to decouple us from our current system, and I like Kate Raworth's effort to do so. I am afraid that the sub-optimisation we see in prisoner's dilemma is a part of human nature. However, when you read Hans Rosling's book *Factfullness*, he describes the original primitive human as living in circular harmony, so we probably have it somewhere within us.

But the difficult question is then: How do we create the framework to activate that part of us? The catch is that while the market economy is bringing out the worst of us, it is also the key driver for development. Thus, the dream scenario is that we design a society that tweaks people to bring out the best in us. This would create a situation where opportunistic motivation could benefit everyone. One example is making sustainable options more accessible and affordable, ultimately benefitting us all. That is also why I believe in the idea carbon tax. Using the financial incentives and penalties is an effective way to regulate human behaviour, at least in the current system. But hacking our current system and behavioural patterns is a difficult task to carry out.

However, I do not doubt that we can move mountains if we all work together. Unfortunately, humans tend to think on a short-term basis. We have become significantly individualised and need more focus on the big picture. So we must start viewing ourselves as part of a larger context and design a world where we understand our history and consider the future, creating a better future for all.

D: Do we then not need to create a new vision? One that is not built on the current system and its embodied contradictions between individual and collectivism and short and long term?

N: Yes, and from my point of view, that is what we have politicians for. Like German sociologist Niklas Luhmann's systems theory and binary logic, I dream that politicians can take long-term visionary decisions and regulate what is difficult for other binary systems, such as the economic system, to do. However, that also sets high requirements for the political system. Conditions that they currently have difficulty fulfilling.

D: What pops into your mind when thinking of Danish design?

N: In my mind, Danish design is a representation of one of the world's best societal structures, and as such, our societal structure is an embedded part of Danish design. One example is that Denmark is known for having a relatively small gap between rich and poor, with a mindset of creating a system that distributes its wealth and other benefits relatively equally which translates to how Danish design is price and quality. When creating a "good" product, you wouldn't compromise on the fundamental qualities, but at the same time, designers aren't interested in pricing their product too high. The same goes for us at GANNI. Despite wanting to be a high-end fashion brand, we have kept our prices reasonably low by international standards, or what you might call an "honest price point" or "democratic price point", which is a reflection of the society we are a part of.

D: Danish artist Poul Henningsen was both a successful designer and founded the magazine *Kritisk Revy* – a magazine dedicated to challenging the status quo in society. In GANNI, you do many projects that engage with the community. Do we need more designers to take part in shaping our culture like that today?

N: As part of the increasing development in our society, we have become more specialised than ever. This has allowed us to become even more skilled within our field of expertise. Unfortunately, there doesn't leave much room to be a multi-artist anymore. But it is still essential to bridge between art, culture, and society to make climate change tangible and enhance our connectedness with each other and our planet.

That is why I am proud of GANNI for our ongoing efforts in creating awareness about sustainability by developing innovative projects and exhibitions. These initiatives, though minor and sometimes even trivial, play a vital role in making sustainability more tangible. They bring back a sense of intimacy and purpose that is otherwise lacking in today's world.

Furthermore, the creations and exhibitions inspire and lead the change we want to see in the world. GANNI sets an example for future brands and individuals, encouraging them to participate. We shouldn't underestimate the importance of our actions, regardless of the scale. I would argue that it is just as essential to creating small initiatives that are tangible and easy for individuals to define. Breaking down the problems is manageable and makes it possible for individuals to relate to them.

Because when we personally connect with a situation, our experience of it becomes profound. This weekend, our children found a frog trapped in our backyard that had been for a while. After releasing the frog, it managed to jump a few times before passing away. This deeply affected my wife, my kids and me, almost bringing us to tears. We relaised that we rarely consider how many frogs die every day for natural reasons or from humans destroying the biodiversity and their natural habitats. The difference lies in our engagement and emotional connection through this personal experience. We tend to overlook the problems unless we experience them personally. But just because we cannot see them does not mean the problems do not exist.

D: Back to Kate Raworth, that correlates with her point on the importance of communicating in pictures rather than graphs only, right?

N: Yes. We need to create that connection, and images are a powerful tool. Imagine if CO_2 was red and sticky, then the problem would suddenly be very real. The physical appearance of the red and sticky CO_2 mass would force us to act and solve the problem immediately. Additionally, everyone would be interested in engaging in handling the issues. But because CO_2 is invisible and abstract, it becomes easy to forget that the problem still exists.

D: What motivates you to want to change the world for the better?

N: Personally, it gives me a sense of purpose to be a part of making the world a better place for the upcoming generations. It can often feel impossible to solve all the problems alone, but it is essential that everyone changes for the better.

As a global society, we are currently at an interesting phase. The increasing focus on our actions' negative impact on the climate has created a situation where companies and brands are starting to transform themselves. Some companies are genuinely motivated to take part in changing the world for the better. At the same time, other companies desire to establish a reputation for being socially and environmentally responsible. This results in an interesting opportunity, as there is a greater demand than supply for sustainable options. This will provide unique chances for new and existing market actors in the coming years.

D: Bigger demand than the available supply sounds like a great opportunity?

N: It is. I believe supply is about three years or so behind demand. Solutions are coming, but they have yet to be commercially available. Hopefully, they are coming soon because it is the CEO's agenda, and budgets exist, so those with solutions to offer excellent opportunities exist. That may also be why things are starting to change. A lot more people are beginning to work on creating sustainable solutions. And again, let's not forget that the business opportunity is gigantic. So, there is a purpose to be found and money to be made – it almost can't get any better for the modern human being.

For me personally, it has been nice in the sense that it brought me back to the bottom of Maslow's pyramid, fighting for our collective survival. This reminds me of what we started by discussing – how people are most beautiful on the way up. Perhaps we can use that and make sure the pyramid we climb is the one that allows us to thrive in unity across generations.

D: In GANNI, you have worked on reducing your negative impact and enhancing your positive impact for a long time. What actions are you most proud of?

N: I'm proud to see what we have accomplished with GANNI so far. We have had some very ambitious and holistic approaches. Even though it's challenging to work with sustainability in the fashion and textile industry, I'm deeply proud of the 44 sustainability initiatives we created in GANNI.

D: What do you still dream of doing?

N: I dream of building a fashion collection, meaning something new, fresh and relevant but at the same time honestly neutral or positive on impact, i.e. absolute sustainability rather than achieved through carbon quotas.

Nicolaj Reffstrup is an entrepreneur best known for Danish fashion house GANNI. GANNI was established in 2000, and Nicolaj and his wife, Ditte Reffstrup, acquired ownership of the Danish fashion label in 2009. Nicolaj served as CEO of GANNI until 2018. It is known for its environmentally responsible fashion and reinventing Scandinavian style, and Nicolaj continues to push the environmental agenda within GANNI, the broader industry, and society. Most recently, Nicolaj co-founded the climate tech venture fund Look Up Ventures to increase funding to green technology.

Question: What do you want to leave behind or take with you, and what do you want to move toward? (See chapter exercise for further explanation.)

References

Bourdieu, P., & Wacquant, L. J. D. (1992). *An Invitation to Reflexive Sociology*. The University of Chicago Press.

Brogger, T., & Marsh, A. (2021). *Big Banks Haven't Quit Fossil Fuel*. Bloomberg. https://www.bloomberg.com/news/articles/2021-10-25/big-banks-haven-t-quit-fossil-fuel-with-4-trillion-since-paris#xj4y7vzkg

Cull, J. (2000). *Living Systems: An Introductory Guide to the Theories of Humberto Maturana & Francisco Varela*. CreateSpace Independent Publishing Platform.

Fitzgerald, F. S. (1936). *The Crack-up*. New Directions Publishing Corp.

Hall, S. (2015). Scientific American, Exxon Knew about Climate Change almost 40 years ago. https://www.scientificamerican.com/article/exxon-knew-about-climate-change-almost-40-years-ago/

IPCC (2022). Climate Change 2022: Impacts, Adaptation and Vulnerability. https://www.ipcc.ch/report/sixth-assessment-report-working-group-ii/

Kuhn, S. T. (1962). *The Structure of Scientific Revolutions*. The University of Chicago Press.

Luhmann, N. A. (1984). *Social Systems*. Stanford University Press.

Smith, A. (1776). *A Wealth of Nations*. W. Strahan and T. Cadell.

European Commission (2019). Turning Challenge into Opportunity on the Course to Becoming the First Climate-Neutral Continent, 13 December. https://ec.europa.eu/commission/presscorner/detail/en/ac_19_6778

Wilde, O. (1892). *Lady Windemere's Fan*. London. Published in 2014 by Start Classics.

World Food Programme (n.d.). Enging Hunger. www.wfp.org/ending-hunger

4

THE TROUBLES WE ARE IN

> Be curious. And, however difficult life may seem, there is always something you can do and succeed at. It matters that you don't just give up.
>
> Stephen Hawking (Joseph, 2018)

I begin with the quote from Stephen Hawking because despite the alarming state of our challenges, there remains a glimmer of hope if we use our ingenuity and take swift, bold action – just like we have been able to in the past. The juggernaut of modernity spurred on by our ingenuity enabled us to fertilise our crops, the invention of the steam engine, the discovery of electricity, the large-scale production of iron and steel, and the unlocking of energy-dense oil reserves, quickly moving us towards the Anthropocene. The first and second industrial revolutions brought prosperity and well-being but also led to rapid changes in our planet's ecosystems and climate over a short period. People put rural and agrarian societies behind them in favour of urban, industrial life, where mechanised mass production was made possible, and labour demand rose quickly. Our use of fossil fuels soared, not least due to the tremendous source of power it is: "A single barrel of oil – about 42 gallons – can do about the same amount of work as a man labouring for 25,000 hours" (McKibben, 2022).

Many of the fundamental structures that shapes our life today were established during this era. They remained unchanged until the onset of the third industrial revolution in the 1980s. The advent of digitalisation has quickly replaced our analogue systems and exponentially accelerated the latest wave of globalisation, this digital revolution still continues.

As you read these words, it is likely that you find yourself in a city. Most of us reside in cities now, and even more are moving towards the urban areas

DOI: 10.4324/9781003261018-4

every day. As such, they significantly represent our modern way of living. They are indeed proof of humankind's most outstanding achievements, yet they also represent the paradigm we must transcend. They were built, renovated and expanded when resources and the labour supply appeared infinite and a powerful demonstration of humankind's seemingly victorious domestication of nature. What was once old and natural have been replaced with new and artificial, and the boundaries of locality have given way to globalisation. As such, cities represent both opportunity and problem. While they are great places for human ingenuity and the development of new ideas, they still demand changes in how we structure and design our cities and society.

Along the way, we stopped respecting our planet and caring for our resources, as evidenced by the current material scarcity and the energy crisis. We grew hyper-confident after the go-go years of industrialisation and globalisation, leading us to be careless with our production and consumption. We started seeing resources as abundant – even endless – and Earth as something that existed exclusively to serve our needs. "Industrialise or perish" was the motto we grew accustomed to during this mega-growth period, and so we did. While this approach yielded many positive outcomes, it also developed our addiction to fossil fuels, putting our civilisation at risk of perishing. Our current system is destructive, inefficient and irrational, yet ever so challenging to change.

Moreover, as the world population, urbanisation and prosperity rise, our need to find ways to reduce climate change and keep global warming in check is continuously accelerated. The key to returning our planet to a restorative and regenerative track is finding new ways to create value without CO_2-equivalent emissions and extracting new raw materials. That is to provide value for people while staying within our planetary boundaries. Industrialisation has undoubtedly led to progress, but it has also moved us into the Anthropocene. The science is clear: Our actions affect the planet, affecting our ability to thrive on earth.

> In short, in just the last fifty years, we have catapulted humanity and the planet out of the previous benevolent Holocene epoch and into the Anthropocene, a new geological period where biogeochemical conditions are dominated not by natural processes but by the palpable impact of human activity. Humans are, for the first time ever, the prime driver of large-scale climate change on the planet. All studies you may read about the Anthropocene epoch point to the unprecedented levels of destruction that we have caused in just five decades.
>
> *Figueres and Rivett-Carnac (2020)*

When Swedish chemist Svante Arrhenius made his groundbreaking discovery correlating the emission of CO_2 to the atmosphere from burning fossil fuels to the temperature rise, he laid the foundation for the goal set at COP21, the Paris Agreement, to limit our global temperatures increase to a maximum 2 degrees Celsius, preferably below 1.5 degrees Celsius (United Nations, 2015). Arrhenius could not have imagined how quickly and how much fossil fuel we would burn. While it is much concerning, it also demonstrates the potential and the capabilities of humankind. It gives hope that the best is yet to come if we start paying attention to what Arrhenius has been saying since 1896 and do the work to transform our systems towards prosperity.

The fact is that our actions have put us into the Anthropocene. When we began burning coal, we entered the first industrial revolution. Rising temperatures of two degrees might not seem significant, but try to recall a past fever in your body and the discomfort that it had created. For example, a 1.5-degree increase in either body or planetary temperature is uncomfortable but can be mitigated; 3 degrees or above are extremely dangerous and potentially deadly. While this book does not delve into the facts of climate change, it draws upon the great work of experts such as Johan Rockstrøm, Christiana Figueres, Vaclav Smil, David Wallace-Wells and the IPCC. I strongly recommend to read their writings. However, I need to explain the concepts of absolute sustainability and the planetary boundaries here.

Absolute sustainability

> It happened so fast. In just two generations, humanity has overwhelmed Earth's capacity to continue stably supporting our world. We've gone from being a small world on a big planet to a big world on a small planet.
>
> *Rockstrøm and Mattias (2015)*

We must care about what we take from our planet and what we contribute to the climate in absolute terms. Nonetheless, we often overlook the absolute numbers when evaluating the problem, and its potential solutions. When will a particular technology be available? How long will it take to scale it? At what cost in terms of embedded energy and resource consumption? And if scaled, how much can the solution deliver regarding absolute sustainability? The fundamental problem is that, to a large extent, we believe we can wait to act on mitigating climate change until we are ready for it. That time is on our side when it no longer is. Instead, we must act boldly, and we must act now. Mother Earth doesn't respond to populism but adheres to the laws of physics. We are yet to see the full effect of entering the Anthropocene, particularly the unstable climate it represents. Considering the vast problems such as COVID-19 and the increase of natural disasters worldwide, including the devastating floods in Germany and wildfires in California, we must exercise caution before disregarding the magnitude of nature's power. One scary fact is that in 2020 alone, twice as much land was burned in California compared to any cases reported in the history of the state.

Fighting climate change is not about magic; it requires grounded understanding of measurable reality. The climate crisis is physical, with absolute boundaries monitored through the natural sciences. It transcends political or moral beliefs and is dependent on the principles of physics and mathematics to mitigate risks. As mentioned in the previous chapter on systems design in the Anthropocene, social constructions have driven us towards the physical boundaries and that new social constructions are needed to fix them. There are absolute boundaries that we must be aware of and respect.

As daunting as they indeed are, we need to get acquainted with a few numbers. Professor Vaclav Smil rightly points out that size matters, and we must enhance our understanding of both the magnitude of the problem and the potential size of solutions. Mitigating climate change is literally by orders of magnitude, the biggest challenge we have ever faced:

> The McKinsey Global Institute, in a highly conservative estimate, puts the cost at $275 trillion between 2021 and 2050. That is roughly $9.2 trillion a year, compared with the 2021 global economic product of $94 trillion. Such numbers imply an annual expenditure of about 10 percent of today's world economic product. And because the world's low-income countries could not carry such burdens, affluent nations would have to devote on the order of 15 to 20 percent of their annual economic product to the task. Such shares are comparable only to the spending that was required to win World War II.
>
> *Smil (2022)*

If there is one message to emphasise, it is that mitigating climate change presents the biggest challenge we have ever faced. It transcends even the achievement of putting a man on the moon, requiring thousands of moonshots. To succeed in overcoming it, we must recognise the magnitude of transitioning from a resource-exploiting fossil fuel-driven society. The great thing is that there is room for many different solutions as long as they help us move towards staying within the planetary boundaries. One key goal is to reduce atmospheric carbon dioxide levels to a safe threshold of 350 parts per million (ppm). In 2021 we have surpassed that level, reaching 417 ppm. It has not been at 350 ppm since the late 1980s. Moreover, the average annual CO_2 emissions during 2010–2019 were higher than in any previous decade. The only positive aspect is that we have managed to mildly slow down the growth rates of emissions. The growth rate between 2010 and 2019 was 1.3% per year, compared to 2.1% per year between 2000 and 2009 (IPCC, 2022).

While a decrease in the growth of emissions is a step towards improvement, it is crucial to emphasise that our focus is not just on our environmental footprint in relative terms, i.e. percentages compared to other factors or times. Although these comparisons can be relevant indicators, but it cannot be the goal. Instead, we must work in absolute terms to ensure the well-being of our planet and thus enhance our ability to thrive on planet earth. This is where the concept of absolute sustainability comes into play, which involves determining the maximum allowable carbon release in relation to the global population. In particular, we must assess the problems we face in relation to identified solutions, considering their potential size and timing.

Planetary boundaries

In anticipation of the United Nations 2009 climate conference COP15 in Copenhagen, Johan Rockstrom and nearly two dozen other scientists published an article in the esteemed scientific journal *Nature* titled "A safe operating space for humanity" with the purpose of:

> If humanity wanted to avoid triggering potentially disastrous tipping points, such as the melting of polar ice sheets, extreme storms, or mass extinctions of wildlife, we argued, then the world needed to know where the boundaries for such thresholds were located, which meant measuring them and tracking them. More positively, we wrote, by identifying these boundaries, humanity could chart a safe path into the future for generations to come, opening the door for greater prosperity, justice, and technological advancement.
>
> *Rockstrom et al. (2009)*

The mapping and surveillance of the nine planetary boundaries by Stockholm Resilience Centre (Steffen et al., 2015) serves as a means to identify a safe operating space for long-term well-being and sustainable value creation. The work has, in particular, been spearheaded by Johan Rockstrøm (one of our modern-day climate superstars similar to Alexander Von Humboldt in his time). While the exact tipping point for the nine planetary boundaries remain uncertain, they offer valuable guidance on the actions we need to prioritise, and emphasise the urgency of taking action without delay. We must continuously strive to improve at working and acting based on the best available information.

The nine planetary boundaries are in random order:

1. **Stratospheric ozone depletion.** When the ozone layer is significantly depleted, it leads to an increase in dangerous ultraviolet (UV) rays, posing risks such as skin cancer and endangering terrestrial and marine ecosystems.
2. **Loss of biosphere integrity.** Popularly known as loss of biodiversity, it is measured by the decline in the number of species of plants and animals and the different DNA strands within each species.

3 **Chemical pollution and the release of novel entities.** This embodies the amount of anthropogenic (human-made) materials and chemicals present in our atmosphere and ecosystems, rather than plastic polluting our waters or radioactive materials detected in the air.
4 **Climate change.** It refers to the long-term changes in temperature and weather patterns brought by an increase in carbon dioxide equivalents per part per million (CO_2e ppm).

When discussing carbon emissions and reductions, we focus on two different types. The first is the embedded carbon which relates to the amount of carbon emitted in producing a given material or product. The second is the operational carbon which is also an essential part of the total footprint of a given material but relates to the energy used or produced during its operation. Both numbers must be taken into account to attain absolute sustainability and measure a given product's level of sustainability.
5 **Ocean acidification.** The number of carbon acids in our oceans is brought by emitted carbon dissolved in our oceans. The decrease in pH value makes it harder for vital ocean ecosystems such as coral reefs to thrive.

We should acknowledge the important role played by oceans in removing and storing carbon. Oceans store the majority of carbon emitted, but there are limits of absorbing a substantial amount, and when surpassed, significant challenges arise for both our oceans and climate in general.
6 **Freshwater consumption and the global hydrological cycle.** Freshwater (non-salty drinkable water) is becoming increasingly scarce due to our immense use in various chemical and production processes, which in turn has an effect on climate change.
7 **Land system change.** This refers to the amount of land kept for nature and forestry as opposed to the land being farmed or urbanised.
8 **Nitrogen and phosphorus flow to the biosphere and oceans.** Chemically created phosphorus and nitrogen have been used immensely since the industrialisation. With leakage to our terrestrial and ocean ecosystems, they negatively influence nature's regulation and ability to regenerate.
9 **Atmospheric aerosol loading.** Atmospheric aerosol has significant impact on earth's climate system, influencing the number of UV rays reaching the world and cloud formation. As it pollutes the air we breathe, this poses a significant short-term health risk, causing many deaths every year.

In developing my methodology, The 4Rs – The Circular Way, which will be explained in more detail in Chapter 9: The Circular Way, I have drawn upon the framework of planetary boundaries. These boundaries are the best available roadmap towards a safe operating space as established by science.

In short, the problem we are facing is immense, and there is no single solution. Instead, we must rely on an ecosystem of solutions, encompassing technological advancement, behavioural change and consumption patterns and our ability to reclaim our power to reimagine a world in which we create value for people while staying within the planetary boundaries.

We are aware that the global efforts to address climate change, such as COP15 in Copenhagen, faced significant challenges Fortunately, COP21 showed some progress and there is still a need for significant improvement. One core reason why it has been so difficult to agree on global action to mitigate climate change is that it cannot be done within the old paradigm of business, consumption and growth. We need to collectively drive the necessary changes and fix this pressing issues.

A map to a safe operating space

Design plays a crucial role in guiding us towards the necessary changes of our world. To ensure we are headed in the right direction, the concept of absolute sustainability must be discussed and strived for the safe operating space. With a steadily growing global middle class and an increasing global population, the earth will be housing 9.7 billion people by the year 2050. As a natural consequence, the demand for everyday consumer goods, housing and transportation will rise enormously, requiring material resources that are currently insufficient. At the same time, we are already facing enormous climatic and environmental challenges that will aggravate if the pattern of production and consumption continues. Should future generations and developing countries continue to pay the price for our mistakes? No. Instead, we need to fundamentally revisit our consumption and production patterns and move from a linear to a circular economy to decouple value creation from CO_2 equivalent emissions and biodiversity loss, enabling us to stay within the planetary boundaries. Thus, we need to adopt an economic system where resources and products are put into circulation rather than thrown out and wasted.

However, the focus on reaching the goal of maximum 1.5 temperature rise and avoiding a massive climate emergency has been mainly on the energy transition from fossil fuel dependence to renewables with an emphasis on energy efficiency. According to the publication "Completing the Picture: How the Circular Economy Tackles Climate Change" by Ellen MacArthur Foundation, 2021, it is to be noted that a perfect transition to renewable energy, renewable sources account for 55% of all accounted carbon emissions. However, the remaining 45% is derived from the production and agricultural sectors, which should not be overlooked. The report shows that even if the zero-goal is achieved in the energy sector by 2100, CO_2 emissions is projected to reach 649 billion tonnes from the remaining 45%. This exceeds the goal set by IPCC of a maximum of 420–580 billion tonnes to remain below the 1.5-degree temperature rise (Steffen et al. 2015).

Thus, designing for circularity is vital, especially considering that in the linear economy, the amount of waste generated per capita is generally

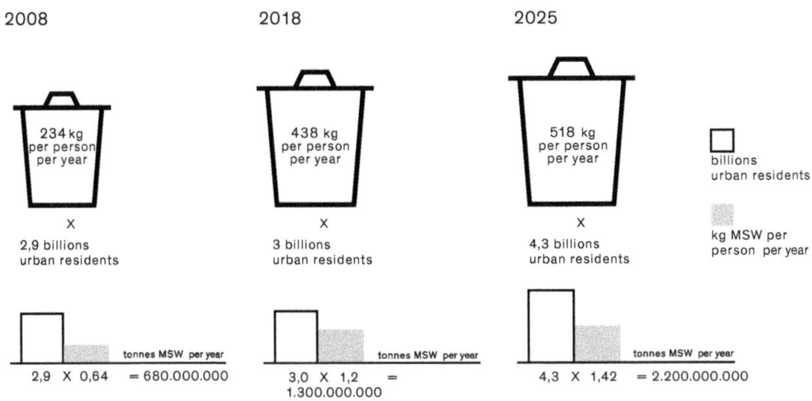

FIGURE 4.1 Growth of municipal solid waste (All The Way To Paris).

determined by factors such as economic development, income levels and the degree of urbanisation. With rapid urbanisation, a growing population and the middle class, we can anticipate the negative environmental footprint to only worsen. An example to support it is that the world generates approximately two billion tonnes of municipal solid waste annually. While only making up 16% of the global population, high-income countries account for 35% of the world's waste. This data clearly indicates a positive correlation between income levels and waste generation. By the year 2050, the world will be producing 3.4 billion tonnes of waste every year if the usual business persists. According to the World Bank (2018; Figure 4.1), a significant share of this increase is due to rapid economic development and urbanisation in today's low- and middle-income countries, which are expected to increase their total quantity of waste generation by nearly 40% over the next 30 years (Ellen MacArthur Foundation, 2021).

Let me explain the problem in our current linear mode of production with an illustration and a quote from the *Routledge Sustainable Design Handbook*:

> The smartphone you cherish, and no doubt have with you right now, weighs 500kg. Let me explain. Put it on the scales, and it will come out somewhere near 200g, give or take a gram or two. But product weight only tells a fraction of the whole product story. The actual weight of the product is only revealed if we consider all the resources needed to bring this product into the world. Calculating the per-unit weight of the whole product story (including resource extraction, material processing, component manufacture, product fabrication, shipping, distribution, retail, use and eventual disposal) weighs about half a tonne.
>
> *Chapman (2017)*

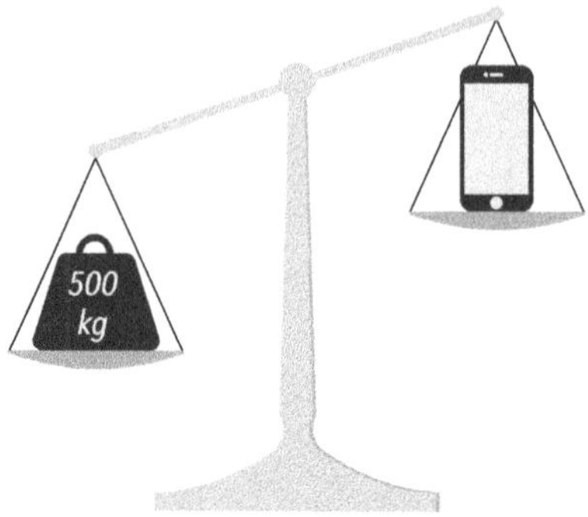

FIGURE 4.2 Resources used in smartphone production (Kathrine Hagemann Snabe, The Circular Way).

Interview with Anders Lendager

> Imagine a world without resource scarcity, where our behaviour doesn't harm our climate, where waste doesn't exist, and sustainability and growth are each other's prerequisites. To us, this world is real.
>
> *Lendager and Lysgaard Vind (2018)*

That is how Anders Lendager and I embarked on our book *A Changemakers Guide to the Future*, which represents the vision of Lendager and all the projects, pioneering the sustainable built environment. Capable of bring his ideas to life, Anders is indeed a doer envisioning things. As Anders asserts in his discourse that insisting on change is challenging and uncomfortable. But we need it now more than ever. In that sense, Anders much resembles the modern-day Poul Henningsen, using his talent and platform as an architect to speak up even when it goes against the norm. Like Poul Henningsen, he fearlessly addresses the issues capitalism and the dangers of its ability to enslave our minds.

D: In three words, describe the world you would design?

A: First, I would use the word regenerative. Because of all that, we need to restore since things are largely broken today. Our task is to restore the world and replace our current systems with regenerative ones. The second word I would use to describe an ideal world is healthy. I hope we can gain the ability to create a healthy world regarding the materials we use and our ability to design based on our natural systems – the goal is to achieve overall health for people, cities and the planet.

The third word is freedom. First, design influences people and creates constraints on our actions and lifestyles. Design can also influence our behaviour towards how we live, work and use materials. However, unfortunately, few designers are conscious of that. Second, the current capitalistic socio-cultural framework makes us all slaves to an incredible number of things that we are not mindful of and, therefore, cannot break free from. This not only poses a problem in itself, but also hinders behavioural change required to mitigate climate change.

D: Freedom is an exciting and relevant choice I had not previously considered. By "freedom", do you mean the ability to look beyond and not be constrained by our social constructions and current structures essentially created and driven by capitalism?

A: Indeed. Because many of the things that are considered not to be possible today are due to the lack of freedom, and we have instead created a society based on acratic norms and structures driven by our self-perception of what is the norm and what we are allowed to do. Hence, I think freedom is significant concerning what it would take to design the ultimate sustainable world. So those who are best at creating something new and innovative have the freedom and ability to think differently and out of the box – metaphorically speaking, to think outside the notion that the box exists.

That is what we try to do at Lendager: To free ourselves from the norms to create solutions that are currently considered impossible. We must rethink all the steps in product development, break free from conventional thinking and turn things upside down. However, there is a paradox within freedom. While the need is for true innovation, ultimately, freedom also challenges the design's success. The road to realisation can often be dark and lonely. The ability to create comes from embracing one's freedom in the context of the solution developed.- It is also tough because the ultimate freedom means challenging the norm, which may lead to failure within the current framework.

D: Perhaps that is the challenge of freedom and breaking free of the existing societal constructions: To self-preserve, the system won't allow it? So regardless of how good your idea is, you must first fight a lonely fight against the system that is ultimately wired to protect itself regardless of what might be holistically best for us.

A: Exactly. If you were to find yourself alone on a deserted island, and you could use three words to describe the world you would create, the choice of words would probably have been quite different from today as you would have the freedom and opportunity to accumulate new experiences needed to create a society without the constraints of current structures and constructions. In that scenario, the premises for creating the future are different from those we have today, and the words to describe it would be different.

D: So, a key element is to be mindful of the systems we are participating in and the incentive structures driving them because if we are aware of them, then we can challenge them as you have done. Because while difficult, you have proven not impossible to "beat" the system and create sustainable innovations. In that sense, The Lendager approach reminds me of the American professor Donna Haraway's notion of "Staying with the trouble", meaning the ability to stay in the uncomfortable problem space. Because as I see it, Lendager operates almost by design in what we could call the "impossibility space", thus embodying the best of the design practice by utilising the impossibility space to both create and realise sustainable solutions that were considered impossible.

A: Yes! But it is crucial to remember how much sacrifice it has cost us. It has been a very long journey towards successfully achieving what we are essentially in the world to do.

This is also at the core of our societal critique: If you can create, why is your purpose as a business than to exploit? That is why we have tried to challenge the existing approach of exploiting resources, capital and people as much as possible by creating buildings that exploit as little as possible. But again, it is difficult to do in a world that does not want to change itself. I mean that there is a demand for new products and concepts. Still, at the same time, the industry lacks the will towards the internal changes in behaviour and processes necessary to achieve the desired sustainable results. So even though people want the result we deliver, we become almost unwanted in meetings because we ruin the good atmosphere and comfort of business as usual.

D: However, Lendager has successfully gone from being a small player to becoming a more prominent and influential company, highlighting that it is possible to grow through sustainable innovation. I think a vital part of the Anthropocene is that we have the power to do good and bad through our actions, so we have a choice. And while we focus on the good choices we make, we are also responsible for the bad ones because a better alternative is available.

A: It is interesting that you mention that. Last night I was reading the new EU taxonomy for sustainable finance. And while intentions are good, there are still way too many loopholes enabling business as usual and limiting radical innovation. Reading it got me wondering who is smart enough to create such a taxonomy? Because, from our experience, everything must be turned upside down for sustainable solutions to succeed. There are no norms. Everything is different. It is a paradigm shift. Yet when the EU created the taxonomy, everything was the same. They chose 35 experts, 30 of whom were from the financial sector and are undoubtedly great at excel spreadsheets but have never produced a single physical item. That is a problem because then we are not seeing the complete picture of what sustainability can nor should be. Where is the knowledge on creating change, the new paradigm, and the creation of radical innovation – nowhere! Instead, it is created by the same type of people who created the problem—leaving no room for necessary change.

So, it will be nearly impossible to create the necessary framework for change before 2030. We need radical change and the people who protest and express their concerns are often overlooked, demonstrations and frustrations can quickly turn to hatred, and climate activism will only increase. How can it not when all we get from decision-makers today is talk, and too few commit to real action? In that sense, I guess all that is left is anarchy. Because we can't wait for change any longer. Our systems are broken, and we need change to survive as individuals and humankind.

D: That is a good point. If we truly want change, we can't entrust the solution to those who created the problem and expect the outcome to change. Systems theory has always provided the answer: The system, and thus its actors, are wired to sustain itself and put the system's survival before anything else. And then it becomes a question of which system we are trying to regenerate? Is the main objective to save the financial sector or society at large? Unfortunately, assigning 30 out of 35 experts from the financial industry points to the fact that the taxonomy will do the latter. And maybe that is the main problem here: We are still focussed on keeping our existing systems intact instead of creating the value necessary for society to regenerate.

A: It could be very interesting to create a parallel and radically different society within Europe. The point is to test what would happen if the structures that prevent change today were removed. So instead of just creating lighthouse projects within our existing structures, this new nation would be a sustainability haven influencing our world by showing how we consume and live can be done differently while still being a part of the system. And it would be interesting to see how this new society would interact with the surrounding world, the goal here being to challenge our existing structures by creating a competing (for lack of a better word) society that brings new meaning to how we live our lives and what we value.

It is an interesting discussion about how self-sufficient the parallel society could become and to what extent they can be left unaffected by the surrounding world. And most importantly, how it could create personal freedom and a framework where you do not negatively impact the globe and the surrounding environment. How would that society look? There is enough money in the world to try it. So why not create the antipodean to tax haven islands? The goal is to create an alternative that is better than what exists.

D: A sustainable haven to exist not decoupled from but as a connected counter-concept. That is super interesting. While writing this book, I have been contemplating whether we can reclaim growth as a tool to do good rather than relying on degrowth, and I see this as a potential tangible solution to how we could do it. There is something natural about the attraction to growth tied to a human urge to develop and evolve. So, is it necessarily the right approach to discourage growth? Or could we instead redefine the concept of growth as not exclusively financial? In a way, back to Adam Smith, who never intended for his economic system to be the only one to guide society. And back to your previous point on the taxonomy, it should be made not only of finance experts but also of society and our systems in general, including the arts and natural science. So the goal is that what we incentivise and encourage is not merely financial growth but instead look at and measure growth from a holistic point of view?

A: In some ways, this is what the New European Bauhaus is about. It is headed in that direction by highlighting the value of aesthetics and culture and setting the capitalistic structure aside by taking a starting point in irresistible cities and societies. Which, as you say, would create a very different response to what the future would look like and, thus, the taxonomy.

D: Yes, the New European Bauhaus is a fantastic initiative, but there is still a relevant question regarding which system is on top? Are we using art and culture to achieve goals aligned with our existing structures, I.e., to create financial growth? Or are we valuing them as essential goals in their own right?

A: Agreed, but there are some basic principles in how we think throughout our entire lives that have been with us since childhood that we tend to overlook. We, adults, are the ones who educate and shape our children, and we play an essential role in what basic principles they grow up with. However, the greed that exists in our society is not something we grownups have created but is something primal, a way we are as homo sapiens fundamentally. Evolution, the need to constantly improve, to take more and to act ruthlessly toward your surroundings to survive are all-natural primal instincts, and they are a vital part of what prevents us from changing. Mainly because that way of being has worked very well for us for thousands of years, but no longer will as we have now become so successful and so efficient that we are cannibalising ourselves. So, it is almost as if a part of our DNA must change: Why is it not good enough to fulfil your needs? Why are there some that can't get enough?

D: I realise that our primal needs and desires shape a big part of our societal structures. This is also a key reason why I look towards reclaiming growth as a tool. However, our social constructions within society also define our ways of being as humans. And that, as humans, we have different things within us that are activated and heightened or kept down by particular social structures. Yes, we have greed within us, but the context, including the culture and social structures we live in, can unconsciously encourage or discourage it as a prevalent trait. So, I think we must find a balance between accepting our primal needs and rethinking the social structures. We should design structures that steer people to benefit themselves and the planet. The Danish societal model and the welfare state are one micro example.

A: The welfare state is an excellent structure in terms of both social and economic coherency. But the damage that our welfare state creates in terms of CO_2 emissions, use of resources, and production of waste, sickness, and more is noticeable. And despite our welfare model, we have not been able to improve our environmental impact per capita. On the contrary, it is very high. But being a small country with many windmills and bike lanes allows us to be perceived as frontrunners in the green energy and sustainable transition, even if our total environmental impact isn't that impressive.

D: Regarding the Danish Design Heritage, what pops into your mind when thinking of Danish design?

A: I would define Danish design as classical, of high quality and as simplistic. Words that are arguably quite boring, which many Danish designs are. Most new designs created today are classic in terms of form and choice of material, and many of them might as well have been designed in the 60s. However, we are starting to see innovation within the production and construction of the products, which is good and the quality of Danish design, especially furniture, is remarkable. So, there is an implicit quality requirement when creating Danish designs. Some elements of fast fashion are starting to appear, but it is not the majority, and most still have a certain level of quality. The last word is simplicity, a key characteristic of Danish design and has been since the original classics.

D: You have talked much about aesthetics for the last few years. How about aesthetic resilience as a sustainability tool: The design we still find attractive years later is what we protect and treasure the most. In some ways, there is unintentional sustainability in aesthetics. So what do you think of that?

A: That is, without a doubt, true. We should not underestimate the power of creating beautiful architecture and design. If you make something that is beautiful enough, it will last forever. But if it were easy to create design icons and masterpieces, everyone would do it. The thing is, it is more than challenging to create art and timeless design. And aesthetic resilience happens when something becomes timeless, not when the object is made. By definition, it takes generations to know if one has created something that is a cultural heritage for posterity and thus becomes timeless. Therefore, an ironic aspect of creating timeless designs is that we will not know what will succeed at becoming timeless in our own time, making it a difficult sustainability tool. Of course, one can also mention historical resilience because we value buildings with historical meaning, even if they lack aesthetic beauty.

D: Cultural history as an equally value-creating parameter?

A: Yes, exactly. And when it is best, the two are interlinked. What I value the most in the Danish Design Heritage is that we have a beautiful variety of schools, rowhouses, libraries, etc., created by some of the best architects of their times, representing our cultural history and still perceived as beautiful today. The ability to make multiple generations value and treasure a design is one of the most sustainable approaches. Creating designs that are so good that they will be preserved forever is the ultimate sustainable design.

The aesthetic value in our world is constantly changing, and the timing of the design should, therefore, not be underestimated. While the cultural history and aesthetics continue to stand the test of time, the functionality can be more difficult. Despite the discomfort I experience due to my height, when sitting in my Swan chair by Arne Jacobsen, I would never throw it out just because I no longer want it. Even if one were to argue that the Swan was badly designed, causing discomfort to sit in or being inconvenient that the leather or fabric gets stained easily, and its high cost, it still holds value. Because it has become a sculpture that we treasure – it has become a cultural heritage through generations and thus still has value in our time. Similarly, arguably most of the buildings that Arne Jakobsen has made do not meet today's indoor climate requirements. I'm not saying the modern indoor climate requirements are necessarily correct. But Arne Jakobsen buildings have poor insulation, resulting in a cold indoor climate with air draft. Due to the design, replacing the existing windows with modern, efficient ones is nearly impossible. Is this sustainable? No. However, if you look at the materials they are made of, the longer the buildings are valued and last, the more resilient it becomes and thereby sustainable.

D: So, your point is that resilience, which ultimately makes it sustainable, happens when it becomes cultural heritage, which, as much as being about aesthetics, is about the historical context and more than anything, it is about the ability to capture a specific moment in time. You are very right. But does that then expand the question of what good design is and what it is not? Because if it is cultural heritage, it entails different elements than just classical characteristics of good design, such as ergonomic or aesthetic expression. It becomes as much about its context, including society.

A: Yes and No. I would say that good design becomes cultural heritage because, in addition to being good, it is made at a specific moment in a culture where exactly that design was the right thing to do. Thus, it perfectly portrays and captures that particular time and context, thereby becoming timeless and cultural heritage.

It is critical to reflect the spirit of the current times in design and architecture at their best. It is the essence of the times. However, it is essential to separate the artistic design that becomes timeless through cultural heritage and craftsmanship. Furniture is a good example. The principles of Kaare Klint on ergonomically creating a chair have retained their value because that is a craft still functional and creates value for today's designs. On the other hand, when making an aesthetic design, we must add another dimension to craftsmanship: the ability to be creative and to form. This captures the exact time and context that inspire the design. These two elements together frame the context and setting for the designer to create the ultimate design. The freedom lies in the creative process, but being grounded in the technique and framework of craftsmanship and context.

So, we can learn from the principle of aesthetic resilience, but it must not be used as a general point to advocate for more classical architecture. For years it was highlighted as the tool for architects to create sustainability: Look at our cultural heritage, just let us make magnificent architecture, and sustainability will follow inevitably. Though theoretically correct, but in practice it is impossible.

D: What actions are you most proud of? And what do you still want to do?

A: I'm very proud that I dared to quit business as usual ten years ago. I didn't know what I was going to do instead. Still, I knew I needed to break free because I was so frustrated about the lack of action and the perception of sustainability as being unachievable. It took a lot of strength and guts to leave my convenient situation, especially as I had started a family and needed stability. Nonetheless, I knew I had to find a way to create sustainability to continue my work as an architect, and today I am both proud and happy I dared to make that decision.

I take pride in the work we have accomplished in Lendager. While I am proud of the successful realisation of projects like Upcycle Studios and the Resource Rows, but they are just a few of the many projects I am proud of. Each project sets new standards and creates a new norm for building, embracing the principle of resource respect. They have become the benchmark for building circular and sustainable buildings that are both beautiful and functional.

Through our projects, we have been successful in driving the building industry to become more responsible. It requires skill and courage because you must be willing to make big decisions and take risks. And I am proud that we so early on saw that if you want to succeed with sustainability, you can't just focus on the outcome; you need to change the process, business model and value chain. It is pretty remarkable how quickly we identified and created a new type of value chain. To achieve this, we had to rethink all our methods and processes, everything from the employment contracts, our problem-solving, to our collaborations and much more that are all unconventional. In order succeed in changing an entire industry, it is crucial to break away from the traditional approaches. That is why I take immense pride in the organisation we have created, including the company's structure and our entire team. I also delightful by our accomplishment in establishing a material production company that has now been spun out to its own company: a:gain.

D: Recently, an employee of Lendager chose to describe Lendager as an "Exemplar" organisation in large due to his belief that what Lendager does is worthy of imitation. I think that is very true, so it is unfortunate that so far, few do. Are architects afraid of getting their hands dirty with materials, or what stops more from taking responsibility not just for the concept and the rendering but the final build like you felt the need to do ten years ago?

A: That's great! Firstly I think quite a few are imitating us. One example is how we moved the concrete industry towards producing recycled concrete because they saw that we successfully did it.

To become more actively involved, changing the mindset is most important. Waste is perceived to be useless then and now. But if we rethink and realise the potential of waste, it can offer endless possibilities. I seriously believe that it is easier to transform waste that has no value into something valuable than to use high-end materials such as marble or oak. –Regardless of our efforts, the outcome will be difficult to match the innate beauty of the material. When we turn waste into value, we bring into use both the materials as resources and our capacity and skill set as architects. Our purpose of life is to create value that did not exist. As a profession, we need to be better at utilising our current resources and be more responsible about how we consume materials. As designers, we possess the skill to create beautiful, aesthetically pleasing, and functional forms. The choice of material to use for the design is just as important. Rather than harvesting virgin materials from nature, we should use the existing resources and create solutions out of materials currently viewed as problems. Through this, we can restore our nature rather than continue our destructive behaviour, thereby, ultimately creating designs that benefit both humans and nature.

Anders Lendager is a Danish architect and founder of the award-winning studio Lendager. The company specialises in sustainable architecture, focussing on circular economy and materials.

Question: What motivates you to want to change the world for the better?

References

Chapman, J. (2017). *Routledge Sustainable Design Handbook*. Routledge.

Ellen MacArthur Foundation (2021). Completing the Picture: How the Circular Economy Tackles Climate Change. https://ellenmacarthurfoundation.org/topics/climate/overview

Figueres, C., & Rivett-Carnac, T. (2020). *The Future We Choose: The Stubborn Optimist's Guide to the Climate Crisis*. Vintage Books.

IPCC. (2022). *Climate Change 2022: Impacts, Adaptation and Vulnerability*. https://www.ipcc.ch/report/sixth-assessment-report-working-group-ii/

Joseph, Y. (2018). Stephen Hawking, in His Own Words, 14 March. *New York Times*. https://www.nytimes.com/2018/03/14/world/europe/stephen-hawking-quotes.html

Lendager, A., & Lysgaard Vind, D. (2018). *A Changemakers Guide to the Future*. Lendager Group.

Mckibben, B. (2022). The persistence of fossil fuels. In G. Thunberg (Ed.), *The Climate Book*. Penguin Books Ltd.

Rockstrom, J. et al. (2009). A safe operating space for humanity. *Nature, 461*(7263), 472–475. https://www.nature.com/articles/461472a

Rockstrøm, J., & Mattias, K. (2015). *Big World, Small Planet: Abundance Within Planetary Boundaries*. Yale University Press.

Smil, V. (2022). Taming the Climate Is Far Harder than Getting People to the Moon. https://spectrum.ieee.org/decarbonization

Steffen et al. (2015). The Nine Planetary Boundaries. Stockholm Resilience Centre. https://www.stockholmresilience.org/research/planetary-boundaries/the-nine-planetary-boundaries.html

The World Bank (2018). What a Waste 2.0. https://datatopics.worldbank.org/what-a-waste/

United Nations (2015). The Paris Agreement. https://unfccc.int/process-and-meetings/the-paris-agreement/the-paris-agreement

5

PARTNERING WITH LIFE: THE ESSENCE OF REGENERATION

An essay

As already touched upon, we need to reimagine our society and more than anything to me, the circular economy serves as a toolbox and a map to stay within our planetary boundaries while providing prosperity for our global population, hence the "way" in The Circular Way. But if that's a means, then what is the goal? It's regeneration. A notion I know none who can explain better than the magnificent Laura Storm. This is the reason why I am so happy that Laura agreed to write an essay for this book highlighting both what it is, why it is so important and what we need to be so very mindful of if we want to get there. I hope you will enjoy reading it as much as I do, and if you want to know more about Laura's work, check out the website www.regenerators.co.

An essay by Laura Storm

The ways of the Homo Sapiens and how they've inhabited this planet and their relationship to the living world has come out of kilter. Since the 1950s we've been through the so-called Great Acceleration – everything from GDP, urban population, total population, CO_2 consumption, fertiliser consumption to the loss of tropical forest, domesticated land use, ocean acidification (I could go on) has been on a steep increase. We are by far out of balance with the ecosystems that sustain all life on our planet. Within a generation we have destroyed more than we can probably ever regenerate. The Homo Sapiens seem to have lost their way.

Across all indigenous wisdom traditions, there's this understanding of being a good ancestor. Many first nation people refer to this as the Seventh Generation Principle – to rely on the wisdom of your past ancestors while

DOI: 10.4324/9781003261018-5

ensuring your actions take care of the seventh generations to come. That all your actions must weave in a legacy that you leave for those to come and that your actions must continue to create conditions for life to thrive in the future. Māoris have the principle of 'Wakapapa' where you envision yourself holding hands with all your past and future ancestors and your main responsibility is to add positively to the legacy. That first and foremost you must be a good ancestor.

Are we as human beings collectively being good ancestors in how we have designed our societies and systems? That is a clear no from me. Not only are earth system trends and socio-economic trends showing a clear picture of imbalance and poor stewardship – our mental health and well-being is suffering immensely and showing the same upward trajectory. Research shows we have never been more stressed, burned out, depressed and anxious as we are today. People who are stressed cannot think in interconnected systems, it's physiologically impossible for a brain in high-beta (the brain wave we are in under stress) to think holistically and systemically. And not only that, it's also impossible for anyone under stress to access compassion and empathy. This says quite a lot, right?

This stress in ecosystems – inner as well as outer – is interconnected and can only be addressed at deep levels through an interconnected regenerative approach. We need compassion and regeneration to guide our society's design going forward.

Thankfully, regenerative leadership, business, design and living is gaining a lot of traction these years. And what does that mean? Regenerative means to heal and replenish through your actions. To continuously create the conditions for life to renew itself and regain its health and vitality. That goes for your inner ecosystems as well as outer. The regenerative leaders with whom I've been fortunate to collaborate with over the years see themselves as ecosystem facilitators where their first priority is to ensure that all of the interconnected ecosystems that create the living system of their business are in great health. That includes the well-being of their employees, greater stakeholder landscape and the interconnected ecosystems upon which their business relies upon. They operate by the notion that we can only be in great health if all who are a part of us are in great health. They look to nature for inspiration and guidance and they understand that this 3.8 billion years of evolutionary wisdom and intelligence is far greater than all human minds combined. Therefore, they respectfully borrow from that wisdom and tap into the potential of biomimicry and circular economy in their design processes and systems. But they do it in a way where circular economy isn't just a new set of metrics and boxes to tick but rather as part of the embodiment of this sacred deep stewardship we ought to have with the more than human world if we want to be here in the long run.

As my co-author Giles Hutchins and I write in the book *Regenerative Leadership*:

> The tree is part of a vibrant inter-relating ecosystem, systems upon systems all feeding off each other, where waste of one becomes food for another. Throughout the year the entire tree is host to millions of microorganisms, bacteria, fungi and insects, all playing their part in the vitality of the eco-system. The tree sequesters carbon, cleans the air, produces oxygen and enriches the soil. Tree blossom enables insects to pollinate and every year we see the beauty of leaves bursting forth in spring, transforming solar energy into tree growth throughout summer. And when the season changes to autumn the leaves fall to the ground, and over the winter they are recycled and reused. No plastic bags littering the streets unable to biodegrade, only leaf-litter that fertilizes the topsoil with rich nutrients for the next batch of production in spring. And ultimately when the tree dies the trunk and its branches, essentially made of water, minerals, and sunlight, will release nutrients for the next generation of trees and for other life-forms to live.
>
> *(Storm & Hutchins, 2019)*

This is nature's wisdom at work. This is what the carpet manufacture Interface taps into when they in collaboration with biologists and biomimicry professionals are redesigning their factories and buildings to mimic the principles of a forest where they turn sunlight into energy, purify water, use regenerative materials as part of a closed loop. They do their best to create ecosystemic impact through their operations and one of their initiatives is to pay Philippine fishermen a fair wage to fish discarded plastic nets from the ocean. These nets are then used in their production instead of virgin plastic contributing to regenerate wider interconnected ecosystems.

Regenerative leaders, however, move further than just aligning their design and production to more life-affirming ways. They know that their ecosystem whether it's a country, city, community or organisation is a living system: an organism. And the inhabitants of those organisms – whether its citizens or employees – are the cells of the living system. If they're not healthy cells, the living system can never tap into full health and vitality, tap into their full human ingenuity, creativity and lifeforce. They will get sicker and sicker before they inevitably die out. Regenerative designers ensure that the final products, workspaces, schools, government buildings, cities and systems they're involved in are designed to enhance the well-being of the users. When we are surrounded by natural materials, or even images of nature, we lower our cortisol levels, are sick less frequently, collaborate better, heal faster and our overall sense of well-being improves (Ulrich, 1984). When we immerse ourselves in nature we become more compassionate, creative, improve our memory and we improve our collaborative and empathic abilities. In cities, researchers have shown how buildings with high levels of vegetation around them had 48% fewer property crimes and 56% fewer violent crimes than otherwise identical apartments with only barren surrounding land. Even modest amounts of greenery were associated with lower crime rates (Kuo & Sullivan, 2001).

Cities are homes to nearly 70% of the global population, yet most cities are designed with little access to nature. They are designed for cars and have an almost hostile approach to all living things – nature and humans alike. And the landscape citizens are surrounded by are dominated by concrete, steel, glass in grey tones and inside our schools and workplaces the surroundings often mimic factories with little natural light or fresh air.

Again I'm reminded of the famous quote by Winston Churchill that "we shape our buildings and then the buildings shape us". We are currently shaping workplaces, schools and cities that make us sick, burned out and depressed.

We, the humans, are the unhealthy cell in the greater interconnected web of life and our only way out of this is to start to align our ways with the principles of life.

If we have to deeply honour our role as ancestors, we must stop in our tracks now and with empathy, compassion and curiosity explore the underlying logic and wisdom of the planet we inhabit and start to design systems, structures, buildings, workplaces, schools and societies in partnership with that wisdom instead of *against it*. Partnering and aligning with life is the essence of regeneration. That is how we can find our way back.

> **Question:** Where and what is your favourite spot in nature? When and where do you miss nature the most?

References

Kuo, F. E., & Sullivan, W. C. (2001). Environment and crime in the inner city: Does vegetation reduce crime? *Environment and Behavior, 33*(3), 343–367. https://doi.org/10.1177/0013916501333002

Storm, L., & Hutchins, G. (2019). *Regenerative Leadership: The DNA of Life-Affirming 21st Century Organizations*. Wordzworth Publishing.

Ulrich, R. S. (1984). View through a window may influence recovery from surgery. *Science, 224*, 420–421.

6

THEORY MEETS PRACTICE AND MAGIC HAPPENS

A few years ago, Carlsberg, a Danish multinational brewery, approached us with a challenge. They had identified a plastic composite waste stream that they wanted to responsibly recycle, but as this was back in 2018, there was lack of know-how, technology and experience in the traditional waste management sector to find a viable commercial usage. So instead, it was trusted upon us to use The Circular Way to find a new purpose and design product, value chain and business model around the recycling of the composite plastic material from their Draught-Master beer kegs. As part of Lendager, our first product design was a facade tile that has since been accompanied by chairs, tables and other products and providing recycled materials for others to use.

What a journey it has been! True to traditional Lendager – TCW fashion, we dived into the challenge headfirst, confident that there were opportunities to recycle the materials rather than incinerating it. This was our first experience developing a material with a waste stream outside the built environment. To our knowledge, it was one of the pioneering efforts to recycle a plastic composite into a high-value product on a large scale. Luckily, improvement has happened in the traditional sector since then, particularly in the field of plastics, a resource recovery sector is starting to prosper. However, we still need to incentivise high-quality recycling and empower the companies and solutions that do quality recycling rather than solely focusing on the quantitative number of amounts recycled, which unfortunately, is the mindset today. That is why I take pride in that we not only designed and created products, but also developing a value chain and partnered with existing industry players and new start-ups. By sharing knowledge and supporting each other, we are working towards our common goal of improving the quality and scale of composite recycling.

DOI: 10.4324/9781003261018-6

FIGURE 6.1A A photo of the chair from the Ocean OC2 collection (Mater).

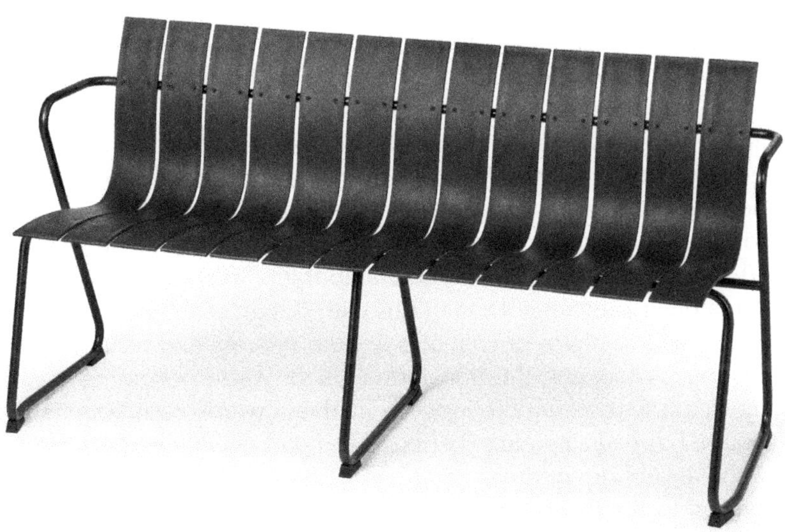

FIGURE 6.1B A photo of the bench from the Ocean OC2 collection (Mater).

This achievement was made possible because we put design at the centre and adopting the Enlightened Action methodology, as described in Chapter 8, questions the status quo continuously, aims for ambitious goals and engages in practical experimentation. Through a cycle of trial and error, we finally succeeded.

While I had experience working with circular economy business models, it was my first time managing a project with such advanced technological development and unexplored territory. It posed a multitude of challenges, including addressing concerns related to strength, fire safety, degradation and potential risks of microplastic pollution to name a few of the developments and barriers. It was an immensely complex challenge that required us to make big decisions and take on many risks. Especially as I am what one might call a theorist caught in practice moving from the realm of Microsoft Office to the real world working with smelly waste (old beer really does smell) in the tool shop is a big shift. Although blessed with a brilliant team far more skilled than myself in regard to the technical aspects of recycling and materials, it was the first time I learned the difference between losing sleep over work due to late night crunching and rewriting a strategy document or repurposing a presentation and losing sleep due to physical properties turning out differently than expected and you need to pursue a different direction than expected. However, it is uncertain where the road will lead us to. Nonetheless, I remain hopeful that we can keep energy and excitement up across stakeholders as we navigate through these challenges, ensuring that the project is not abandoned due to technical roadblocks. It is important to accept that no PowerPoint can change the physical capabilities and the results of a fire test. Therefore, unable to sleep when the technical tests initially did not provide the results we hoped for, nor could I personally fix it. I don't mention the lack of sleep to scare you off from creating tangible solutions and innovation, rather to encourage collaboration and support as we collectively help each other move out of our comfort zones and take action.

Ultimately, a presumption of possibility and stubborn optimism made us succeed. It helped immensely to have a diverse team of cross-professions from design, engineering and business, as well as a high degree of external collaboration from both science and industry with individual areas of knowledge. This collective knowledge and collaboration ensured our ability to act and ultimately create tangible solutions with design as the core driver. While the process had its share of challenges, both process and results have been so gratifying. Witnessing the transformation of waste becoming a valuable resource again and seeing the industry evolve towards even better solutions in the future has been a great experience and part of what enables me to continue to be a stubborn optimist.

However, technological barriers were just one part of the innovation process to be mindful of. Therefore, I decided to build our design and innovation process on MIT's innovation model of Market, Implementation and

Technology. This helped create our version and navigated us through our resource innovation journey of recycling a plastic composite waste stream avoiding incineration. It gave a new life that could compete on market terms. In the following sections, I will share our experiences with the hope that they can inspire and guide others to overcome similar challenges.

By prioritising design, we began by addressing the fundamental question: **Is it desirable (in the market)?** We can design a product and a business model that is attractive enough for people to choose it over traditional alternatives. Through trial and error, we initially explored different modes of production for the facade tiles. We discovered that because the material was a composite, the main problem for the existing plastic recycling industry from a design and an aesthetic point of view, provided an opportunity to create new value. It is necessary to differentiate between mono and composite plastic materials in plastics. Mono materials consists of one type of polymer that, in unity, creates the plastic. In contrast, a composite consists of different kinds of polymers that, in unity, make up the plastic. Composite plastic poses greater difficulty to recycle because each type of polymer has different technical capabilities and will respond differently to processing. One key factor is the difference in temperature in which they melt. Due to this being a plastic composite, the material changed colour when processed with heat leading to variations in appearance and a marble-like aesthetics, which is often associated with luxurious materials. We were able to create attractive products by combining aesthetics with the unique storytelling of a circular product and the growing trend and thus increasing demand. As mentioned earlier, also it is imperative to make sure that it was possible to do this from a technical perspective, thus answering the question: **Is it feasible (technically)?** This is where we met the most challenges, ensuring the high quality of the material without adding unnecessary additives, to avoid compromising circularity (that it can be re-circulated again after we used it) and increasing the environmental footprint. At the time, it was not a common ask in the industry for sustainable additives or fire retardants. I remember one situation when I pushed for sustainable alternatives and met with resistance from the sales representative from a large chemical producer, sarcastically suggested sitting under a tree instead. Fortunately, industry is evolving, and there are now emerging commercial options for new additives, including ones derived from biogenic materials. Achieving this outcome took much effort, and the team became leading experts in the process due to our unwavering belief that it was possible and thus persistently ask questions and eventually make it possible.

Interestingly enough, during our testing and experiment, we discovered that there were actually low-tech solutions available to help turn the material back into a valuable resource. That also had a positive advantage: We could share the knowledge we had gathered from our feasibility study and apply it in a refugee camp in Uganda, where very little technology was required.

This initiative not only helped them gain skills but also helped solve two of their biggest problems: waste pollution and lack of building materials. In fact, when Lendager was commissioned to design the Danish Pavilion at the Milan Design Week, for the construction of temporary chairs we witnessed the use of the Re-Plastic material. Furthermore, the roofing was bought from the refugee camp where they used our low-tech method to mitigate there grand plastic waste problem and make money turning it into a viable resource sold for use in Milan.

Lastly, we had to ensure the implementation of our solution was feasible, taking current infrastructure, regulations and existing value chain capabilities into account. We put the question: **Is it (implementation) viable?** Fortunately, it was and Re-Plastic is now used in production for several products. One of my personal favourites is this series of chairs, tables and lounge sofas for outdoor use designed by the great Danish designer Nanna Ditzel and manufactured by Mater using our draught master Re-Plastic material. These products are currently available for purchase under our spinout company a:gain (https://again.dk/), which operates under a resource recovery business model specialised in providing a variety of reused and recycled materials for the building industry. For more on Mater's great work combining the Danish Design Heritage with the opportunities of today to push toward global sustainability, explore their case in Chapter 2 on the Danish design classic chair by Børge Mogensen, now produced with recycled biogenic materials.

Perfect must not be the enemy of improvement

We need to, and we will design our way out of the problem from its root by ensuring that new products are made and used to prevent them from ever becoming waste. But first—right here and now—we must find intelligent ways to use the immense waste we have already generated. We will most likely continue to create waste in the transition period to a circular economy. That's why I have focused on resource innovations where waste is turned back into value and kept in circulation, the fundamental goal being to reduce the upfront carbon necessary in new products. Creating Re-Plastic (now part of a:gain) as an innovation, collaboration, and a company has been a great and meaningful experience. In this regard, I would like to share a few of those learnings from a personal point of view and how it has shaped both my thinking and actions.

In Chapter 9, I will delve into the details of my methodology, the 4Rs – The Circular Way, where I will address the shortcomings of recycling. If we want to create a prosperous future for both people and the planet using the circular economy as the tool, it is an absolute necessity that we get much better at reducing and reusing waste. However, Rome was not built in a day, and recycling will play a vital role in the short to medium future. As technology and renewable energy advance it might also play a role in the longer term if we are successful at finding ways to recycle without reducing quality and without the need to use fossil-based energy or chemicals in the processing. Through our journey, we faced and overcame both technical and commercial barriers, which proved to be quite challenging/ The level of insecurity was more than high, setting the bar high for the team's resilience and their unwavering belief in the potential of our efforts. **We were continuously presuming possibility** trying to achieve our goals even though there was not always a clear road to success. We were stubborn optimists. I learned that we needed to not only come to terms with but also learn to thrive in an environment where action comes before strategy. Deviating from the traditional types of documents is necessary and desirable to reach the full potential of the innovation. That does not mean that it is not helpful to have a strategy and that all strategy documents are useless (albeit my gut feeling is that about half of them are). However, as I will discuss the methodology Enlightened Action in Chapter 8, we need to prioritise action and place it at the core. We must shift our mindset from valuing strategy documents higher than action. Action must always take precedence.

I also learned something unexpected, being called a greenwasher. While the vast majority of responses to Re-Plastic have been very positive, there were one or two accusing us of greenwashing and being on the wrong side of improvement. I am fully aware that recycling a composite, whether for a high-quality second life or not, is far from the ideal solution. However, it represents essential steps towards improvement. First, it has a direct positive effect on reducing CO_2 emissions and a reduction in waste incineration. Second, rather in Denmark or in the refugee camp in Uganda, it is part of creating the infrastructure and value chains that enable increased and improved resource recovery. And last but not least, it inspires through a tangible example on how waste can and should remain a valuable resource. Defending our solution is not my primary purpose in sharing my experience of being called a greenwasher. This experience emphasises the importance of nurturing and supporting one another as sustainable changemakers. We are part of a collective and a larger ecosystem, and although our solutions may differ, we rely on each other and each other's solutions. If we turn against each other, the only beneficiaries will be the existing industry exploiting resources and relying on fossil fuels, while we will all stand to lose. There is no silver bullet for fixing the dire crisis we face today. Instead of allowing the race of perfection get in the way of good and focusing our energy on what is wrong with a particular solution, let's acknowledge the work we do and the effect on improvement that it has, pooling our knowledge and efforts to drive sustainable change.

Our solutions are far from perfect, but it took much effort and risk from our partners and us, and we need more of that because achieving absolute sustainability is a journey. So when the great climate activist Greta Thunberg

(2022) says, "either you are sustainable, or you are unsustainable", she is correct. However, there is a difference between how unsustainable or close to sustainability you are, and that matters. It matters to our planetary boundaries and to our well-being. So, the challenge is how do we encourage the journey towards creating value for people while staying within our planetary boundaries and, at the same time, avoid greenwashing and inaction? There are clear examples of greenwashing that should just not be tolerated. However, I believe that the conversation should continue and allow for different options, as long as tangible actions are taken towards the real goal. It is essential to acknowledge when we are off target and redirect. The case of recycling concrete is an example from my journey, which I will share in Chapter 13: Building The Circular Way. We discovered that the CO_2 reductions from recycling concrete were minimal. Instead, continuously sentising the harmful use of cement, a material that in its production emits an extremely high amount of CO_2 mainly through the chemical reaction that happens when lime is heated and turned into the cement. Instead, we are focusing on scaling the reuse of load-bearing concrete components rather than recycling, eliminating the need for use new cement to bind the concrete. I will delve into the toolbox of the circular economy and the difference between reuse and recycling and its ability to keep us within the planetary boundaries in Chapter 9: The Circular Way.

> There are no perfect solutions in a perfect storm.
>
> *Guterres (2023)*

So let us focus on nurturing each other, helping one another act and improving our actions to take further steps on our journey towards improvement continuously. The experience inspired me to create the 4Rs – The Circular Way, highlighting that some things are better than others. Yet, even small steps can make a significant difference in moving us in the right direction and helping us stay within our planetary boundaries.

Question: What actions are you most proud of?

References

Guterres, A. (2023). UN Secretary General, WEF. https://www.un.org/sg/en/content/sg/statement/2023-01-18/secretary-generals-remarks-the-world-economic-forum

Thunberg, G. (2022). *The Climate Book*. Penguin Books Ltd.

7

MANIFESTO

Design in the Anthropocene

Does the world need another design object? Yes, it most certainly does. However, unfortunately, a large part of the designs made today could have very well been without. This is mainly because it has been made to drive exchange rather than use value. Owing to limited problem-solving and improvement for the user and society and its focus mainly on high gains for the financial sector as a driver for sales, the reality of design is questioned. Do we need that new colour?

Design and designers are at crossroads, faced with a choice. They can be perceived as a mere embellishment or recognise their indispensable role in shaping of the rules of material, product and system development. Designers can rethink the rules of the game and create new solutions, not just minimising harm but also creating improvement whilst staying within our planetary boundaries.

Furthermore, as we enter the Anthropocene epoch, reality dawns upon us that we have the power to destroy. Therefore, it is our choice as an industry and as individuals if we wish to stay on a trajectory of destruction and despair or to reclaim our power and use design as a force for good and pursue repair and reimagine a regenerative world, using the unique abilities of design to shape the future. Therefore, essentially, the question before design is: Whether it aspires to be a world maker or a world breaker?

You can guess what my answer is. Inspired by the likes of Kaare Klint and his philosophy of combining tradition with new practices and innovation, I crafted this manifest of ten principles for design in the Anthropocene, bringing together the collective wisdom of the Danish Design Heritage, my practical experience and the insights of current designers and progressive system

DOI: 10.4324/9781003261018-7

thinkers such as Donna Haraway. It paves the way for design to be a world maker. Thus, the manifest **is a nexus between the heritage and the challenges and opportunities of the current**. I created it to revive human ingenuity to spark creativity and action. It serves as a guide for designers to use, to impart knowledge and inspire the society and business to enhance advancements across various professions. Despite the challenges we face on global scale, it is crucial to acknowledge that it is also an opportunity for us to regain our creative force. As we already learned from the Danish Design Heritage, social purpose can be a positive, creative constraint. Tactile designs raise the level of ambition and achieves even better design solutions that create global prosperity within our planetary boundaries.

Manifesto: Design in the Anthropocene is:

Stubbornly optimistic

Imagination is the first step towards creating. Believing in the possibility of positive change is the initial step to improvement. I first came across the expression "stubborn optimist" coined by the brilliant Christiana Figueres (Figueres & Rivett-Carnac, 2020). It highlights the essence of staying optimistic in dire situations and continue working to reverse the situation. It is also

FIGURE 7.1 A chair in a tree (All The Way To Paris).

important to acknowledge that being optimistic requires hard work and it is a driving force for innovation and citizen engagement to move from despair to repair and, ultimately, reimagination. We are making the required societal transformation not just about what we need to get away from but, more than anything, what we want to move towards.

Staying with the trouble

We are undeniably facing significant challenges, and to overcome them, we must be willing to face these problems and take the time to analyse them holistically before seeking quick fixes. That process may not necessarily be pleasant, but through a design approach, we can turn it into a valuable experience. It ensures that the solutions we create are well thought through and tackles problems not just on the surface level but addresses their root cause. This process includes questioning the norms and systems we take for granted as being natural, while they are social constructions. Rather than trying to fit in with existing systems, we should not hesitate to challenge the status quo and reflect on the system itself. Thus, design in the Anthropocene can ask questions without being afraid of not knowing the answers.

The notion of "Staying with the trouble" comes from Donna Haraway, who, in her book *Staying with the Trouble*, describes it as:

> In fact, staying with the trouble requires learning to be truly present, not as a vanishing pivot between awful or Edenic pasts and apocalyptic or salvific futures, but as mortal critters entwined in myriad unfinished configurations of places, times, matters, meanings.
>
> *Haraway (2016)*

Design enables us to do just that: stay with the trouble and change the rules of the game not just to treat the symptoms of the current systems but to create systemic change and a regenerative society for all to thrive in. By staying with the trouble, design enables us to question our choices, constraints and previous beliefs and perspectives. This allows us to view the world through different lenses, seeing opportunities where once we would only have seen obstacles.

Views the planetary boundaries as positive creative constraints

The Danish Design Heritage exemplifies the equilibrium of social purpose and aesthetics that raised the ambition and result of the final design. With the severe state of our climate, I observe that design talents are rediscovering that equilibrium and learning from nature how we can harness the power of creativity to bring harmony between people and the planet. Inspired by the Danish Design Heritage and the newer Danish design cases highlighted throughout this book, sustainability does not have to compromise aesthetics, convenience or price. Instead, it can be a positive, creative constraint that heightens the level of ambition and ultimately ensures better solutions for people, profit and the planet. As such, staying within our planetary boundaries should not lead to compromises but be a means to heighten the final design solutions, much like fulfilling a social purpose improved the overall ambition and design in the Danish Design Heritage and for Danish businesses.

Natural

Learning from and mimicking nature via biomimicry as a design philosophy and the tactile use of biomaterials is a grand opportunity to move from despair to repair and ultimately towards reimagining our buildings as a tool to regenerate our planet. If we dare to use it, there are opportunities in abundance to harness within mycelium, algae, seaweed, etc. To create genuinely positive buildings smartly capturing carbon in a way so simple, it is indeed the ultimate form of sophistication we as humans and technologists can only hope to dream of (so far). A great starting point is always to look towards nature and biomimicry and the incredible solutions, materials and systems nature continue to create. So the essence lies in remaining connected to and collaborating with nature.

Furthermore, bioengineering is gaining force, providing new ways to scale and accelerate the use of our natural materials and solutions.

Collaborative

From nature, we also learn that, much like Gaia, we are all connected and part of a larger ecosystem, and our actions and futures are interlinked. Hence, we must remember connectedness with nature and each other across geographies, professions and demographics and learn to collaborate. An important aspect is thus to be mindful of one's capabilities to put them into play, but just as essential to make room and allow different abilities and professions to cast their magic to ensure the best possible holistic approach and effect. Just imagine the possibilities if we collaborate and combine our global efforts and start working together across industries and geographies and design in a way that accelerates and scales the journey towards regenerative products, buildings and cities in harmony with nature.

Most likely simple

Simplicity is a crucial trait of the Danish Design Heritage, and one can find many design examples reflecting minimalist aesthetic. However, it is essential to recognise that simplicity is as much a design philosophy ensuring that:

- form follows function, leading to improved design solutions through their synergy
- solutions are transparent and mainly composed of mono materials

- the end output is understandable, not only to the experts but also to people in general
- it entails the ability to achieve more with less

While complexity may be required in certain cases, too many things are covered in unnecessary complexity without creating value, instead decreasing transparency and connectedness while increasing material usage and carbon emissions. In this regard, less is truly more, and there is talent and craft in keeping things simple. Interestingly, the more complex the problem is, the simpler the solution it often requires.

Relevant

Business and design are here to solve problems and create value for users and society. The essence of design is problem-solving and shaping a better world. Whether at micro level of individual product design or at a macro level of grand systemic design, when done right, no profession is better than design at the art of shape making and thus holds the ability to shape the unknown future.

In this context, the focus shifts from solely considering exchange value and more about the tactile effect of your solutions. Success is measured not just in profits but in the use-value and the improvement it creates. Hence, a simple question to remember is whether the design creates value for the user while staying within our planetary boundaries.

Is imperfect

This is both about practicality and philosophy. Practically, so many materials and products are wasted due to an unnaturally high threshold for perfection. If we make room for more quirkiness and that things don't have to be exactly alike, we can quickly reduce a lot of waste.

On a more philosophical level, it is also about not letting perfection stand in the way of good. Instead, realising that we need to be willing to experiment, fail or even fall short of our goals, is perfectly acceptable. Failure is an integral part of the journey towards success. If we are to be victorious at mitigating climate change promptly, we must dare to raise our ambition and move to unchartered waters, which requires the willingness to fail. What matters is that we have taken the first steps, acted towards improvement and continue to do so.

Is caring

Caring is a trait instilled and inspired by the craftsmanship of Danish design. We take our time to care about the quality of materials, craftsmanship and aesthetics to ensure the designs stand the test of time.

There is an inherent possibility to care in the design process due to the choices we actively make. A colour, an object, a specific shape: Our decisions are never random but always thought through, rational and questioning the status quo. Therefore, design embodies functionality. It enables intentionality. Unfortunately, today we know the opposite of using intentionality for good all too well – that is, to design for obsolescence, which must never be the intention.

Thus, it is also essential to acknowledge that storytelling and the power of design as an opportunity and responsibility that can make or mar the possibility of a better world. While taking the time to care sounds so simple, but it has become increasingly difficult for our society. We struggle to prioritise quality of solutions, materials, craftsmanship, aesthetics and care for each other and our planet as a collective. It is vital to emphasise caring throughout the entire design process – caring about the process, the product, the behaviour and usage it promotes, and the importance of designing for thoughtfulness rather than thoughtlessness among users and society at large. For instance, we should design durable and timeless products that can be treasured for generations.

Is not sustainable

Design is a craft and a methodology that can create improvement and lead us to regeneration. We must always appreciate the importance of skills and tactility in the design profession. The combination of technical know-how, a social purpose and artistic sensibility has made the Danish Design Heritage so successful. The ability to shape forms and design solutions regardless of being analogue or digital and use tactility and understanding of materials as well as user needs to improve functionality and solve problems is a much-needed unique value of the design trait. This trait only gains importance for design as a world maker rather than a breaker that creates solutions shifting us from despair to repair and ultimately to reimagining. I don't believe in sustainable design as an individual discipline separate from design in general. What matters the most is a designer or changemaker's ability to craft good design and put the methodology of design to good use.

Furthermore, "sustainability", or lack thereof, depends on its effects in its context. A "sustainable" concept or rendering must be measured on its tangible or intangible impact. Thus, good design always considers its context and the responsibility and opportunity that the Anthropocene gives. Moreover, overusing the notion of "sustainable design" leads to challenges rather than achieving meaningful progress. This results in distraction from the needed action, desensitise users, and slows down the necessary improvement through "sustainable" consumption. That, in reality, has minimal effect. So the question remains: Whether or not the designed solution enables us to create value while staying within our planetary boundaries or not?

Question: We are all individuals and so are our journeys toward change. What other personal principles would you add to the manifesto?

References

Figueres, C., & Rivett-Carnac, T. (2020). *The Future We Choose: The Stubborn Optimist's Guide to the Climate Crisis*. Vintage Books.

Haraway, J. D. (2016). *Staying with the Trouble: Making Kin in the Chthulucene*. Duke University Press.

8

THE PURPOSE OF BUSINESS IS TO SOLVE PROBLEMS

The current linear system, which focusses on exchange value rather than use value, poses a significant constraint to your business and prevents you from making a positive change at a global scale. It is as simple as that. Industry plays a key role in scaling the necessary solutions globally in a timely manner with the circular economy as the toolbox. We can change the game radically and pave the way for a new vision where current obstacles become future opportunities. That is the reason why you see sustainable business icon Vestas adopts the concept of circular economy to future-proof their operations, as described in the case later in this chapter. As already discussed across this book, there is an excellent potential for businesses to be inspired by the philosophy of the Danish Design Heritage and use the principles presented in Chapter 7 Manifesto: design in the Anthropocene as a tool to drive improvement on a global scale. Businesses have the opportunity and necessity to lead the change by creating innovations that demonstrates to the public and politicians the feasibility of changing the status quo.

From a Danish perspective, the role of business as a societal problem solver delivering both innovative solutions and income via taxes to fund public spending is widely acknowledged. This concept forms part of the societal contract not only in Denmark but also across the Nordics. As we explored in Chapter 2 on the insights from the Danish Design Heritage, the social purpose elevated the final product and created superior solutions. Look at some of our largest corporations today: Novo Nordisk, Ørsted, Vestas, Christian Hansen Holding, Danfoss and Grundfos, all created in that perfect interlink

DOI: 10.4324/9781003261018-8

between societal problem-solving and commercial viability. This highlights that strategically integrated sustainability makes viable businesses and businesses drive sustainable development. It's a straightforward yet powerful principle.

I started The Circular Way in 2015 to help businesses claim their role in the transition towards improvement. Since then, I have learned a lot regarding practical experience breaking down technical and commercial barriers. These insights are shared as cases in this book. and they have been further shaped by the evolving state of our world and climate. The "old" purpose of the circular economy, centred on decoupling growth from carbon emissions, was one small part of the problem and opportunity for our global solution space. I now know a much dire truth regarding how bad a situation we are in and how quickly we need to improve. This chapter is an effort to share the methodology I developed to help guide our decision-making from an entrepreneurial perspective. I do still believe that business provides the best way to get us from despair to repair and ultimately reimagine our society to one that creates value while staying within our planetary boundaries.

After establishing The Circular Way, I later created Lendager TCW (The Circular Way) with Anders Lendager to reclaim business as a powerful driving positive societal change by utilising a cross-disciplinary skills approach to spearhead the creation of a regenerative society for all to thrive in by enabling business and climate to be each other's prerequisites. The most significant change was to expand my Microsoft Office consultancy realm with the laws of physics in the tool shop. We need to act and create genuine innovations capable of competing commercially while reducing the environmental footprint significantly and highlighting that improvement is durable. Later some of those waste-to-resource innovations were spun out to be part of newly established company a:gain, an independent entity we created with external capital to scale the material innovations to accelerate the use and effect of the innovation. Therefore, in this section, I will share our experience and describe the tools used to achieve the goals, hopefully giving you valuable inspiration and insights to help you ACT and scale your impact.

Given the direction our world and climate are moving, the only way forward is to raise the level of ambition, strive to achieve aspirations and find ways to create value at scale while staying within our planetary boundaries. This entails moving beyond a benchmark approach of doing "less bad" and towards regenerative value creation. In that sense, I see three types of businesses:

1 The regenerative business, where the business model and use of materials and products enable the business and environment to be mutually beneficial.
2 The responsible business strives to minimise the negative impact. Still, it operates within a linear business model, making it difficult to decouple its growth and value from CO_2 emissions and the use of virgin materials.
3 The stranded business lacks the need or the opportunity to operate differently. Instead, it remains trapped in a traditional structure where business and the environment remain each other's worst enemies.

This highlights that 'doing less bad' by outperforming the current benchmark or being the leader within an industry is not enough. Admirable as it may be, these achievements are not enough for the society or your business, especially if you wish to gain or maintain a competitive edge. It is only when sustainability becomes intrinsic to your core business, enabling you to increase the value you give to your clients and users, you will make a real improvement and gain that competitive edge. That is when you measure your success on your ability to create value for people while staying within the planetary boundaries. A good starting point is to account for the actual cost of your carbon equivalent emissions and continuously measure and work to improve your return on carbon.

But to become a *regenerative business*, simply looking towards financial targets and defining success in one's ability to make money is not ambitious enough. Remembering that business is about solving problems, not just creating returns, we must do more and create use value. The financial sector can put results in a spreadsheet and show their investors they generated a return higher than the benchmark. Undeniably, returns are necessary, and as an investor, I expect returns. They are a means to an end, not the goal itself. Ultimately, it should be about problem-solving. Currently, the elephant in the room across industry at large and the built environment, in particular, is that it is not any more. We have forgotten that capitalism is meant to help and improve society, and it should not be society working for capitalism but the other way around. So much like designing The Circular Way and the duality of having to work towards both utilising the waste we have today and at the same time designing a world without waste. Similarly, we must also work to create more responsible and ultimately regenerative businesses while challenging and changing our societal structures to become sustainable and achieve a regenerative world truly.

We must ask ourselves: What matters the most, short-term financial gains or long-term prosperity? Most would intuitively say the latter, but the problem is that we have structured our society to incentivise people, businesses and even nations to do the opposite, that is to choose the short-term win. While making the improvements we need today, we must never forget the importance of imagining and creating a new societal structure incentivising long-term societal prosperity rather than short-term gains benefitting the very few.

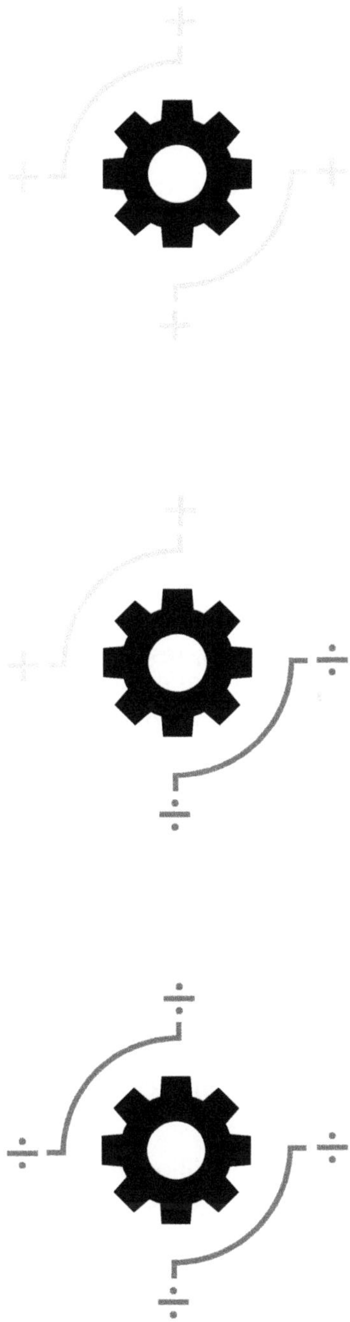

FIGURE 8.1 Three Types of Businesses (All The Way To Paris).

This is not an argument against capitalism; it is simply an argument against how we have structured our society with a one-sighted focus on quantitative rather than qualitative economic gains as the sole definition of value (GDP). In short, growth and development are powerful enablers of change. Just as it has always been in nature, but this is only true if we make sure that the growth we hope to create is a means to an end – and not an end in itself. What we grow matters. When we explore both circular economy and technology as part of a business's toolbox for improvement, they can either be a tool for disruption and paving the way for the new paradigm or be of service to business as usual, helping to uphold the existing through incremental change.

The magnitude of the challenge is immense. We have built our modern world in a stable environment (the Holocene). We find ourselves in a world with an increasingly unstable climate (the Anthropocene). We must address this situation by not using our so far essential tool – fossil fuels. It means there are many different parts of the solution, and we will encounter failures before we get it right. So it is vital that we support each other in navigating these failures and share the good and the bad, so we can learn quickly and adapt.

We *need* to change the rules of the game and redesign the system to address the challenges before us. Currently, we have privatised all benefits, socialising all costs of pollution and emissions, resulting in significant shift in societal values and the methods of measuring them. Putting a price on externalities through a carbon tax is a great starting point for fixing this, but that alone will not help us bring the comprehensive change that we aspire. We must consider the structures in society, including the cultural norms and mindset that have developed over time. It is important to break free from the harmful habits and behaviour. When you think about it, how odd is it that culturally we perceive the capital market as a force of nature out of our control but the planetary boundaries as social constructions we can control and thus wait to act upon until we find it convenient? The need of the hour is innovations, enabling prosperity for all without compromising our climate, and creating value for people whilst staying within our planetary boundaries. We must reclaim business as a stellar force to solve societal problems. For the future of industry, the slogan must be **that the bigger the impact, the better the business**.

If Mother Earth walked in with a million dollars

For years, science has been trying to tell us what we must move away from. In particular, we must stop using virgin resources and fossil fuels excessively. However, we have not given much heed to it because the use of fossil fuels contribute to a country's prosperity, and many things we treasure are taken for granted today. Neither of those things that we either treasure or take for granted are things we are keen to live without. Especially not since business has continuously told us first that we can't and lately that we don't have to. This narrative is misleading as a change in consumption patterns and in business models is equally essential although technology plays a crucial role in finding the solutions as well.

We need a fresh approach to communication driven by science in collaboration with the world's best communications director or the likes. Imagine if Mother Earth walked in with a million dollars to the world's best creative agencies. What if the combination of scientists and creatives together joined forces to craft a compelling narrative, one that captivates and inspires to work towards a better future?

Advertising has been tremendously successful at changing our behaviour and altering our desires. Let us take a scenario where the client walking into the creative agency is Mother Earth asking them to employ all the tricks they know to get us to behave in a way that saves rather than deteriorates our planet. The goal is to foster harmony between humanity and the Earth. Together we can create a narrative that brings out the best and most beautiful aspects of humanity, empowering us to ACT, question our existing systems and find new ways to generate value for people while staying within the planetary boundaries.

Storytelling and the ability to create a compelling narrative that encourages and enables us to take in the facts and, most importantly, act upon them are significantly important, and we must get much better at it to succeed.

As explored throughout this book, I believe the way to do that is to make the story of climate change less about what we need to leave behind and move away from and much more about what we aspire to achieve. In this regard, the Danish Design Heritage serves as a source of inspiration to strive towards and engage us in crafting a narrative that allows for optimism and empowers us, Rather than pacifying us by fear or greenwashing. Although there is plenty of data that can make us lose hope and paralyse us, we need to see beyond that. And instead, design a new narrative for mitigating climate change—a **narrative balancing climate urgency and empowerment**.

Such a narrative is best created via consilience, which combines creative professionals and scientists. Creative professionals have decades of experience successfully influencing our actions and choices. The scientists have persuasively conveyed the message of what we should avoid.

> We do not appropriate what we need but what we desire … This is why arts and all the other things we do with other people are the most powerful agents to preserve a liveable world. Nothing can change humanity's basic needs, but arts can change our desires, which are the source of most of our impact on Earth's environment and biological diversity.
>
> *Rosing (2020)*

As Danish design legend Poul Henningsens tried to call to action back in the 1950s, mass production had successfully occupied our minds, as referenced in Chapter 2 on the Danish Design Heritage. It is an important reflection point on the dangers of cultural and societal structures gradually imposing and pacifying us as citizens in reigning societal structures. I, for one, do not wish to be reduced to being a consumer. Yet it is precisely what we collectively have often fallen to this role. It is now time to reclaim the power of storytelling and take back the narrative. This is important because we are greatly influenced by strategic storytelling today without realizing the powerful impact it has on us. As the first public relations mastermind Edward Bernays, who made a career out of helping businesses ensure a steady flow of demand by driving consumption, so clearly put in his book *Propaganda* back in 1928.

> The conscious and intelligent manipulation of the organised habits and opinions of the masses is an important element in democratic society. Those who manipulate this unseen mechanism of society constitute an invisible government which is the true ruling power of our country.... We are governed, our minds are molded, our tastes formed, our ideas suggested, largely by men we have never heard of. This is a logical result of the way in which our democratic society is organized. Vast numbers of human beings must cooperate in this manner if they are to live together as a smoothly functioning society.... In almost every act of our daily lives, whether in the sphere of politics or business, in our social conduct or our ethical thinking, we are dominated by the relatively small number of persons...who understand the mental processes and social patterns of the masses. It is they who pull the wires which control the public mind.
>
> *Bernays (1928)*

So, what would happen if Mother Earth did walk in with a million dollars to the world's best creative agencies? Not a whole lot with the one million dollars alone. That is at least not as long as billions of dollars are still poured yearly into advertising campaigns to make us do the wrong things. And unfortunately, billions of dollars still are! That is why we need to change the system and bring back the purpose of business. The knowledge from both Barneys and Henningsen nonetheless highlights that our short-term consumerism behaviour could be different. What if we designed the system towards use value and regeneration rather than exploitation?

The purpose of business

In 1970, the economist Milton Friedman wrote an article titled "The Social Responsibility of Business is to Increase its Profits" published in *The New York Times Magazine*. As the title suggests, he argued that "the sole purpose of a business is to generate profits for its shareholders" (Tepper, 2020). A notion widely used and which sentiment has become a fundamental logic within the financial sector. But for one, he forgot that business is connected to and part of a larger context. That is why the notion of Stakeholder capitalism proposed by Klaus Schwab, the founder of the World Economic Forum, is gaining momentum (Schwab, 2021). As author Thomas Friedman expresses it, Mother Nature and Father Greed need to collaborate (Friedman, 2019).

The purpose of business is not just about generating profit for shareholders, but the purpose of business is to create use value by solving problems and doing that well enough to make a profit. Not the other way around. As already shared, growth should be a means to achieve improvement rather than a goal in itself. So how do we reclaim growth as a means to our societal ends? First, we must remember to use the planetary boundaries as creative constraints and take the time to care. So we make sure we always have our real goals with us, the ones we took the time to reflect upon, where we haven't been afraid to stay with the trouble to reimagine and find the goals that truly create value and matter as guided by the principles presented in Chapter 7 Manifesto: design in the Anthropocene. Your starting point and what unites you is your vision and a collective answer to the question, *Why?* What problem(s) do you solve, and why does it matter to your user and society at large? Reaching for the stars and not being afraid to be ambitious, as I will share more on in the methodology Enlightened Action in the section below.

Reiterating the purpose of business, you need to think long and hard: about what you actually do Sure, you may be selling a product, but instead of fixating on that, start by looking at your value proposition: What are you providing? What value do you give your users, and how can you enhance that? Why does this matter? Being able to find the answers to all these questions enable you to create a new type of financial incentive structure, making it possible to increase value based on longevity and the quality of the innovative products. Before starting The Circular Way, my journey into the realm of circular economy was when I invested in the Danish baby clothing company VIGGA, built as a service rather than selling clothes. Users subscribe to a service that regularly provides them with clothes for use during a specified time frame, after which they are returned to VIGGA to be checked, cleaned and recirculated. That changes the rules of the game by providing a product benefiting consumers and the planet while finding its sweet spot between cost and value. Luckily, we see more and more of this kind of value innovation.

This brings me to our next point. Take the time to be inspired to learn from others within your industry, alternative industries, and other geographies. In that sense, the concept that holds good is *Local is global* and vice versa. What trends are happening, and what innovations are being brought to market? Can you use some of these from either a business model or a technological perspective? Or in a new way? You don't have to reinvent the wheel. Learn from others and build upon it to apply value within your area of expertise.

Chances are that you, too, can recover resources from elsewhere and use them as your supply chain. Or you may have dormant resources internally that you can reactivate to increase your innovation's value proposition. In fact, the process of recovery and reuse does not only apply to innovations. It is relevant all across your production line. And it is not just about the reuse and recycling of materials and products; it's as much about finding new business models to reduce the necessary input and replacing fossil materials with new and better materials altogether. Therefore, it is recommended to use the 4Rs – The Circular Way as discussed in Chapter 9 to guide you on your exploration.

It is crucial to focus on problem-solving and creating use value rather than exchange value as society needs it. In doing so, it gains a positive aspect presenting a grand opportunity for you to do good for the planet while doing good business. Starting with why and using design to question the status quo and our existing structures enables you to see and explore ideas that most others have yet to experience. We should fearlessly experiment as *trial and error* is an essential part of the process and key to accelerating your development. So if you have the opportunity, don't let yourself be brought down by the lack of equipment, financing, know-how, etc. Instead, use the fact that you have dared to trust your vision and intuition and have dared to go your own way. You must continue to follow those instincts. Remember that the only constant is change and in a world where traditional market segments are becoming blurred, where limits are constantly broken, and technology develops at unprecedented speed, the ability to look beyond norms and to ask questions is essential.

Above all, this means prioritising action and being proactive, not reactive. You need to be a stubborn optimist to create your own and our collective future. You do not have to blindly follow the rules of the current market and the economic macro trends that affect it. Essentially, success depends on the ability to innovate and to ACT to deliver value continually. The next section presents my framework, Enlightened Action, created based on our learnings to put the action at the centre and enable the doers.

Enlightened Action

> Opportunity is missed by most people because it is dressed in overalls and look like work.
>
> *Edison (cited in Hilimire, 2017)*

A remarkable quote by Thomas Edison that highlights the importance of action and not being afraid of accomplishing tasks. So now, let's embark on an interesting journey and get things done! Enlightened Action means placing action at the core and enabling the doers to prioritise their tasks and letting strategy and the countless "productions" in Microsoft Office or similar take second place in service for the doers who take action. I am very well conscious about my action in "producing" this book at the realm of Microsoft Office. However, the goal of this is to inspire and empower more to take action and that ultimately the value of this book should be measured in just that: the action it enabled. Reflecting our entry into the Anthropocene and the dire problems we are in, it is evident that we have the opportunity as humans to move from despair, repair and to reimagine. However, there is urgency to take action swiftly because with any and every rise in temperature that window of opportunity decreases. This is the reason for enabling Enlightened Action as my methodology for moving from theory to practice prioritising action and at the same time enabling the best possible and most enlightened conditions therefore. To guide you on this path, I present four principles:

- with both eyes open
- reach for the stars
- trial and error
- local is global

With both eyes open is a reference to the "Use Less" group of scientists at Cambridge University that coined the phrase whilst working on their project and book *Sustainable Materials: With Both Eyes Open* (Allwood and Cullen, 2012). Their point is that with energy efficiency, we open one eye towards the opportunity of doing less harm by optimising our existing systems; with the circular economy, we get the toolset to open both our eyes to the chance to reimagine and create new solutions that enable business and climate to be prerequisites rather than opposites by turning problems to opportunity and ensuring that sustainability is at the core. From a business perspective, it is about moving your business from doing less bad to doing good. So start by making sure both your eyes are open for opportunities and the barriers prohibiting you from moving from despair to repair and ultimately to reimagining. The book *Sustainable Materials: With Both Eyes Open* is highly recommended and available for free download.

Reach for the stars inspires you to be bold, to dare to dream and set our ambitions high – so high that we continuously strive to get there. When I present the methodology of Enlightened Action, I always have a picture of the moon landing in the background of the first slide because it perfectly reflects what we need to do. That is what American president John F Kennedy meant when he said that he wanted to put a man on the moon. He gave direction and empowered the public and private sectors to work towards the common goal of putting a man on the moon. When he set the goal, no one knew how to do it. By literally reaching for the stars and having the courage to set an ambitious goal, it became possible for people to work together towards that common goal and jointly piece the puzzle together to ultimately not just find the way how to do it, but to act and do it. If we want to succeed with the transformation and ensure our solutions are future-proof, we must learn from that and set our ambition aloft.

One checkpoint is: Do you know how to reach your goal? If you do, you need to push yourself to go higher.

Trial and error is about reaching the necessary improvement at the speed we need it. Author and environmentalist Bill McKibben so rightly said: Winning the climate crisis slowly is, unfortunately, the same as losing (McKibben, 2017). Therefore, speed, as well as ambition, is the essence to make the necessary changes and improve our human and planetary well-being. That requires a lot of trial and error, and we must get much better at it. That is daring to be tactile and experimental. Celebrating the wins as well as accepting failure is a part of the process towards success. In that sense, discussing and celebrating our failures and to learn from them is a must-do. So, start testing your idea by creating a mockup and making it tangible in any way possible. Take it to a test market and gather user feedback. Though it may be difficult to hear the initial user feedback, it is crucial to listen to it. Delaying the process will not make it any easier or better.

On the contrary, continued testing saves you valuable time. In our experience, making your product development and thought process tangible provides many insights that benefit and accelerate the entire development. I cannot recommend it highly enough. Another critical point is that we must encourage and support each other on the journey of trial and error because currently, it is always the easiest not to act and instead stay behind the comfortable desk. Let's work to change that. We must celebrate those who dare to try, even when they fail. It is all part of the journey towards improvement.

Local is global, the greatest advantage of globalisation and our technological and digital advancements is that we can now work together globally and harness our collective work and brainpower towards improvement. This means we can and must look for global solutions and experiences to use and learn from rather than think we must reinvent the wheel in every project, company, city or country and instead harness our collective efforts to increase the effect and ensure amplified impact at scale. It also clarifies what nature has known all along: We are connected, and our local actions have a global effect. It is our responsibility and opportunity that the result is for the better.

Lastly, the list of five insightful points to remember are some specific practical learnings of The Circular Way contributing to the methodology. In no way is it to scare you from working with the Enlightened Action methodology, but on the contrary, to increase your chance of success by ensuring you are mindful of the barriers you must overcome.

1 Doing things differently is not only fun, but also challenging. Nonetheless, it is precisely what we need to do. So, we must change the rules of the game and start creating businesses and buildings that give more than they take.
2 The goal is to reach for the stars and make sure that your solutions are not only doing less harm than traditional business but that they are part of the solution – contributing positively to our global well-being. Simply put, we must give more than we take, and strive to create solutions that are not only doing less harm – in terms of using resources responsibly but also facilitating the sustainability of our physical and mental health, our communities, and the way we create regenerative urban environments.
3 Strategic alignment across the value chain is necessary. Don't underestimate the value of being strategically aligned. Instead, you must ensure that your stakeholders and the required actors are aligned with your vision and share your motives, and, most important, that they are ready and willing to support you when reality hits and the going gets tough.
4 Innovation is not "business as usual". No matter what your idea is, innovation is never business as usual. Identify the potential barriers, whether they are regulations, lack of partners, old habits or perceived impossibilities. And if you are successful, the added value should far surpass the potential downside of doing something new.
5 Similarly, without compromising on the final result, be aware that you might need some wiggle room (that is, flexibility) to figure out the best way to implement your innovation. Be sure your stakeholders are aware of this in advance.

From Danish design to global sustainability

Denmark is, of course, part of a larger global context, and with the continued integration in the European Union a part of a strong regional collective. Danish design has always been very aware of the global community, leveraging it to strengthen solutions through inspiration and collaborations internationally.

This approach provides the opportunity to create solutions delivering high value at a global scale. In fact, with fewer than six million people, we need to share, learn and collaborate globally to achieve success.

Throughout my research for the book, the welfare state has been brought up continuously as part of the success of Danish Design Heritage and why coherency, transparency, and, in particular, quality is such a large part of the tradition. Due to the relatively equal distribution of means in society, there has been a sizeable middle class willing and able to buy quality. The Danish furniture was costly but still affordable, as the quality was demanded in our welfare state. With the new design renaissance brought on by the dire troubles we are in and thus the need to stay within the planetary boundaries while creating value for our growing population, the creative forces have once again been released, elevating the ambition and serving as an opportunity to improve the overall design and focus on use rather than exchange value benefitting the user, society and the designer. Therefore, I count my blessings for being Danish and having the perspective gained from growing up in Denmark, with quality design and multiple examples of businesses combining quality, sustainability and commercial viability. Purpose-driven businesses are the norm rather than the exception. A key area where Denmark continuously provide sustainable value at global scale is within systems design, and in particular, with regard to water, energy and heating systems. One example being Danish giant Danfoss who provides solutions within energy efficiency, electric vehicles and as is in this case with waste water management. According to the UN, waste water management still accounts for 8% of global energy consumption. A typical European municipality still uses between 30% and 40% of its total electricity consumption on water treatment. So, it is significant that with the help from Danfoss the Danish city Aarhus have not just managed to reduce that amount significantly, they have actually turned their water management plant, in the area of Marselisborg where the royal Danish family resides during summer, into a surplus enterprise producing 90% more energy than it consumes. This is just one of many great examples of Danish systems design that provides global solutions while being good business creating some of the largest corporations in Denmark. So, I would say the Danish mindset and understanding of the business opportunity when combining green technology and our world-class aesthetics and industrial design is worth sharing globally. Another key area is, of course, renewable and in particular wind energy. I will conclude this chapter by sharing a case of a Danish company that is the embodiment of moving from Danish Design Heritage to global sustainability: That is the iconic Danish windmill manufacturer Vestas, that in 2022 was ranked the most sustainable company in the world by Corporate Knights.

Case 8.1 Vestas

FIGURE 8.2 Vestas Wind Systems Wind Turbines (Vestas Wind Systems A/S, Vestas).

The Danish wind adventure, particularly windmill maker Vestas, is an excellent example of The Danish way. It combines industrial design, green technology and commercial viability to create a business at a global scale, and as such, a perfect example of how business and climate become prerequisites rather than opposites as business and the renewable energy transition are just that: prerequisites. It also tells a great story of what visionary policymakers can accomplish when they dare to set the ambition high and reach for the sky to create new sustainable demand and industry – creating the way for both Vestas and the ecosystem around from small parts manufacturers to global windmill parks developers such as Ørsted and Copenhagen Infrastructure Partners. A true story of how the Danish Design Heritage can turn into global sustainability.

The story of Vestas originates in 1898, when the 22-year-old Hans Smith Hansen bought the local blacksmith workshop on the windswept west coast of Denmark, in the small farming town Lem. However, it was not until 1945 that he, in collaboration with his son Peder Hansen, established Vestjysk Staalteknik A/S, which soon after was shortened to Vestas. The first experiments with wind turbines were carried out in 1978 and by 1979, with the help of two blacksmiths, Karl Erik Jørgensen and Henrik Stiesdal. Vestas successfully sold and installed its first turbine. After being on the brink of bankruptcy in 1986, the company decided to focus exclusively on its goal of making wind energy a viable solution to meet the world's energy demands. Much of the group got sold, and a new company, Vestas Wind Systems A/S, was born.

Technological innovations have always kept Vestas at the forefront of the wind industry despite growing competition. By 2012, Vestas reached the milestone of having installed 50 GW of capacity worldwide, by now that number has more than tripled. In 2020, Vestas became the first company to have more than 100 GW of wind turbines under service and is now servicing +123 GW in 71 countries worldwide. On top of that, Vestas has successfully helped its partners avoid more than 1.7 billion tonnes of carbon emissions over the past four decades.

While sustainability is at the core of Vestas' business, the company has realised that it must become truly sustainable throughout the organisation to meet the growing expectations from customers, partners, investors and employees. Therefore, in January 2020, Vestas launched its Sustainability Strategy, *Sustainability in Everything We Do*. The strategy is based on four key goals: (1) Carbon neutrality in Vestas' own operations by 2030 without using carbon offsets and reducing the CO_2 emissions from Vestas' supply chain by 45% per MWh generated by 2030, (2) Producing zero-waste wind turbines by 2040, (3) Becoming the safest, most inclusive, and most socially responsible company in the energy industry, and (4) Leading the transition to a world powered by sustainable energy.

To achieve these goals, Vestas has, among other initiatives, introduced its pioneering Circularity Roadmap. The roadmap marks an evolution of the previously announced ambition to produce zero-waste turbines by 2040 and showcases one of the first times any company has attempted such an ambitious approach to waste reduction. The roadmap outlines circularity pathways for Vestas' entire value chain by setting new targets across three key areas: design, operations and material recovery. Through its ongoing circularity journey, Vestas aims to accelerate industry wide adoption of circularity practices by fostering a close collaboration with all stakeholders across its value chain, and by leveraging its industry-leading scale, and extensive supply chain network.

Vestas' sustainability efforts have been highly recognised by leading sustainability ratings, such as the CDP ranking, the Dow Jones Sustainability Index

Europe and most recently by Corporate Knights, where Vestas was named the most sustainable company in the world as part of the 18th annual Global 100 ranking.

Building a more sustainable future for our planet, demands that we do more. As the energy transition accelerates, Vestas is dedicated to making sure this transformation unfolds sustainably. Through establishing sustainability as a priority across the entire value chain, including its supplier network, Vestas has created many more opportunities for collaboration, and for driving maturity and scale for the renewables industry. Although there is still a long journey ahead, Vestas is proud to be paving the way for renewables to expand without compromising the interests of future generations.

Question: What problem would you like to solve via business?

References

Barneys, E. L., & Crispin Miller, M. (1928). *Propagangda*. Ig Publishing.

Friedman, T. L. (2019). The Green New Deal Rises Again. It was a good idea that didn't catch on in 2007. Now we're running out of time, 8 January. *New York Times*. https://www.nytimes.com/2019/01/08/opinion/green-new-deal.html

Hilimire, J. (2017). Opportunity Is Missed by Most People Because It Is Dressed in Overalls and Looks Like Work, 18 May. jeffhilimire.com. https://www.jeffhilimire.com/2017/05/opportunity-missed-people-dressed-overalls-looks-like-work/

Corporate Knights (2022). Vestas Named Most Sustainable Company in the World. https://www.vestas.com/en/media/company-news/2022/vestas-named-most-sustainable-company-in-the-world-c3488428

McKibben, B. (2017). Bill McKibben: Winning Slowly Is the Same as Losing: The technology exists to combat climate change – what will it take to get our leaders to act?, 1 December. Rolling Stone [online]. https://www.rollingstone.com/politics/politics-news/bill-mckibben-winning-slowly-is-the-same-as-losing-198205/

Rosing, M. (2020). Biodiversity. In Krogh, M. (Ed.), *Connectedness: An Incomplete Encyclopaedia of Antropocene: Views, Thoughts, Considerations, Insights, Images, Notes & Remarks*. Strandberg Publishing.

Schwab, K. (2021). *Stakeholder Capitalism: A Global Economy That Works for Progress*. People and Planet.

Tepper, T. (2020). Milton Friedman on the Social Responsibility of Business, 50 Years Later. https://www.forbes.com/advisor/investing/milton-friedman-social-responsibility-of-business/

Allwood, J., & Cullen, J. (2012). *Sustainable Materials: With Both Eyes Open*. UIT Cambridge Ltd.

9

THE CIRCULAR WAY

Essay: A fairytale of circularity

H.C. Andersen and Klods-Hans teach us an important lesson: That rather or not it be dead crows and a glob of mud – when seeing treasures where others see waste, significant victories are won.

The contemporary business concepts such as circular economy, upcycling, disruption, innovation, lean management, etc. are mostly considered slightly hyped and buzzword-sounding terms. Renowned Danish storyteller Hans Christian Andersen was a forerunner of today's organisational oracles and savvy consultants when writing one of his many stories back in 1855.

The stories of Hans Christian Andersen are not just great fairytales but also show a deep understanding of human nature and how we operate as a society. And I continuously see an approach to innovation and business development greatly inspired by H.C. Andersen's famous fairytale "Klods-Hans" (translated in English as "Jack the Dullard" or "Blockhead Hans"). The protagonist is the typical underdog who exceeds everyone's expectations and overtakes his two brothers, his father's favourites, in winning the princess and half the kingdom. While both siblings are awed into speechlessness when they see the princess, Klods-Hans charms her by turning a dead crow into a royal meal, a wooden shoe into a frying pan, and a handful of mud into a delicious sauce and in classic Danish design style creates value with less.

The story teaches us an important lesson about the circular economy. While I am not advocating that dead crows, wooden clogs and a glob of mud should

DOI: 10.4324/9781003261018-9

literally be seen as top-notch recyclable resources, by seeing treasures where others see waste, large victories are won, and innovation often means doing what others have deemed impossible.

Although disrespected by his two self-confident brothers and mocked for going against the established norms, Klods-Hans surprised everyone by winning the kingdom and marrying the king's daughter. Thus, we learn that success depends on having courage when seeing possible failure and remaining steadfast when confronted with disdain and disapproval.

Klods-Hans was not just unique in his way of thinking; he also ensured that the most important stakeholder – the princess – would buy into his vision and see things from his perspective. So breaking with tradition and winning depended on having a coherent story and communicating it clearly and persuasively. After all, if no users are willing to listen to your pitch, your impact will be limited, no matter how good your ideas are.

In the best Klods-Hans style – waste can become resources and be reused or recycled. In my work and at Lendager, it is the norm, and we do this with a genuine desire to make sustainability both understandable and appealing to people at large. We aim to inspire by demonstrating that we can do things differently.

But, all too often, the distance between the visionary idea and the measurable result is too big for even the most ambitious companies. That is where Klods-Hans come in because the world needs more out-of-the-box thinkers like him.

It's about celebrating diversity, seeing flexibility and ingenuity as strengths, and celebrating those who excel at seeing possibilities rather than obstacles and achieving success by pursuing it step by step. To be a modern-day Klods-Hans, you must be willing to challenge convention and break the existing framework.

Indeed, you have to see the barriers and the risks, but you can't accept them as roadblocks. On the contrary, for your business to succeed, you must identify the structures, rules and regulations that stand in your way to overcome them! Only then can you – with your unique idea that satisfies an unprecedented need – identify problems needing solving and turn them into business opportunities, create sustainable improvement and position yourself in an advantageous sweet spot with limited competition.

Beginning The Circular Way

Imagine a world where houses are grown using fungal networks, shoes are made of plastic waste and yarn picked up from our oceans, T-shirts are created from recycled polyester and homes are built using old newspapers and champagne corks. Products such as lamps and baby clothes are designed to create value for many users through a product-as-a-service model, instead of being sold to an individual consumer and eventually discarded. These examples illustrate how designing for circularity changes our consumption patterns, and there is much more to explore. It is a necessary transformation from exchange to use value and part of the solution to the challenge of the globe's rapidly growing population that consumes and depletes its dwindling resources. To ensure we utilise the full potential of circular economy as a disruptive tool requires moving towards a user-centric design of value creation for society. This entails not just considering the material or product but also its context, including business model and the systems it is embedded in. It is an opportunity we must not miss. When done right, designers' creative ability to think across traditional materials, methods, sectors and professions, and produce attractive products, can deliver impactful global change.

The core objective of a circular economy is to prevent waste generation and stop materials from ending up in a landfill. Achieving this goal requires a two-fold approach. In the long term, the focus is on designing products in a way that prevent them from ever becoming waste. Currently, we have to find new, innovative ways to repurpose the substantial amount of waste that has already been generated and most likely will continue to create in this transition period. The challenge here is to implement the two approaches at once. To fix the problem in the short-term, we must adopt waste-to-resource innovations, while keeping our focus on long-term resolution of designing to eliminate waste from the start and accelerating that transition is a priority.

The circular economy is a fundamentally new way of looking at resources and returning to nature's way, where everything is used. From a practical perspective, it means ensuring we use our resources better and to their full extent through design. We think that this is how we usually use our resources, but unfortunately, it is not the case. With industrialisation and technological advancement, we more or less unintentionally came to build our international society and systems on an abundance of natural resources, a need for speed, and a desire to conquer unknown technological opportunities. Ultimately, this leads to incentivising speed and change over quality and improvement, consequently resulting in extreme resource usage and waste production, hurting both our climate and biodiversity and entrapping our global population in a spiral of consumption. Therefore, while the circular economy has traditionally been described as the process of decoupling growth from materialisation and CO_2 equivalent emissions, I propose a changed focus, expressed as the process of decoupling value from exceeding our planetary boundaries, which focusses on quality rather than quantity, content over numbers and ensures that our designs create holistic solutions taking its systemic context into account. Though countless reports have been made on the theoretical potential of circular economy highlighting numerous small-scale pilot projects and targets set by governments and large corporations, the absolute tangible effects of the circular economy have so far been limited.

The limited implementation of circular economy principles can be attributed to several factors, such as lack of scale and its predominant use to support business as usual by doing a little less harm through recycling and reuse schemes used for branding in a linear business model. In that sense, it is both a blessing and a curse that circular economy, on the surface, fits so well with the existing economic mindset and system. On the one hand, it opens the door for a conversation on material, product and business model innovation. Still, on the other, it is currently at high risk of becoming sustainability sprinkles disguising a traditional exploitative business model. So like designers at large, as circular economy entrepreneurs, we must ask ourselves: Are we servicing business as usual, or are we part of paving the way for a new realm?

We must move from sustainability being about doing less bad and instead focussing on creating processes, and solutions that do good and give more than they take. The circular economy provides a toolbox for achieving this goal. However, it is crucial to recognise that activating that potential requires a comprehensive approach that considers not just materials and products but also business models and systems. Otherwise, there is a potential risk that the circular economy is used to keep business as usual; unfortunately, such instances are in abundance.

The Circular Way of design goes beyond streamlining existing products or creating additional sustainable benefits it involves redesigning products and business models from the start. The aim is to create value for our global population decoupled from our current immense co2e emissions and exploitation of new resources. Without compromising aesthetics or quality, this approach enables a new type of value creation where citizens are viewed as users rather than consumers, moving business from a focus from exchange to use value. As such, established brands and startups have equally much to gain from the circular economy, mainly the ability to create the future we need. To me, that is the real end game of the circular economy.

The key to unlocking the opportunity and moving towards creating value for our global population while staying within our planetary boundaries lies in the combination of a circular economy with design and innovation. By combining these three elements, we can transform ideas into value innovation that can be brought to the market. In Denmark, we see multinationals such as LEGO, Carlsberg, Danfoss, Vestas and Novo Nordisk starting to explore this idea. Novo Nordisk, a pharmaceutical company, has embraced a Circular for Zero strategy that emphasises the importance of the circular economy to reduce greenhouse gas emissions, as set out in the Ellen MacArthur Foundation's report titled "Completing the Picture: How the Circular Economy Tackles Climate Change" released in 2021 (Ellen MacArthur Foundation, 2021).

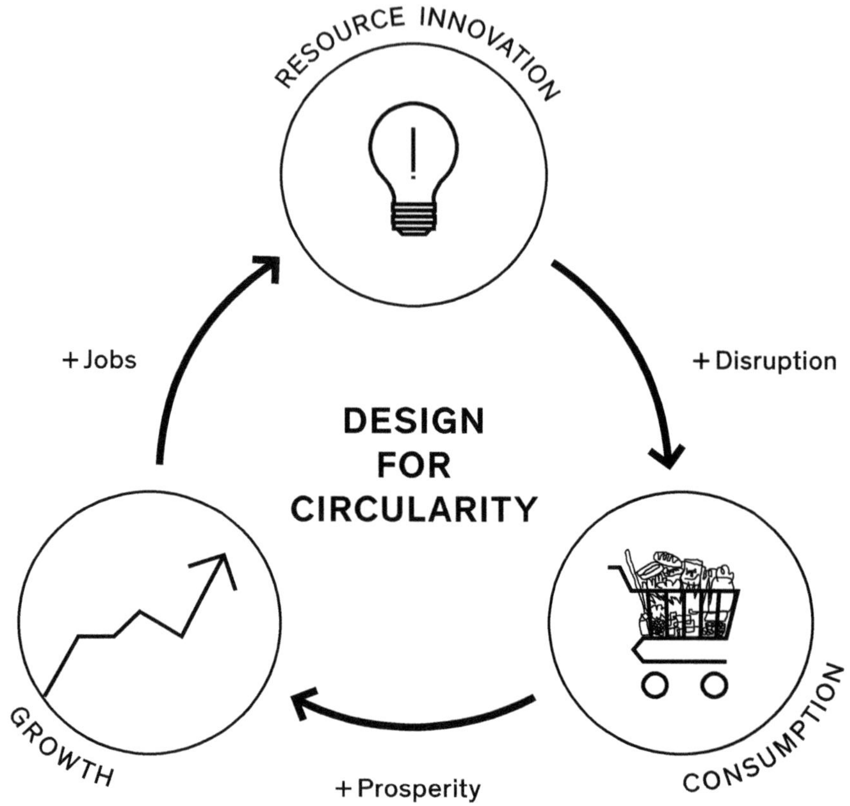

FIGURE 9.1 Design for circularity (All The Way To Paris).

The question is, how can we increase value to ensure livability and prosperity for our global population without exceeding our planetary boundaries? So before we move on to the details, let me clarify that the fact that circulation does not inherently create value, therefore, a circular economy is not a goal in itself. Instead, **it is a toolbox that enables us to act to find a way forward**, delivering value and global prosperity while staying within our planetary boundaries. I call it The Circular Way because it is a map of several paths from where we can move closer towards achieving the goal of a regenerative world to enable both people and the planet to thrive together. (For more in-depth exploration of regeneration, I recommend you to refer to the insightful essay by regeneration specialist Laura Storm in Chapter 5.)

The Ellen MacArthur Foundation says, "A circular economy is restorative and regenerative by design, and seeks to keep products, components and materials at their highest utility and value at all times" (Ellen MacArthur Foundation).

While solving our climate and biodiversity crisis, different types of solutions will emerge, all incredibly important to ensure a prosperous future. However, it became apparent that exploring and testing how the circular economy and designing for circularity can help ensure a prosperous world in which all of us can thrive staying within our planetary boundaries. In 2014, I decided to leave my consultancy day job and immerse myself in the complex and pressing issues of sustainability and climate change. I pursued to gain more knowledge and established a niche consultancy that helped companies use the circular economy. Embracing this approach helped increase their value and gain a competitive edge while also benefitting people and the planet. From there came the collaboration with Lendager Group and the creation of Lendager The Circular Way, where new materials were created from waste resources that are now part of A: GAIN, a product and material producer servicing the built environment in particular. But the goal has always been the same: To design the world of tomorrow with the waste of today while working towards designing a world without waste. We have now realised that virgin materials are becoming scarce, the materials we have already extracted, used and thrown away have not disappeared. Indeed, they are still accumulating, waiting to be put back into use again and in the meantime polluting our ecosystems. It's high time we acted on the problem and seized the opportunity, moving from waste to resource, from exchange to use value.

4Rs – The Circular Way

The great potential of the circular economy has been significantly discussed for years, and countless reports highlighting the theoretical potential have been made. Yet much too little has happened. I see two primary barriers to that. First, from a systemic and societal perspective, as explored in Chapter 3, we are still operating from an outdated paradigm. We are wired to incentivise short-term gains rather than long-term value creation. The other barrier is more tangible, specifically the need to make the circular economy more operational.

By exploring the methodology **"The 4Rs – The Circular Way"**, I have been able to translate our experience into a tangible toolbox that effectively addresses climate change mitigation without compromising on value. This approach provides tactile actions to rethink our mode of production and consumption, moving from our current state of despair toward repair and ultimately reimagining our global society.

The first three Rs, Reduce, Reuse and Recycle, are commonly used terminology within the circular economy and widely used for their effectiveness. However, in practical application, the three Rs need to be combined with a fourth R "Replace" to include "new" biogenic materials as part of the solution space. Thus, it helps create the framework of the 4Rs, Reduce, Reuse, Recycle and Replace. To design effective solutions, it is important to identify the points of inflexion. This involves examining the new types of biogenic materials entering the market in the recent years and assessing them holistically as part of the opportunity space alongside reduce, reuse and recycling that enables you to create value within the planetary boundaries.

Let's dive deeper into the methodology and start with the R that is not a part of the four operational Rs, that is Rethink. The reason for its exclusion from the four is not that it is not essential; on the contrary, it is the fundamental basis on which the 4Rs can be put to use. The circular economy is about design, intentionality and active choices. Therefore, if we aim to create better models for reuse, we need to start by rethinking. For example, when Starbucks Coffee tried to make a more sustainable straw but ended up rethinking and asking if there was even a need for a straw? They shifted their focus from using replace or recycle to reduce as their design tool. I recommend you to explore Chapter 16 Trust the future for a broader perspective on systemic rethinking that emphasizes on the importance of imagination and the ability to reimagine.

However, let's remember that rethinking does not mean we can't learn from the past. On the contrary, it encourages us to question existing structures and challenge our minds to think outside the boxes, current silos and mindsets. It prompts us to think creatively without even having a box in the picture. **So, to be conscious, always start with Rethink** and keep the user's actual need in focus when exploring which of the 4Rs is the best tool for you to progress within the particular situation and context with a bias toward use rather than exchange value. And in the process, it is crucial to assess that we do not caught up in the "how" of things, ignoring the "why" (trust me, speaking from experience, that can happen).

We must understand why we should choose one of the 4Rs as our guiding star when making the decision. The purpose of the methodology and the tool it aims to be is to decouple value creation from the use of virgin materials and, most notably, from CO_2 equivalent emissions and negative impacts to stay within our planetary boundaries. You may previously have heard a similar version, but with growth rather than value creation as the goal. Focussing on value creation does not mean opposing growth. It is however essential to differentiate between means and ends (goals). Growth is a means that has historically been an important tool to create prosperity, and if we can continue to use growth to create prosperity and we are mindful of what that prosperity looks like and what value needs to be created, then it is by all means beneficial to grow. As nature has always been growing, it is crucial to be aware of what and how we grow things. Therefore, I have expanded the purpose of the 4Rs – The Circular Way to not just avoid emissions and virgin resources, instead I have chosen to expand the things we should focus on to the nine planetary boundaries with a particular focus on climate and biodiversity as guided by Johan Rockstrøm.

But back to the 4Rs – The Circular Way. What does each of them stand for, and how to choose? As you see in the model, the 4Rs can help you move towards a safe operating space within the planetary boundaries and can all be viable tools. However, some are more certain to move us closer to a safe operating space. Throughout this book, you will find that I have focusses on

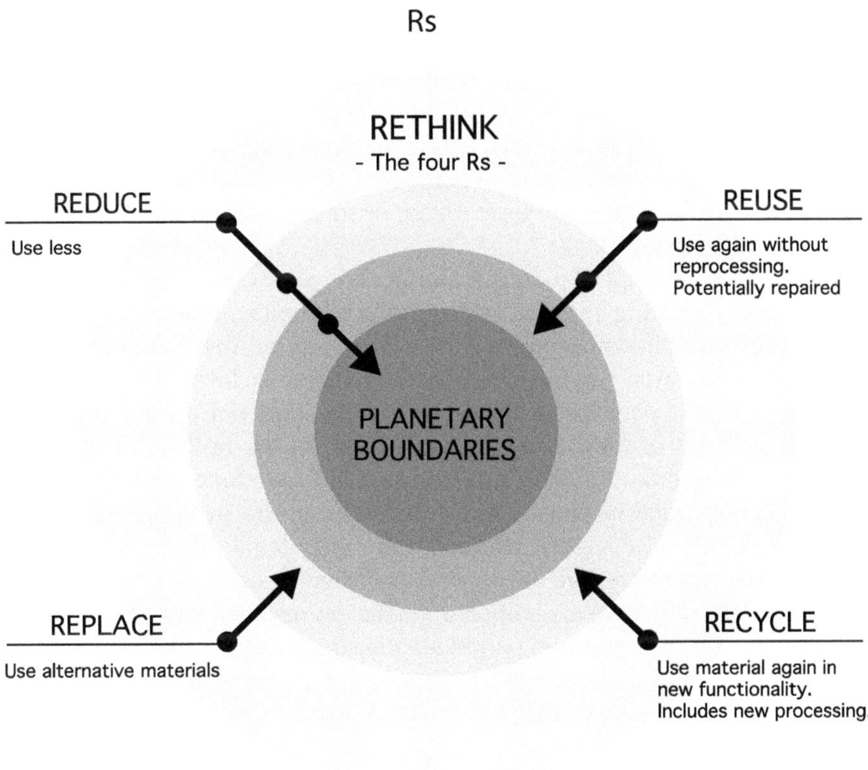

FIGURE 9.2 A model of the 4Rs (Kathrine Hagemann Snabe, The Circular Way).

creating solutions within the realm of recycling. I believe that we need to find solutions that tackle the waste we have today. For long-term sustainability, we must increase the solutions within reuse, replace and reduce as they are more likely to keep us within a safe operating space. So, I continue to push myself to expand my work within the solution space within the other three Rs as well.

Take apparel as an example. Recycling as well as reusing through selling old clothes via online platforms and thrift stores, are usual ways to prolong the life cycle. But it's also a type of damage control. We squeeze the most out of a product flawed by design. We are not changing as much as we should until we begin designing clothes of lasting quality from the get-go and a business model and systemic context incentivising longevity. In an actual circular model, products are made to last as long as possible in a way that makes it possible to separate and reuse the different materials repeatedly, because it is the smart business move. Thus, it is no longer about producing and selling as many products as possible, instead, producing the best possible quality so that the product can be kept in circulation and rented out as long as possible, shifting the focus from exchange to use value. And if you one day find yourself in Schiphol Airport in Amsterdam, you might have the opportunity to experience this model yourself. The Dutch airport no longer buys lamps and bulbs to light up the many gates, terminals and shops inside: They lease energy-efficient lighting systems as a service from Signify (formerly Philips Lightning). They now have a completely different incentive to design durable products that can be reused as they are dismantled, or so each part of the product gets a new product life cycle.

Reduce. The concept of reduce is simple. It involves using fewer resources and materials, resulting in a direct decrease in harmful emissions. It can be often achieved without compromising the value creation. There are various levels at which reduction can be achieved. On a materials level, it can be about redesigning a food package container so that less material is used to contain the same amount of food. On a product level, in the built environment it might include optimal building site management to reduce wasted products during the construction phase, and thus lowering the overall material use and reduces CO_2 equivalent emissions. On the systemic level, reducing the number of square metres we use as well as designing our cities to reduce the number of cars can have a significant impact on resource consumption and carbon emission. By promoting and incentivising bicycling and investing on infrastructure design that supports transportation as explored in the cases of Biomega bicycle design and infrastructure design by Dissing+Weitling highlighted in Chapter 15, we can reduce our dependence on cars and create more sustainable urban environment.

FIGURE 9.3 A drawing of a bathtub (Kathrine Hagemann Snabe, The Circular Way).

> When your bathtub is about to overflow, you don't go looking for buckets – you start by turning off the tap.
>
> *Thunberg (2022)*

As Greta Thunberg rightfully illustrates in the her quote, the strategic starting point should always be to ask: Can I reduce? If you remember the description of the grandness of our problems in Chapter 4: The troubles we are in, it is clear that in the foreseeable future, we will need to look at ways to reduce. Just look at renewable energy. Great things are happening, and solar and wind, among other renewable energy sources, have become not just technically viable at scale but a preferred commercial solution as well. However, even though that is the case, renewable energy is and will continue to be a scarce resource. So reducing our total energy usage via energy efficiency is also a part of the solution and will continue to be. From a material scarcity perspective, reduction is also of the essence as particular metals are in high demand for both the build-out of renewable energy infrastructure and our digital infrastructure and products.

While it might seem a bit of a bore to design with a guiding principle of reduction, it does not have to be. Instead, we can be inspired by the classic Danish design principle of simplicity and the notion that less is more, as explored further in Chapter 7 Manifesto: design in the Anthropocene. As such, designing for reduction is the most challenging and ambitious discipline requiring an excellent skill set within creativity and innovation.

Furthermore, while it is about doing less, it is also about exploring new systems and business models that incentivise reduction. The exciting question is how do we design business models that make a reduction in consumption an attractive business model? One part of the puzzle is the product as a service business model (PAAS), as explored later in this chapter.

Reuse. This approach ensures direct reuse of your product by increasing the first customer's usage as long as possible or ensuring that another user reuses it. More straightforward repair and refurbishment might be necessary, but the product more or less stays the same and does not need energy-intensive processing before it can be passed on to the next user. Take-back schemes and product-as-a-service business models are used to ensure continued circulation. As highlighted in this chapter through the Bang & Olufsen case and my initial experience with the circular economy through the baby clothing startup VIGGA designing and delivering the clothes via a product-as-a-service business model.

When talking about reuse, the context really matters, i.e. if the product is replacing something that is currently in use as a single-use product, the new product designed for reuse should preferably be introduced in a product as a service business model or at least with a viable take-back model as we otherwise risk designing for reuse and thus higher quality which tends to have a higher amount of embedded carbon (the carbon used in production) but the result being that it is still consumed in a single use scheme.

Of course, on the other hand, plenty of products are not currently in use as single-use products but are at risk of becoming one. Just think of the coffee cup you might have in your hands while reading this. Not many years ago, there would be no question as to whether or not a coffee mug would be used time and time again – but unfortunately, that is no longer the case, and single-use coffee cups to use on the go as well as at the office and even in some cases at home are significantly on the rise. When we look at clothing, particularly fast fashion, the trend worsens, with an alarmingly high amount only used once or twice and very little recycling. So when possible, always design for reuse rather than recycling. My experience with the Lendager building with A: GAIN building materials for Upcycle Studios, which I use as a case in Chapter 14 has also been a critical eye-opener. There it was evident that while there was a great reduction in CO_2 emission when reusing the glass from old windows in new frames – the recycling of concrete aggregate, on the contrary, had very little – mainly as the process required using cement to bind the recycled concrete aggregate.

Recycle. The term "recycling" can have multiple meanings to different people. In my definition, recycling involves reprocessing the material to be reused on material rather than product level at the highest value possible while at the same time ensuring that it stays within the circle and can be recycled again. This means waste-to-energy process is not a part of recycling. As highlighted in the case on Re-Plastic in Chapter 6 Theory meets practice and magic happens, as well as the build environment cases from Lendager and A: GAIN on Upcycle Studios and the Resource Rows, I have extensively worked with recycling and continue to do so. However, it is critical to acknowledge that recycling is not the ideal scenario. We should avoid products and materials becoming waste via reduce and reuse whenever possible. However, especially in short to midterm, we will need recycling to reach the necessary scale, but what is essential is that we innovate to ensure that we always recycle to the highest possible quality and that the system to ensure quality recycling is in place.

Furthermore, within chemical recycling, we will see important innovation within recycling technology, moving from high energy-intensive solutions achieving scale but compromising on quality towards higher quality, restoring the original functional capabilities and, at the same time, with an increased focus on energy intensity reductions. We need those because we need all those resources already in use to return to circulation. One example is the innovation in closed-loop recycling of windmill wings.

Replace. Speaking of windmill wings, the wind industry as a replacement to fossil fuels plays a vital role in the Danish Industrial Design Heritage, as explored in Chapter 8 discussing Vestas, Danish windmill manufacturing company, as the case. The initial Danish windmill design has played a vital role in positioning Denmark and the Danish industry in the transition towards an economy less reliant on fossil fuels and closer to staying within the planetary boundaries.

But it is not just about replacing sources of energy. Here replace also refers to replacing our current materials with new and better ones, particularly biobased materials where many interesting materials are being commercialised, allowing for new and better materials while staying within our planetary boundaries.

A few things to be mindful of though is if the biomaterial can be reused or recycled staying within our planetary boundaries. Ensuring a safe operating space is about biodiversity as well as climate, so, particularly within biobased materials, it is essential to look at land-use and ensure production is not at the expense of biodiversity. Fortunately, lots of materials such as mycelium, coffee grounds, algae, seaweed etc. are brought to the market.

The case from Danish furniture company Mater in Chapter 2: Learning from Danish design, on how they use a biopolymer made of coffee grounds to produce a new version of a Danish classic Børge Mogensen chair is an example of the opportunities within Replace, but all of the developments within mycelium, algae and eelgrass etc. are incredibly interesting as well, as will be explored further in Chapter 10 Nature's playbook.

Case 9.1 Bang & Olufsen – designing for longevity

Writing this, I am listening to music on the Bang & Olufsen stereo I inherited from my grandmother after her passing in 2013. I am confident that in technology terms, that makes it ancient; however, through a minor update, it has excellent functionality, aesthetic quality and, not least, emotional value for me; in my experience, that is the rule rather than the exception for B&O continuously creating technology products such as stereos and televisions with an aesthetic resilience that enables their designs to stand the test of time and become true icons in Danish homes. That is why I am glad to include them here and have them share not just their work designing for aesthetic resilience but also how they use the circular economy as a tool to ensure that technology improvements can be made continuously to increase longevity and ensure that the full potential of the high quality of both design and function is reached.

Enduring magical experiences since 1925

The Danish luxury audio and visual entertainment brand Bang & Olufsen was founded since 1925 and have over the last 96 years been recognised for its design-led approach to creating long-lasting products based on uncompromised craftsmanship, high quality, and consistently innovating the way that magical music and cinematic experiences can be provided.

Building a case for a lifetime of music

For many years, Bang & Olufsen has been striving for adding timeless qualities to its designs and the way music and cinematic experiences are consumed. Looking several decades back through the design heritage of the brand some of the designs from the 1960s, 1970s, 1980s, 1990s and all the way forward to today are still subject to high levels of desirability and recognised as appreciated design classics from the world outside of Bang & Olufsen.

However, a long lifetime of products in the consumer electronics and audio industry has been strongly challenged in the same time period because of radical change in music formats from vinyl over CD to digital and streaming services and technological transformation of connectivity technologies from wired to wireless, which have made technology obsolescence the main barrier for longevity.

The current situation with radically reducing life cycle durations and concerning increase in electronic waste generation at global scale, is a key challenge for the long-term existence and growth opportunities for the industry. As a company operating in the industry, Bang & Olufsen also see themselves as part of the problem.

However, Bang & Olufsen is also committed to become part of the solution by showing that there is another way. A way where longevity can be brought back in the game and circular principles can enable products to circulate longer through service, repair, upgrade, remanufacturing and recirculation of materials. A way where we innovate for the better and a way where we strive for the ultimate goal of providing a lifetime of music.

A new definition of the old and the new

In September 2021 Bang & Olufsen launched the moveable wireless speaker Beosound Level as the first Cradle to Cradle Certified® consumer electronic product ever made. It was from the very beginning created with the intent of providing at least a decade of music experiences. Furthermore, it was the ambition to create a product architecture that redefined the product life cycle away from a static definition of old to a dynamic cycle of evolution that allows the product and experiences it provides to develop and appreciate over time.

The speaker was designed with durability, high-quality and performance excellence in mind for a long lifetime, but it was also created based on modular principles with the purpose of integrating flexibility in use, future-proofing, customisation, serviceability and easy disassembly into one holistic package.

It was created with planned over-engineering in a way so that it only uses 50% of its processing power out of the box to allow for evolution over the product life cycle through software updates offering new features, improved performance, and adaption to incremental changes in connectivity standards. Technology development can be difficult to predict many years ahead, for which reason Beosound Level has been prepared for hardware update of the streaming module, which can be replaced by service professionals many years from now in case of radical changes to connectivity or streaming standards, which cannot be adapted to through software updates.

It was, furthermore, created with customisation options to allow users to dynamically changing the visual expression of the product to adjust to changes in personal taste or interior design trends over time to stimulate emotional durability. The modular approach has also been used in relation to power management, where the battery-pack has been engineered to be replaceable by the end-customer as a do-it-yourself solution to prevent obsolescence from eroding battery playtime after several years of use caused by limitations in current battery technology. The modular approach has also made easy maintenance, service and repair possible together with efficient disassembly, sorting of material fractions and recycling.

A future created to be recreated?

When looking at the goal of designing for longevity we face the interesting dilemma of creating something which is relevant in the present, while at the same time cater for relevance and new opportunities in the longer term. The consequence of this is that how we design the products today will be shaping the world we will inhabit tomorrow.

In the light of this perspective, the modular approach used for Beosound Level could potentially offer future innovation opportunities for extending the product life enabled by the art of re-creating through multiple life cycles, where the speaker could be taken back after its first useful life cycle and be remanufactured, upgraded to latest technology and redistributed as a 'new' product with no compromises to performance and quality.

Perhaps this potential future business model could offer an even more desirable history than a brand-new product from the factory assembly line can provide. One thing is certain: A more circular and long-term sustainable future for the consumer electronic industry will call for a new definition of the old and the new and a shift from linear to circular.

FIGURE 9.4A The Beosound Level (Bang & Olufsen).

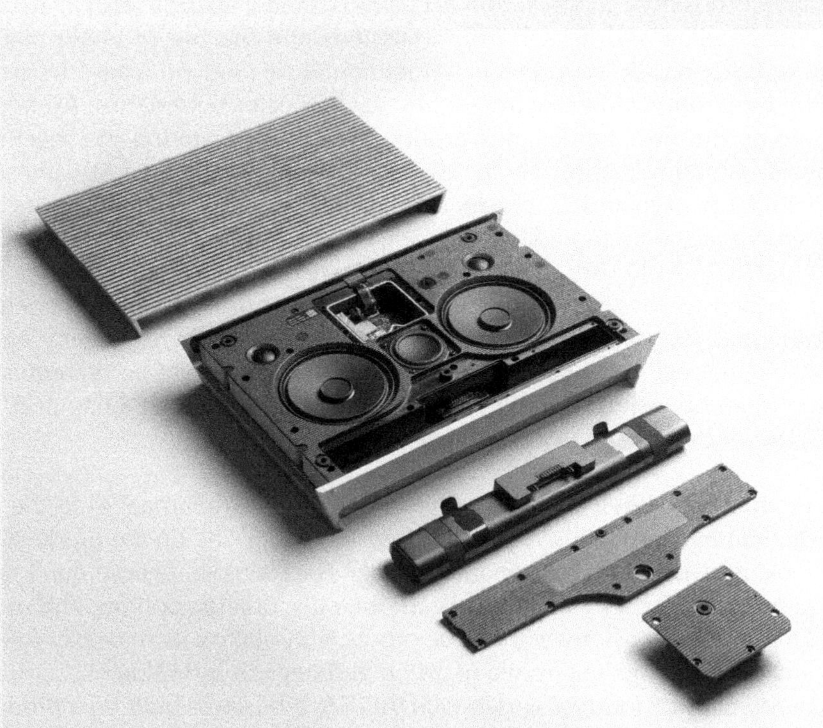

FIGURE 9.4B The Beosound Level (Bang & Olufsen).

Beosound Level is certified at Bronze Level according to the Cradle to Cradle Certified Product Standard version 4.0, which was introduced in March 2022.

Beosound Level is a wireless speaker, which is made to be anything else than static. It is made to move, it is made to evolve and it is made to last.

Beosound Level has been awarded with the Cradle to Cradle Certified® Bronze Level status as the first consumer electronic product in the world.

The speaker has been designed for longevity, enabled by strong modular design principles with the purpose of setting new standards for customisation, serviceability, upgradeability and disassembly to show a more circular way for the consumer electronic industry.

Designing circular business models

As you have gathered by now, the best chance of achieving success in transitioning to a regenerative society, especially in a timely way, is to connect business and the environment synergistically. But there is only value innovation with a market and real circular economy with viable circular economy business models. For a business model to be circular, it must decouple value and growth from emissions and the use of virgin materials. More precisely, as previously mentioned, it must be a tool to create value for people while staying within our planetary boundaries. A circular economy business model thus produces value by fostering the regeneration of natural resources while striving to maintain the highest value and functionality of materials, products or components for as long as possible. As shown in the methodology 4Rs – The Circular Way, it is about Rethinking via Reduce, Reuse, Recycle and Replace, and what follows here is a comprehensive overview of typical circular economy business models to enable that, which I have divided into seven sub-themes for inspiration on how circular economy can enable business and climate to be prerequisites rather than opposites. For more on the role of business, see Chapter 8 The Purpose of Business is to Solve Problems.

1. **Product as a service.** This is about providing new alternatives to the traditional model of "buy and own." Instead of focusing on the product, we look at its functions and people's needs. For example, people don't need lamps but light; they don't need cars but transportation options, and so on. One or many customers then use products through a lease or pay-for-use arrangement, moving from a focus on exchange to use value.

   My circular journey started with VIGGA, a business built on a product-as-a-service business model. I saw first-hand how the business model incentivised the quality of materials, craftsmanship and aesthetics, much like in the Danish Design Heritage. Because the better the quality, the more times it could be circulated between subscription takers, thus the better the business from a financial perspective.

   About the 4Rs – The Circular Way, this business model can help you achieve reduction and reuse.

2. **Product life extension.** Repair, remanufacturé, and upgrade existing products to keep them in use for longer. It can be both physical and digital updates. One example is upgrading current products to fit with circular materials, new energy requirements, etc., instead of disregarding the existing products for new ones.

   About the 4Rs – The Circular Way, this business model can help you increase reuse and possibly reduction.

3. **Circular supplies.** It is essential to establish a high-quality circular supply chain. One goal is to replace all new or virgin materials with fully renewable and recyclable resources. Other goals are to eliminate waste generation and reduce general material usage, decreasing the total input in your production, whether it consists of new or reused resources. But looking

at a new supply stream can create a high effect at a relatively low implementation barrier as potentially the only thing you have to change is your supplier. So start by mapping available circular supply alternatives to your current traditional supplies. For example, suppose a circular supply stream is yet to be readily available. In that case, you can look into cross-industry partnerships, particularly industrial symbiosis, where you partner with others to exchange waste resources in a closed loop, ensuring a steady supply of circular resources. The Kalundborg Symbiosis in Denmark is an excellent example of how businesses can benefit from entering into a cross-industry industrial symbiosis.

About the 4Rs – The Circular Way, this business model is mainly used to recycle and replace but could also be used to reduce.

4. **Take-back systems.** As the name indicates, this is about extending the life of your products and assuming responsibility for them and their materials by taking them back in various ways. By systematically doing so and reusing products, components or materials in your value chain or passing them on to others, you have gained an outstanding opportunity to increase customer loyalty and create new sales channels and side-business activities. Compared to Resource Recovery, the business model described below, the resource will most likely be kept at a higher value via a closed-loop take-back system than traditional resource recovery.

   The model is gaining traction because it allows you to interact with your users at the end of their product journey, which is most likely also when they are looking to acquire a new product, and not least due to the global resource scarcity for new materials.

   About the 4Rs – The Circular Way, this business model is used to reuse and recycle.

5. **Resource recovery.** It enables a company to eliminate material leakage, maximise the economic value of product return flows, and provide others with fully renewable, recyclable or biodegradable resource inputs that underpin circular production and consumption systems. In short, it is building a business on access to waste materials and the ability to turn them back into valuable resources. Globally, an increase in waste tariffs increases the attractiveness of the business model.

   About the 4Rs – The Circular Way, this business model is mainly used to recycle but could also be used to reduce.

6. **Data.** Technically not a business model but big data and digitalisation have the potential to help us accelerate other circular economy business models. This is based on the prospect of creating more transparent supply chains and having a better understanding of resource flows, consumer

behaviour and product availability. Thus business models that use data to enable a circular economy at scale are critical.

7. **Sharing.** Sharing is caring, to use an old cliché. By developing platforms for collaboration among product users, individuals or organisations, can utilise already existing products and materials much more efficiently. The digital revolution became effective here as apps and social media connect people and units better than ever.

Question: Looking at the 4Rs – The Circular Way, what products do you use regularly that fall under each of the four categories?

References

Ellen MacArthur Foundation (2021). Completing the Picture: How the Circular Economy Tackles Climate Change. https://ellenmacarthurfoundation.org/topics/climate/overview

Ellen MacArthur Foundation (n.d.). The Circular Economy in Detail: Deep Dive. https://ellen-macarthurfoundation.org/the-circular-economy-in-detail-deep-dive

Thunberg, G. (2022). *The Climate Book*. Penguin Books Ltd.

10

NATURE'S PLAYBOOK

We are a part of nature, not a part from it. Thus, learning from and mimicking nature via biomimicry as a design philosophy, as well as the tactile use of biomaterials, is a grand opportunity to move from despair to repair and ultimately towards reimagining how we might go about regenerating our planet. Because if we dare to use it, there is an abundance of opportunities to harness within mycelium, algae, seaweed, etc., to create genuinely positive materials smartly capturing carbon in a way so simple it is indeed the ultimate form of sophistication we as humans and technologists can only hope to dream of (so far).

In design, in general, and architecture, in particular, there is a growing trend and use of biogenic materials. At scale manifested via the uptake in wooden constructions materials such as hemp, seagrass, straw and clay are fortunately increasing significantly in use as well. While the increased use of biogenic materials represents a new and improved practice compared to how we have been constructing buildings and producing construction materials within the last five or more decades, it is not as such a new way of doing. Instead, it is going back to previous ways of doing and relearning the wonders of biogen materials not just in regard to CO_2 emissions and staying within the planetary boundaries but also from a health and well-being perspective where, among other things, the ability of the material to create natural ventilation can improve indoor air quality and avoid the degassing that plastics and chemical additives, etc. typically releases in your household. As such, I see the ongoing progress of replacing our current materials with biogenic materials as **innovation by remembrance**. Just visit (or revisit) *Biomimicry: Innovation Inspired by Nature*, the incredible book by Janine Benyus, published

DOI: 10.4324/9781003261018-10

in 2002 (Andersen, 1835), in which she describes how humans have copied nature's models to solve problems in our industrialised world.

In awe of technological development and in a frenzy to conquer unknown scientific territory and explore human capabilities, part of industrialisation came to be that by design, we sought to move as far away from nature-based solutions as possible to prove human superiority, but ultimately instead leading us astray from human improvement. In the new scientific revolution, where we acknowledge that our actions have consequences for the planet, which affect our ability to thrive on Earth, an opportunity arises for an industrial revolution brought by human ingenuity in synergy with the wonders of our natural world, much like how Kaare Klint saw that future opportunities came from combining the accumulated knowledge of tradition with the possibilities of the present. Tradition and, in this case, nature's solution are not holding back our innovation and creativity; they are tools to heighten both ambition and final results. Because when we use our human ingenuity to work with rather than against nature, our collective abilities are accentuated. Just as Alexander Von Humboldt saw it when he spoke of consilience and the importance of combining science with the arts, combining nature's intelligence and human ingenuity and embracing the beauty and connectedness that follows. Silk as a material is one example of the beauty that can come from our natural solutions albeit most of us give little thought to the fact that the material is created by silkworms when they spin themselves on their journey to becoming silk moths. A material now being explored in combination with technology and particular robotics to create pavilions made out of silk material with technical capabilities strong enough to become a functional structure for the pavilion.

I refer to the above materials in use as first-generation biogenic materials, and while there is great potential for creating value for people while staying within our planetary boundaries through the use of first-generation biogenic materials, where I get excited is when looking at the great potential of next-generation biogenic materials that is the use of bioengineering and biomimicry to learn from natures playbook to create superior solutions. One example is Biomason, an American company now active in Denmark because they have gotten strategic funding from Novo Nordisk Holding, and the venture fund 2150 whom rightfully sees the synergy to life science and thus the opportunity to leverage their knowledge within biotech and life science can be leveraged in the future of materials. Biomason is inspired by nature, mimicking how the coral reefs create lime in the ocean to produce a biocement to replace the existing cement industry, thus avoiding the high CO_2 emissions when making traditional cement. Also it is a great example of the change in innovation and research perspective and an early indication of the scientific revolution towards an understanding of the fundamental difference of now living in the Anthropocene. That is the difference from moving away from a mindset where synthetic and exploring the outer boundaries of chemistry was the most interesting, with plastics being a good representative thereof, as explored in Chapter 12 to the continuously growing interest in natural materials and replicating our biological systems.

Similarly, we are in the early phases of understanding the great potential that mycelium presents as a material, with primary commercial applications being leather replacements for the fashion industry and acoustic panels for the built environment, but with a wide range of research and innovation into the use of mycelium, among other things, to create load-bearing structures for buildings. As I will highlight here, there are just some of many first and next-generation biogenic materials in total, making me very optimistic and confident we are in for a treat in the coming years with many new material innovations making their way to commercialisation and whose functionality and applicability will leave us continuously positively surprised and in awe of nature's capabilities. And a possible new Danish fairytale of using businesses to create global prosperity while staying within our planetary boundaries through consilience that is bridging life science with design, architecture and the craftmanship of the build environment is in the making.

FIGURE 10.1 The fungi network (All The Way To Paris).

Biogene materials have great potential in many industries; however, through my work, I am particularly exposed to building materials and also see a good amount of application within packaging and fashion. And it is through that lens, the list of materials should be seen.

The biogenic materials I am most excited about are:

First-generation biogenic materials

Wood
In particular, when used as load-bearing structures for buildings. For the smaller pieces, wood fibre is a great natural alternative to insulation as it has, among other things, good moist transportation capabilities.

Straw
The leftover material when oat, wheat and rice etc., are harvested. It can, among other things, be used as an inexpensive construction material with excellent insulation and natural ventilation capabilities.

Hemp
The material has been used to create textiles, bioplastics and building materials such as hempcrete (mixed with lime), among others. Its advantages are its ability as a binder and its rapid growth and regeneration of the soil it grows within. One of the first to recognise the advantages of hemp as a material was car maker Henry Ford who used hemp fibre composites to make the first Model T cars; however, as it was sourced from a cannabis plant (albeit different than the one used for marihuana) it ended when American president Richard Nixon banned the farming of all cannabis crops.

Seagrass
As the name implies, it is a water plant, and the material used is primarily the leaves when they naturally come off and wash ashore. Among its potential applications are as a bioplastic and acoustic or insulation material. One of the most common types of seagrass is eelgrass, known for its outstanding properties to capture CO_2.

Cork
Primarily comes from the bark of the cork oak tree and is a widely commercially used material but with increased use for interior and exterior building material, including facade cladding, using not just part of but the entire material.

Next-generation biogen materials

Mycelium
The fungi consist of two parts: the mushroom that grows above ground and the mycelium, which is the network of roots that grow below ground. First,

studies of mycelium networks have shown incredible levels of intelligence and resilience that are mimicked in network theory in use for organisations, movements, etc. Second, mycelium as a material is showing great promise in various applications, from the ability to clean waste streams such as plastic to its use as a load-bearing structure for buildings. Early commercialised applications including mycelium is an acoustic and leather replacement material for the fashion industry. It can be cultivated at industrial plants in sterile environments.

Alges

We are used to eating algae, but the opportunities within algae are much more significant. One area that is gaining a lot of interest is that algae can achieve many of the same capabilities as naphtha (the material used for creating traditional fossil-based plastic) and thus has the potential to become a bioplastic with great strength and functionality, among others.

Carbon

We know carbon for two things. As an element, it is part of all known types of life on Earth, from humans to plants and more. We also know it as an emission we want to avoid, and it is that stream that can now become several valuable products. Some exciting applications are using captured carbon to produce biochemicals and building materials. Still, an excellent amount of early-stage technologies and applications are currently being developed.

Work in bioengineering is also ongoing with all of the above first-generation materials, with innovation going on to improve functional capabilities and scaled production ability. Furthermore, more is coming from materials such as cellulose, seashells, grass, bagasse, clay, soil and organic waste streams. It is commendable that much innovation is ongoing. Still, it also means that we need to be mindful that our natural resources are put to use as the highest value application possible, which is why 4Rs – The Circular Ways should be used for guidance to make sure that you do the best thing possible and remember to ask the question what would otherwise happen if I don't use this material and just as important what should ideally happen?

With constant change being the new norm and significant innovations and thus competition coming from unexpected places, prepare yourself by taking a page from Nature's playbook ensuring resilience by agility. To me, biogen materials and bioengineering are one of the most exciting opportunities within our global solution space towards creating value for people within our planetary boundaries.

Essay: A fairy tale of complexity

> "But he has nothing on at all," said a little child at last. "Good heavens! listen to the voice of an innocent child," said the father, and one whispered to the other what the child had said. "But he has nothing on at all," cried, at last, the whole people. That made a deep impression upon the emperor, for it seemed to him that they were right; but he thought to himself, "Now I must bear up to the end." And the chamberlains walked with still greater dignity, as if they carried the train which did not exist.
>
> Andersen (1835)

Taken from the short tale *The Emperor's New Clothes* written by Hans Christian Andersen, about two frauds who pretend to be weavers that can create the most beautiful clothes for the emperor, but what is even better is that the clothes serve as a test of intelligence and worthiness because as they convincingly claim only those who are genuinely first-rate intelligent can see the clothes. Therefore, if one cannot, it means they are incompetent and not worthy of their position in society – while in reality, they make no clothes at all. Nonetheless, neither first the noblemen working with the emperor nor later the society at large dared to speak up out of fear of exposing their incompetence. Instead, the weavers successfully deceived everyone by creating unnecessary layers of complexity as a cover-up. That is until a child finally says it as he sees it: The emperor is wearing nothing at all.

Surely, we are smarter than that today, right? Willing and able to speak up against wrongdoings and incorrectness? Unfortunately, the dire state of the world today tells a different story. For a long time, our global scientific community led by the United Nations Intergovernmental Panel on Climate Change has been trying to draw attention to the increasing problems. In contrast, the response from policy and business has been incredulity or, as of later, greenwashing. So much like they believed the weavers in the fairytale, so too have we, to a very large extent, chosen to believe it when politicians and traditional industry tell us everything will be okay. We just need to make sure we put our trash in the right bin and buy "sustainable" products. A few adjustments here and there will do the trick; therefore, don't worry; nothing will really have to change. Complex future technology with great intangible potential will fix it for us.

Suppose we don't understand their expensive consultancy-developed decarbonisation roadmaps and plans to innovate groundbreaking technology of power-to-x and carbon capture storage, etc. In that case, we are just not intelligent enough. Because if that many people, magazines, ESG rating agencies and even NGOs applaud these plans, I must be at fault for not understanding it, right?

All the while, the fact is that we have caused more harm knowingly than we ever did unknowingly. Since the United Nations Conference on Environment and Development, Rio de Janeiro, Brazil, in 1992, we have burned more fossil fuels than we ever did before. The conference is popularly known as The Earth Summit because it was the first time global nations came together and turned our attention to the troubles of climate change caused by burning fossil fuels. That is, we have burned more fossil fuels since 1992 than we did between 1992 and their first use in 1880.

Therefore, you are not at fault for not understanding their overly complex net-zero roadmaps. Instead, we should never be afraid to ask questions and demand transparency. Because now more than ever, we need to call out the fraud weavers using pretend complexity to greenwash their solutions and cover up the great damage it does to our climate and biodiversity and face up to the need for systemic change because right now, the fraud weavers of our time have it much too easy.

Instead, we need a system that benefits the doers and creates solutions that solve actual problems that benefit both people and the planet. And lastly, like in the fairytale, we need to start listening to the young boy or girl (hallo Greta Thunberg) who tells it like he or she sees it and dares to go against the norm and speak truth to power: We need to ACT today. That it will require change and that technology cannot fix everything. It makes no sense that we push a tremendous amount of money into developing technology to capture carbon artificially whilst globally, we are cutting down forests and ruining our marine ecosystems, both of which have a remarkable ability to do the same. That is to capture carbon, but unlike the technological fixes, it is not in the future, and it does not take extreme amounts of embedded energy; instead, it can be done today and with no risk. Quite frankly, it is that simple.

If we look at mobility, the picture is the same. We have become so fixated on cars that the land area used for parking lots in Los Angeles could fit San Francisco six times. That is prime real estate that we use for storing vehicles that more than 50% of the time are not used. Surely we can quite simply do that smarter? Yet the solution seems to be vast amounts of money and embedded energy going into creating the future of mobility through self-driving cars, etc. Rather than asking what we actually need? And solve the problem by improving our infrastructure and design for bikes, pedestrians and collective transportation in our urban landscape. A straightforward solution that improves our environment and human health at little to no cost or risk. So why don't we?

Because while it might not require complex technology, it does require a change in mindset and a new way of doing. As we will learn from the emperor later in this essay, such an endeavour to change one's mind can seem daunting and uncomfortable. Right now, the idea that we can fix the problem through technology without changing our behaviour at all is simply too convenient.

A few adjustments here and there will do the trick, so don't worry; nothing will really have to change. Complex future technology with great intangible potential will fix it for us.

Another example is the many advertisements from traditional industry promoting "sustainable consumption" when in fact, it is, at best, a slight decrease in a still much too large environmental footprint and most likely a claim made due to a purchase of carbon offsets at a much too low price, thus still economically incentivising the destruction of our planet. While simultaneously paralysing the individual buying the "sustainable" product by making them believe they are acting to safeguard the Earth. Much like the weavers did, deceiving them into believing and buying that recycled swimsuit made of rPET (recycled plastic bottles) is a positive contribution to solving our dire problems – a solution they desperately want to be a part of. When in fact, it is primarily a marketing effort created to drive sales, while we most likely could have done without that extra bathing suit, and the plastic should have been recycled back into plastic bottles or other food-grade material.

Going back to the methodology of the 4Rs in Chapter 9, *Reduce* as a tool is the most effective way to stay within our planetary boundaries. While all four are important, a reduction is the best way to improve your individual environmental footprint. Again, the solution is that simple.

But more than anything, we need to stop believing that we can safeguard our planet and thus our ability to thrive without a fundamental systems change, putting the cart back before the horse and focusing on the problem-solving necessary to ensure global prosperity for society at large is placed before the interests of the financial system and fossil fuel-based industries.

What you see is what you get

How does it relate to Danish Design Heritage and Global Sustainability? First, because one of the wonderful traits of the Danish Design Heritage is that it is the exact opposite of the weavers' strategy of deceit through layers of pretend complexity. Instead, a key trait is simplicity, and at its best, Danish Design is intuitive, easy to understand and appreciated not just by the special few but by the general public.

You do not need a trained eye or years of practice to recognise whether it is good design or not. Instead, due to its notion of form follows function, minimalism and, perhaps most importantly, care for materials, craft and the user, what you see is what you get. Transparency and simplicity are valued rather than considered lesser worth than more complex solutions, such as what the two fraud weavers are trying to mimic in the tale of *The Emperor's New Clothes*.

Of course, some are complex, and we do need deep tech solutions too, especially due to the dire situation we are in and how long we have let the problem go on without calling out the frauds and start working to fix it, but it is the exception rather than the rule.

Too many things are covered in layers of unnecessary complexity without creating value and instead decreasing transparency and connectedness while increasing material usage and CO_2 equivalents. **In that sense, less is truly more, and there is talent and craft in keeping things simple.**

Alas, simplicity does not mean lesser ambition. On the contrary, most likely, the more complex the problem, the more simple a solution it requires. The fairytale is still important in our present time, as the title of this essay suggests, that we have been caught up in a fairytale of complexity. We need to relearn the trait of valuing simplicity as something to strive for and see the ability to create simple solutions that matter as smart if we are to reach global sustainability and improvement towards regeneration.

And it is not just about the Danish Design Heritage; we can look to nature and biomimicry as well: Nature does nothing in vain, and more is in vain, when less will serve; for "Nature is pleased with simplicity, and affects not the pomp of superfluous causes" as Isaac Newton (1687) wrote in *The Mathematical Principles of Natural Philosophy*.

Just think of how simple yet impactful growing a tree or eelgrass in our oceans is – and the immense impact it has as a solution to our climate crisis due to its ability to capture carbon without the necessity of people spending vast amounts of resources and embedded energy on building factories made of concrete and precious metals. It exemplifies the concept of innovation by remembrance, where we learn from our past natural systems and combine them with the opportunities and needs of our current. Because the more wicked the problem, the more simplicity in the solution is required, and the true champions are those that can create solutions so innovative that they don't need to be wrapped in unnecessary layers of complexity and are instead inspired by the craftsmanship of Danish design we need to take our time to care. This sounds simple, yet it seems to have become something we as a society find challenging to do: That is taking the time to care about the quality of the solution, the materials, the craft, and aesthetics, as well as care for each other and our planet as a collective. Caring about the process, the product, as well as the behaviour and usage it promotes and the importance of designing for thoughtfulness rather than thoughtlessness to ensure solutions that stand the test of time and solve our problems at the root cause, not just cover the issues visible from the surface with layers of complexity.

Let's take the built environment as an example: Buildings and materials have become more complex, meaning that mono materials have been replaced with composite materials. Most things are now glued rather than screwed together, making it impossible to see what the materials consist of and, just as importantly, impossible to repair or recycle – the increase in complexity has been at the cost of the quality of the solution.

A change of heart

But that is not the only thing we can learn from the fairytale; another critical lesson from Hans Christian Andersen's story is the emperor's reluctance to change course even though he realised that he had been fooled by the pretend weavers and their layers of unnecessary complexity. It goes back to Machiavelli's *The Prince* on our power structures and how they favour the existing:

> There is nothing more difficult to take in hand, more perilous to conduct, or more uncertain in its success than to take the lead in the introduction of the new order of things. Because the innovator has for enemies all those who have done well under the old conditions, and lukewarm defenders in those who might do well under the new'.
>
> Niccolò Machiavelli, *The Prince*, 1513

Breaking down existing structures is difficult because it requires people to have a change of heart and question already made decisions and current beliefs – and not least investments. Just like the emperor had invested a great deal of capital in having the fraud weavers create his clothes, have we as a society spent an enormous amount of money investing in the wrong solutions. The reluctance to realise that and depreciate the investment is a great barrier for progress, perhaps the biggest of them all – far more significant than technology or the economy in itself. Hence quite simply, another reason why we need honest and straightforward solutions is that they are intuitive to understand, and we cannot rely on the existing system alone to ensure that the best possible solutions are chosen; instead, we need to empower each other to make the right choices and like the young boy in the fairytale dare to speak up when things stop making sense even if it means we have to acknowledge past failures. It is part of the journey towards improvement.

We need to move away from our desire to add complexity as frosting to just about every solution and instead remember our past greatness and that of nature and combine it with our current opportunities and future needs to create transparent solutions for longevity. We must move away from the fairytale of complexity to the value and opportunity of simplicity. I hope this thought-provoking essay will help improve the balance and shift from a world that has become complex and theoretical that we forget the value of tangible action and the importance of transparency if we are to rethink and truly deliver improvement.

Question: Take a walk. What natural wonders do you see, and how might they inspire your work?

References

Andersen, H. C. (1835). *The Emperor's New Clothes*. https://andersen.sdu.dk/vaerk/hersholt/TheEmperorsNewClothes_e.html

Machiavelli, N. (1513). *The Prince*. Simon & Schuster.

Newton, I. (1687). *The Mathematical Principles of Natural Philosophy*. https://books.google.dk/books/about/The_Mathematical_Principles_of_Natural_P.html?id=Tm0FAAAAQAAJ&redir_esc=y

11

TECHNOLOGY

Friend or foe?

The fourth industrial revolution has been responsible for a paradigm shift characterised by new technologies that blur the lines between the physical, digital and biological realms. Technology – such as artificial intelligence (AI), additive manufacturing (AM), quantum computing, bioengineering and more – has had a tremendous impact on the way we interact with one another and with our surroundings. Therefore, our lives and opportunity space are transforming. At the core of this development lies global connectivity through digitalisation: The connection between human and human, human and machine and, not least, between machine and machine. While the previous industrial revolutions have mostly empowered companies to accelerate the unsustainable linear economy, this new wave of technology holds the key to a rapid transition to the circular economy. Technology cannot only scale and replicate; it can also empower our ability to reimagine and shape a better future. But as explored in Chapter 10 in the essay A fairytale of complexity, it needs to be about actual improvement, not just because we technically can nor use a smoke screen for inaction.

As every part of our lives, from our buildings to our bodies and brains, is becoming increasingly integrated and extended by technology; we are at a crossroads. Will we use technology to disconnect from each other and our natural surroundings or the opposite? Change is inevitable, but will we use it to reinvent our relationship with natural resources, nature and each other?

Businesses are moving forward increasingly fast, driven by the fourth industrial revolution of innovative technologies. Although it might seem unthinkable, these changes will occur at a constantly increasing speed. This will make

DOI: 10.4324/9781003261018-11

the sustainable transformation towards creating value while staying within our planetary boundaries even more necessary. On the one hand, technological progress is an essential enabler for scaling the new solutions we need to create improvement and regeneration. on the other hand, it can also speed up all the activities driving us away from our planetary boundaries, as such progress within technological development is a primary reason why the shift from a linear to a circular economy is so timely. How so? Well, just like many other notoriously great inventions, technology, in general, has an enormous power to change the world for good. But, depending on how this power is channelled, the result could also be horrific because while technological development enables us to speed up the implementation of sustainable solutions it also makes it possible to scale the negative consequences at rapid speed. Consequently, the positive outcome depends on our intentionality and whether we consciously choose to use technology correctly and whether we have the proper systems. If we do not, the development risks becoming a high-speed runaway train (with us on board) heading off the planetary cliff and creating the crash of our civilisation.

At the same time, we are facing a rapid demographic change globally, including an increase in the global population and the middle class, which will entail an increasing demand for basic goods, housing and transportation. The million-dollar question is: How will we simultaneously meet this demand and reduce our negative effect on the planet? How do we come to create value for people while staying within the planetary boundaries? We know that centuries of lean mass production and automation have not only met our needs but brought radical life improvements for billions of people. Due to our systemic integration and use of technology, we have also wreaked havoc on our environment, put our climate under immense stress, left far too many people behind in poverty and participated in creating unnecessary needs and a cultural addiction to excess. Every year millions of tonnes of plastic end up in our oceans. Temperatures are rising, and the resources we have been using lavishly to pay for our mass consumption are becoming scarce. The story of modernisation is the perfect example of how, thus far, the technological revolution has had an enormous downside. Fortunately, the climate emergency and the need to solve the climate and biodiversity crises have become essential to the global agenda. Global unprecedented financial and talent resources are working to solve those obstacles. And while resources are dwindling, we have also developed innovations unimaginable just 30 years ago.

To get there, we need technology. One of those technologies is the physical counterpart to the philosophy of quantum mechanics – quantum computing as explored alongside other technologies that hold a grand opportunity to help us achieve prosperity for people within our planetary boundaries – IF we use them right.

Separately, circular economy and technology represent new producing, consuming and living paradigms. The interplay between the two will change the nature of human behaviour and present a significant opportunity for almost every part of society. The new digital opportunities are already helping take the circular economy from a manual and sometimes slow process to an accelerated, streamlined and efficient one. Creating new circular resource flows and consumption patterns, which will extend a product's life cycle while cutting its CO_2 equivalent emissions, is essential to developing the future of industry and society. Tremendous potentials exist in the interface of technology and the circular economy, and we must press on to unlock them as tools to mitigate climate change. If we do not, we risk the opposite effect.

To unlock the circular economy's tremendous opportunities, gaining information about resource usage along the entire product life cycle and every step of the value chain and knowledge about material specifications for products is critical. Doing so enhances value retention in every design, manufacturing and marketing decision. Technology is the key to unlocking this potential. In the field of circular economy, value is created by extending the life of the product, maximising the utilisation of an asset and creating one or multiple loops for the product's components and materials. Digital solutions provide value by gathering data about an item's location, condition and availability; by easing access to products and services; increasing the traceability of materials; and making processes more convenient and efficient. The interface of circular economy and digital solutions thus provides a fertile ground for innovation and value retention. Danish newcomer Stykka, whom you can read more about in this chapter's case, is an excellent example of how technology can enable both circular solutions of high quality at a low price and the ability to scale the good solutions quickly.

On a final note, thanks to technological development, we now have an unprecedented opportunity to scale circular economy-based business models to larger audiences faster than ever before. But the gain also entails risks, and we must act quickly and utilise technological advancements for good. The relationship between circular economy and technology is still in its initial phases, both fields are still maturing, and their potentials are yet to be fully discovered and utilised. When accessing a new circular or technological solution, a key question is what and who does it benefit? What does it incentivise us to do, and is there a risk it is gaining traction simply because it is convenient as it allows us to continue business as usual? One example is chemical recycling. How can it be helpful to achieve absolute reductions of CO_2e, and when is it of interest mainly as a way to continue business as usual and extract fossil fuels? Hint with the wide range of technologies available today – both answers can be accurate, but so far, most available solutions do the latter. Still, new and improved technologies are in R&D and or pilot scale. But again, the context in which we use technology is most important. Though we do need it, but it can't be a stand-alone solution. It needs to happen in synergy with systems and behavioural change in a combined ecosystem driven by a common goal of achieving prosperity for our global population while staying within our planetary boundaries.

Moreover, if we are smart about it and use it right, in that case, it has the potential to create a source of new value for society and an opportunity for businesses to replace our current 'make, use and dispose' kind of linear economy and help redefine production and consumption in the 21st century. What do I mean by that? The best way to explain it is to share a few of the opportunities to be excited about.

Additive manufacturing, known as 3D printing, is a paradigm-changing technology. Imagine grinding down your old garden furniture at your local 3D-printing centre and producing a new design from the old material in less than a couple of hours. The technology also has the potential to distort the industrial production landscape fundamentally. 3D printing allows us to design for circularity, achieve new forms and shapes, mass-customise these and redesign, repair and remanufacture products. We are also already seeing 3D printing with biogenic materials, such as bagasse.

Blockchain enables greater transparency, enhanced security and improved traceability, which provide the necessary trust and openness to scale resource sharing and circulation. Transparency is essential to increase the sharing and circulation of resources on a business-to-business level and between individual users. Blockchain technology provides the opportunity to build global, decentralised trust. Whether it is a public Blockchain for resource sharing or a private Blockchain circulating a particular resource within a value chain, distributing resources has become much more manageable. Thus, we can design the best global value chains to keep resources in circulation and upcycle what has otherwise been deemed waste.

Artificial intelligence (AI), among many other uses, can provide an overview for waste to become resources. Imagine that, within milliseconds, you could determine the potential value of a waste resource if recycled and ensure it is constantly recycled at the highest value possible. AI provides the opportunity to quickly close the funding gap between the cost of collecting and processing the waste and the profit of the end resource. Furthermore, AI allows us to analyse data with higher accuracy; source correctly; increase resource quality, efficiency and productivity; enable predictive maintenance and open up further untapped potentials.

The Internet of Things (IoT) will intensify the connectivity between units and increase the performance of the circular economy. In terms of connectivity, humans have long been outcompeted by machines. For example, 10 billion physical devices are connected through IoT already, which might grow to almost 50 billion by 2050. As this vast inter-network is getting bigger, devices are constantly collecting and exchanging data about our resources' location, condition and availability. This will open the implementation of "smart" energy systems and infrastructure in cities allowing us to adjust, reduce, streamline and automate our resource flows and consumption patterns.

Bioengineering provides optimised natural solutions. The realm of bioengineering is well-known within life science, where living cells are produced and optimised to help our bodies recuperate and ensure our overall health. The same can be said within food, where bioengineering is also gaining traction to ensure increased longevity and health. But we are on the cusp of understanding the power and scaled opportunity bioengineering truly is. With reference to the framework The 4Rs – The Circular Way in Chapter 9, some promising areas are enzymes' ability to clean waste fractions and enable high-value recycling as well as the next-generation biomaterials such as mycelium and algae to replace our fossil-based materials in use today.

Quantum computing is a rapidly-emerging technology that harnesses the laws of quantum mechanics to solve problems too complex for classical computers. Or, quite simply, computer superpowers, which can be used to take large manufacturing data sets and, with algorithms inspired by quantum mechanics, can analyse and solve complexity with highly rapid speed.

Data collection, technically not technology but the ability to collect and interpret data about the flow and traceability of resources, plays a vital role in our global transformation toward improvement. The relevant data points typically cover user habits (i.e. the type and quantity of waste, the type and amount of food purchases) or product life cycle data (i.e. origin and life cycle stages of every product component to better determine the end of a lifetime). But as data has become an increasingly powerful commodity, it becomes more challenging to establish ownership of and access to data. To build circular economy business models based on data, the business must either buy the necessary data or collect it themselves.

I take the time to explain some of the technology I am excited about because while technology today is as much a part of the problem, I believe we must embrace technology as part of the solution space. Otherwise, we risk simply reproducing the structures of the existing system by leaving no support for the good tech while the bad is supported by the existing system. Good tech suffering and bad tech prevailing benefitting from the lack of transparency. Furthermore, we must also differentiate between technologies that provide short-term symptom treatment or if it is providing a solution to the root cause of the problem. While we should fight the technologies that are nothing but a smoke screen created to ensure inaction, we must find the balance between the technologies that provide short-term fixes and long-term solutions because we need them both, given the dire state we are in today. One example is that tech such as carbon capture can be necessary not because they are solutions moving us towards regeneration but because they are required problem solvers in the short-term.

Our choice is rather to use technology as a friend for improvement or as a foe to accelerate the negative impact of linear business and give false hope for future quick fixes to do the trick and mitigate climate change without any systemic or behavioural change. Instead, we must realise that it must be behavioural changes via design of new systems and utilise technology. Why? Because the challenge is that grand, and once we start to grasp the actual size of the challenge, it becomes eminent that we need to use all possible tools available to succeed at delivering prosperity for our global population while staying within the planetary boundaries.

Case 11.1 Stykka – Danish design meets Industry 4.0

Stykka is a young Danish company trailblazing the built environment by combining design and technology to provide quality constructions in wood at a compatible price highlighting the opportunity to use technology to increase quality and use value and that when done right, the built environment is open to change and ready to adapt to new and improved solutions. Much like the Danish Design Heritage, a case for how the quest for sustainability can be a positive, creative constraint that, in this case, enabled a high-quality product at a democratic price point benefitting both users and the environment, which is why I am thrilled that they have agreed to share their work here.

Accounting for 40% of global energy-related CO_2 emissions and 30% of global landfill waste, the construction industry plays a significant role in our planetary crisis and is by far the most polluting sector. Stykka is a Danish startup on a mission to make the construction industry a part of the solution rather than the problem, by providing circular kitchens and built-in interiors designed to last a lifetime.

Stykka has digitised the whole process from design to manufacturing and maintenance of kitchens. All products are designed for disassembly and made from high-quality FSC100-certified plywood from responsible forestry. Everything is produced through Stykka's digital manufacturing platform via a distributed network of factories. The digital manufacturing process allows Stykka to produce everything made-to-order and hence avoid overproduction and minimise waste in the manufacturing process. The whole supply chain has been optimised to lower costs, eliminate overproduction and minimise CO_2 from transportation by producing closer to the client.

Each product comes with its unique digital twin, which, along with computer chips on each part, helps keep track of all elements in the product. As a user, you can access the information through a QR code and get access to Stykka's online maintenance platform, where you can order replacement parts or kitchen fronts in a new colour, should you be tired of the old ones. The component-based approach is an essential part of being truly cyclical and sustainable. If any part should need a replacement for some reason, you can order a new part and replace it easily. You don't have to throw out the whole piece, and you can maintain your kitchen for a long time. Damaged or worn-out parts can be returned to Stykka for repair, remanufacturing or recycling.

Stykka believes that the construction industry has an outsized impact on the environment, but it also has enormous potential to be at the forefront of change. The firm wants to challenge the fact that when our buildings are meant to last 100 years, the kitchens – the part of the interior of the home that is used the most – we put inside them last for only ten years. This way of thinking does neither the economy nor the environment a favour.

FIGURE 11.1 Stykka Kitchen.

Interview with Philip Battin, Google

With rapid digitalisation and development within technology and globalisation, the requirements for and usage of design have changed. In this interview, Philip Battin, one of the most successful Danish designers in Silicon Valley, addresses the importance of design and the role and responsibility of design and designers in a global context.

Danish design is easily seen as being about the era following the World War II, and it is but not only, most importantly it is about designing new types of processes, products and business models and, more than anything, about designing new ways of being and ensuring that they are applicable at a global scale. Philip Battin is a true testament to that. He is a brilliant designer with a background in the arts as well, now deploying his talent and skill set at a global scale at Google. Thus, I am thrilled that Philip agreed to participate here. Both because he is an excellent example of how Danish design can create value in our modern-day global world also because he has a perfect mix of knowing the industry and sentiment from the inside also having been away from it for long enough to gain a unique perspective of both opportunities and obstacles.

D: In three words, describe the world you would design?

P: I would use three words: inclusive, diverse and sustainable. Inclusive because designers often tend to design for themselves as the target audience. But this is a narrow scope, thus targeting a niche segment that, unfortunately, often results in large groups of people being overlooked. It is a problem we need to address and something I have become much more aware of, personally and by working at Google. When billions of users use your product daily, it's essential to take responsibility for the design by becoming aware of its users and their needs. Especially when designing digital products, designers must remember to make them accessible to everyone. Unfortunately, accessibility is often overlooked or postponed to one of the last tasks of the design process. This results in the solutions for disabilities often compromising on aesthetics and convenience. Instead, Microsoft adaptive Xbox controllers are a good example to be inspired by. For example, they made a computer console that can be used even if you have a disability. Finally, they incorporated accessibility from the start, making it part of the design.

D: That's interesting because it is the same thing we see when designing The Circular Way. It needs to be embedded in the design from the start to create value successfully.

P: The second word is diverse, as it is such an extensive discussion at the moment for good reason because current ideals of good design have evolved under a western gaze which builds on a primary western view of art history. In other cultures, beauty and aesthetics are looked upon differently. One example is how European modernists have entirely discounted the use of ornamentation in modern design at the expense of other cultural contexts. Working in a diverse team with design for a global audience has made us question our approach to design to achieve a more varied understanding of good design.

D: And I guess for any designer working in a global context, it is something to be mindful of both in terms of aesthetics and consumption patterns – and that's quite a challenge not just designing solutions for our own culture but for a global world view. How do you think we should approach this task?

P: Yes, a common approach for companies has been to send a group of people to an area to observe the local patterns and environment. Based on these findings and conclusions, they develop the design that will be incorporated into that region. However, the people observing the environment bring their own perspectives and assumptions from home. Instead, we should work more authentically and focus on empowering the local community. One way to do that is through co-creation and participatory design. In Index Design Award, a Danish-based global design award that celebrates design that improves life, we generally see that the solutions anchored in the local community have the most significant potential rather than solutions created for these by outsiders.

The last word is naturally sustainability. Moving to California created a personal sense of urgency around climate change. When experiencing natural catastrophes such as wildfires, drought, flooding and much more firsthand, it becomes impossible to ignore. Nonetheless, we are still consuming immense amounts of products, and it's about time we act and take responsibility for the future, and designers play a crucial part in this transition.

D: Agreed; what impact do you see design having?

P: Designers tend to assume that sustainability is a top-down strategy. But we quickly forget how extensive the design process is. Usually, leaders and companies are only presented with a few decisions made regarding the design. Hence, most design is based on the designer's judgement and decisions. One example is the choice of using glue or screws for assembling enclosures. We've seen many products transition to glue as it results in a more seamless design, but the side effect is that it makes it impossible to service and repair the device. The impact of a designer's day-to-day decisions is immense, and designers must become aware of their personal responsibility and ability to create change in the transition to a more sustainable future.

D: When talking about the importance of being mindful of environmental and societal impact within the design industry, I often meet the assumption that it negatively limits a designer's creativity and freedom. Does it limit you, or do you think it is possible to view it as a positive creative constraint?

P: I absolutely recognise that sentiment in the industry. However, designers are incredibly good at working within constraints. Because what we should never forget is that design is a craft, and the fundamental part of design comes from art and the ability to form. We need designers to put their skills to work on how to make products made from less desirable materials feel desirable. For instance, Nike's space hippie shoe, made from waste materials from their factory, is a good example of how designers can make the most out of the most challenging materials.

D: One of the reasons why the Danish Design Heritage can give valuable learnings today is its ability to create desirable products without compromising on sustainability. Hopefully, serving as a tangible example for designers today on how aesthetics and positive environmental and societal benefits do not have to be opposites; instead, sustainability can be a positive, creative constraint. Regarding the Danish Design Heritage, what pops into your mind when thinking of Danish design?

P: When thinking about Danish design, my initial thoughts are classic designers such as Hans J. Wegner, Jørn Utzon and Jacob Jensen. As a more organic take on functionalism, I'm very proud of being a Danish designer, especially when working abroad. I notice how well-received Danish designers are, as Danish Design Heritage has international prestige.

However, because we're so proud of our heritage, I feel it has made us afraid to evolve Danish design. A lot of the new designs in Denmark have identical appearances to the old well-known designs because they approach design with many of the same philosophies, tools and materials that have been applied to design for generations. We can't change the design without changing how we design. To continuously advance and deliver, we must rethink our approach using new technologies, such as additive manufacturing, 3D printing, machine learning, AI-aided design and more.

D: In this book, I have looked back at the old tradition, the beginning of modern Danish design, starting with Kaare Klint's Faaborg chair and the Furniture School at the Danish Royal Academy. When reading his original teaching material, he always started by having the students deconstruct an existing chair to learn the craftsmanship while encouraging design to embrace the new opportunities, which I rephrased as modern Danish design developed in the meeting between tradition and the opportunity of the current. That sounds like what you are also asking for. Instead of focusing on the traditional design philosophy, including the importance of challenging the status quo and adopting new technology in our design processes, we have become too focused on using the old methods and literally doing the same thing. And unfortunately, that means we have not fully explored the possibilities that digital tools and new technology give us. Especially because Danish design strives towards minimalism and simplicity, I could imagine that emerging technology would work very well to achieve a minimalistic look.

P: Yes, but personally, I think minimalism is coming to an end. It's nearly impossible to make it simpler than it already is. And how many materials, colours and patterns can we remove and still be inspired? It has become so minimal that we, in some ways, have forgotten the beauty of design. The incorporation of ornaments and the details of craftsmanship have been neglected in our pursuit to achieve the simplest and leanest expression. It will be interesting to see how the next design phase will turn out. Will beauty as a function have a revival, and will design for longevity rather than obsolescence become the norm and bring back timelessness and slow design as a goal?

D: That's interesting. Because talking about designing for longevity and slow design relates very well to the Danish Design Heritage. Still, if we look at Danish furniture designs today, brands like Muuto and Hay are the most commercially successful. Who has moved towards the fashion industry and created growth by continuously designing new collections, adding new colours, etc.? How do you think the Danish social model, where everyone is reasonably well off economically, has influenced our design tradition and today?

P: I am often asked why Danes have great taste and focus so much on design. I think it is because we have a large middle class who can afford to pay for design. This has resulted in a massive market of mid to upper-premium quality design goods. Danes prefer to buy a beautiful chair that can last many years, instead of purchasing a lower-quality chair that might need to be replaced a year later. In contrast, the US market is divided into value and luxury brands, leaving a significant gap in the middle of the market.

D: Maybe the global market greatly affects the current Danish design tradition. This brings me to my next question. Two levels of design influence sustainability: the product level, where design and materials, etc., are chosen and then a systemic design which considers consumption and business models. What do you see regarding not just the product but also systemic and business model design?

P: We need to be mindful of the system we are part of as designers. I am not too convinced about the idea of recycling. Plastic does not disappear when we recycle it; it is just used in one additional cycle. In the end, it still eventually becomes waste. Instead, we need to ensure that the designer and producer of a product are responsible for the entire product life cycle. Before that happens, we will not see real change happen. Ideally, the producer does not sell the product but sells the hardware as a service. Instead, they should ensure the product is repairable throughout its life cycle and be responsible for it afterwards. This forces producers to consider the whole life cycle and creates economic incentives to become more sustainable and make products that can be appropriately disposed of or upcycled at the end of life.

D: I completely agree. Will we look back at today and wonder how little we used our things?

P: Yes, I think that will be the case. Powertools, for example, is only used for 13 minutes on average throughout their life cycle. However, everyone still owns one. Transitioning to sharing economies for commodities like this will help us find a more sustainable balance between consumption and utilisation.

D: Have we started valuing newness rather than longevity as a functional and aesthetic design principle?

P: Yes, and by striving to the point of obsession for perfection and flawless products, it is partly the designer's fault. Instead, we could start appreciating product imperfections, perhaps inspired by Wabi-Sabi, the Japanese design philosophy, where flaws or unexpected outcomes in the production phase are valued because it makes the product unique, for example, Bang & Olufsen had a campaign for a speaker promoting patina, explaining that every dent and scratch over time is the result of an experience and should be celebrated rather than a reason to upgrade to a brand new speaker.

D: What gives you hope?

P: One thing that gives me hope is watching the younger generation: Generation Z. They are a lot more woke and progressive than the previous generations. They display higher awareness around global warming, and I've seen reports about how this generation is becoming more conscious consumers. Additionally, their creativity and use of new tools and media are remarkable. Furthermore, I'm glad to be part of Index Awards and "see" good news and inspiring designs and solutions. It gives me a sense of hope to see how big of an impact design can have seeing the great ways design can make a difference for the better.

D: What actions are you most proud of? And what do you still want to do?

P: I am proud of our recent project on Google's new design systems on-screen in Android 12.The new design is reaching a vast audience and has the potential to impact accessibility and energy consumption. We're making the operating system more personal by allowing users to change colours, contrast, sizes, etc., to make it more adaptive to their needs and abilities.

Secondly, we decided to use dark mode as the standard setting for the display in the Android system, as it consumes less energy which is good for the battery life and environment.

D: Cool, interesting to hear about the opportunities when actively combining product design with behavioural design and choosing sustainable features as the standard setting.

P: Yes, the design responsibility becomes apparent in how the design can nudge its users. With great power comes great responsibility!

Question: Is technology a friend or a foe? Explain.

12

PLASTIC NOT SO FANTASTIC

Today, our oceans contain 51 trillion plastic particles – outnumbering the number of stars in our galaxy by 500 times (Parker, 2017). By the time you read this, it will be even more. Because every single year, around eight million tonnes of plastic waste find their way to the oceans. If that continues, there will be more plastic than fish in the sea by the end of 2050 (*The Economist*, 2018). Take a moment to think about that.

This is the story of how plastic became so successful that it became a problem. It is a relatively new material invented sometime in the late 19th century and didn't get its proper international breakthrough until the 1950s. Yet, by 2015, humankind had produced 8.3 billion metric tonnes of plastic (Knapton, 2017). Worse, most of that plastic is no longer in use. A total of 75% – 6.3 billion tonnes of plastic – has already become waste. In addition, 12% of this waste has been incinerated, while only 9% is recycled. That leaves us with approximately 4.9 billion tonnes of plastic waste either piled up in landfills or spread throughout nature, from our rivers to the world's deepest ocean trench, most still entirely unaccounted for. From a purely economic point of view, we are missing out on €480 billion to €720 billion in lost plastic material value. And if that's not reason enough to feel appealed, the physical consequences sure are.

Recently, a 10-metre-long whale washed ashore in southern Spain. Cause of death? Killed by plastic. Doing what a whale does best – swimming in the ocean – it had swallowed 29 kilos of primarily plastic and a few other waste streams, including an entire gasoline dunk. As a result, the whale could no longer digest and process its food.

Hence, more than any other material in the world, plastics tell the story of how even significant innovations and improvements are unsustainable

DOI: 10.4324/9781003261018-12

and problematic in our current system design and traditional linear mode of operation. Just as brilliant as a material it has proven to be to humankind, it has also proven to be devastating to our surroundings. And if that was not bad enough, research shows that in 2050 plastic will be responsible for up to 13% of the total "carbon budget" – equivalent to 615 coal-fired power plants. While it is a problem that plastic waste is polluting our marine environment, it is not our only plastic problem. The amount of embedded carbon used in production is a significant problem. For example, it takes more than two litres of oil to produce one kilo of plastic, which is also why most plastic-to-oil chemical recycling facilities are far from ideal.

In fact, plastic as a scientific discovery is genuinely a tremendous technological advancement and human achievement, mainly due to the technical capabilities of plastics. Without great innovation and technological improvement, it would never have happened. With plastics, we have been able to preserve and provide healthy food and beverage to our global population. Plastics have also helped in producing tools, goods and constructions that have made us prosper as a society. Parachutes, lightweight transportation, computers, airbags, medicine and incubators are a few examples.

Nevertheless, plastic has almost been too successful within the current linear economy and is now on a trajectory of outdoing itself. And that is a significant problem. The truth is that, just like with other major innovations, we haven't managed to comprehend how to utilise plastic without harming ourselves and nature. Or maybe we just haven't cared before now. This untypical double-edged relationship between man, nature and innovations is best summed up in Susan Freinkel's book from 2011 titled *A Toxic Love Story*. In an interview on her book, she explains the following:

> Plastics are amazing materials, though that can be hard to remember when you're looking at photos of seabirds with bellies full of plastic trash. But plastics freed us from nature's limits and gave us an unprecedented ability to make things that we need and want—and for relatively little money.
>
> *Freinkel (2011)*

And that's still the case today. With the alarming prospects of bigger chances to catch plastic than fish in the ocean, people have indeed begun to focus on the adverse effects rather than the now taken-for-granted advantages. Questions are arising. Is plastic really that helpful? Can we replace plastic with other materials? Should I instead use a cotton bag when carrying home my groceries? Why is plastic so hard to recycle? Plastic's pros and cons are weighed against each other in a public debate based on whole and half scientific conclusions, and the result is often more confusing. And unfortunately, the use of plastic is still on the rise. Among other reasons is that the traditional oil industry hopes to increase plastic demand as we move from using oil for energy towards renewable energy. Thus, continued investments in petrochemical infrastructure, that is, the production capacity to turn oil into plastic, is increasing. Once again it highlights the need for systems change and a scientific paradigm shift towards understanding the consequences of our actions and working towards creating value for people while staying within the planetary boundaries.

Interestingly enough, the oil companies are once again at risk of becoming obsolete due to the renewable energy industry with the increased focus on producing Power2X (p2x), a technology that, via electrolysis, can turn electricity into fuel with the benefit being the high-density, and has naphtha (the input product to create plastic) as a byproduct that might once again replace oil. But remember, there are no silver bullets, so even though new and better materials are being made, reducing our current consumption will still be part of the solution.

And unfortunately, that is far from the case today. While plastic waste is continuously piling up in our nature and landfills all over the world, the demand is still increasing. Over the last half-century, plastic production has increased by a staggering 2000% – from 15 million tonnes a year to 311 million tonnes a year today. And that number is expected to double over the next 20 years. That amount of plastic from fossil fuels, i.e. oil, is not okay and will not be feasible within our planetary boundaries. That's why we must adopt The Circular Way's 4Rs to find a path enabling us to cater to global demand while staying within our planetary boundaries through a reduction in use, increased reuse, quality recycling, and, not least look towards the many exciting biobased polymers starting to enter the market such as algae, mycelium and byproducts from agriculture. An area where I truly believe that we have just scratched the surface of the wonders of nature's materials and their capabilities.

It's the system

Looking at plastic in a greater context, we quickly understand how deeply intertwined many of today's global challenges have become. Food waste is an important example. Plastic is crucial in preserving food and ensuring prolonged durability and quality.

The growing global population causes an increased need for food. However, every year, one-third of the food produced for human consumption does not get eaten – it ends up as waste or is lost in the process. Producing the food, transporting and handling the food causes significant CO_2 emissions. When producing food, much CO_2 is sent into the atmosphere. Proper packaging can prolong the food's life and lower the percentage of food that ends up being wasted. And remember, plastic does not have to come from fossil fuels.

So biopolymers can create it, and one very interesting thing we are starting to notice is that biobased packaging from materials such as seaweed improves the function of food packaging because its natural ability enables it to absorb moisture and thus further increases shelf life.

Similarly, plastic can be of great use in medical equipment and many other industries. So plastic can be of value, but is it enough to justify the increasing amounts of waste? Obviously not, but it visualises how difficult it can be for us consumers to understand the costs and benefits of a material and how two global agendas can sometimes conflict. Luckily, there is a way to avoid clashes between important agendas: The Circular Way. By decoupling the adverse effects of plastic CO_2 emissions and pollution, we can hopefully unite the goals of eradicating hunger, reducing greenhouse gases and ensuring life on land and underwater. Still, there are no quick fixes, and it will not come easy. Instead, it requires systemic change. So how do we tame this two-faced creature of industrialisation? How do we regain control of innovation on a course of self-destruction?

First, we can start looking at the input from which we produce plastic, using biogenic materials instead of petroleum. Second, we can use designing for circularity as a tool to create materials, products and business models that incentivise the reuse of plastics and make it financially viable to collect and reuse the material globally. Sounds too good to be true? It does not have to be.

Around the world, politicians, businesses and citizens are starting to take action and demand new solutions. Globally, new agendas are forming, and increased packaging and waste-handling restrictions are being implemented. The corporate world is ditto moving ahead – fast in its ambitions to meet increased customer awareness and demands. One example is Danish plastic toy maker LEGO and their announcement that they will spend $400 million in sustainability research adding to the work they already do to improve their plastic footprint. A current example is that now all LEGO sets are made from plant-based plastic – that is biobased plastic (Replace in the methodology the 4Rs – The Circular Way). And in 2022, the first global United Nations treaty fighting plastic pollution was passed (United Nations, 2022). Politically, the EU launched its European Strategy for Plastics in a Circular Economy (The European Union, 2018) at the beginning of 2018 because, luckily, there are alternatives to our current damaging use of plastic. And now, all member states are at the final stage of implementing the extended producer responsibility for plastic packaging.

As explained more deeply in Chapter 6, an example is Re-Plastic, an innovation Lendager created The Circular Way and now part of a:gain. While it has recently been spun out to be an independent company, it is based on us being tasked with reutilising a composite plastic waste stream that would have otherwise been incinerated. By looking through the lens of design, we were able to find desirable and feasible new applications for the waste stream and turn it into new commercially viable design products such as tables and chairs while still innovating to utilise the waste stream to the highest value possible continuously. At the same time, others in our collaborative ecosystem of improvement are looking at innovating it from ever becoming a waste stream.

However, right now, research shows that at least 30% of the current plastic packaging has to undergo fundamental re-designing for it even to become recyclable. That's partly because of the many different types of plastic and the difficulty of recycling them when put together in various combinations. On the other hand, that means 50% of the current plastic packaging will be economically attractive to recycle if we adjust minor design and collection structures.

The key to the solution is found in the circular economy, where we design and produce plastics that can be reused and recycled repeatedly. So when choosing what to do, remember to look for the 4Rs – The Circular Way for guidance on what the best course of action is, as some things are better than others, and when it comes to plastic recycling (particularly chemical recycling) some things are outright damaging and should not be done. So it is a matter of asking whether we are moving towards creating value within the planetary boundaries or if it is this simply increasing our dependence on business as usual.

From my experience working with plastics and packaging The Circular Way, I have found that the following tips provide good guidelines to get started.

Here are a few starting tips:

- Mono-plastic materials should be chosen rather than composite materials, as it makes it difficult to recycle and reduces the material value.
- It is often best to choose PE, PP and PET materials, as these are the most uniform quantities.
- Additionally, it is crucial that it is easy to clean the packaging for labels, covers and contents.
- Biogen plastics that can be reused and recycled together with traditional plastic should be prioritised.
- Most importantly, however, remember to reduce and reuse (the 4Rs methodology).

It is critical to reduce the amount of plastic used and wasted. Reusing that comes from reducing our plastic use and designing new products, business models and systems enables the material to stay in circulation rather than being disregarded. There is a long way to go, but if we collectively work together, we can create better solutions, providing value without the excessive use of fossil fuel-based virgin resources and without harming our environment. Finally, and most importantly, the demand for sustainable packaging and plastics has never been higher. This also means that new technology development regarding waste management and recycling has significantly improved within the last few years and will continue to do so.

CRITERIA / QUALITY	MAIN COMPONENT (container, bucket, tray, bottle, foil)	SUB-COMPONENT (closures, lid, inserts, seals)	DECORATION (cover, print, glue and labels)	EMPTYING (by consumer)	EXAMPLES
HIGH	Main component is in mono-material: PET, PE or PP. Shall tolerate washing to a suitable degree.	Sub-components are in the same material as the container or completely separated from the container in use.	Cover and labels are entirely removed in use or simple dismantling. There is no coloured print on the container, only on the cover or labels.	The packaging can easily be entirely emptied of residues after normal use. Only needs a light rinse with water (e.g. meat tray).	rPET can for example be used for new bottles, food trays and food tubs. rPE and rPP can for example become pipes, buckets or containers for non-food products.
MODERATE	Main component is of mono-material: PET, PE or PP. Or a minimum content of compatible material (cf. Appendix A). Main component is coloured.	Sub-components are not separated in use but are of materials that are compatible with the main component (cf. Appendix A). Sub-components are coloured.	Cover and labels are not separated from the container but are of the same material as the container or compatible materials (cf.Appendix A). There may be printing on the cover, labels or container.	The packaging is only partly emptied of residues after normal use. However sub-components are easily separated so that the consumer can rinse the packaging. (e.g. ketchup bottle)	rPET can for example be used for fibres for textiles. Can also be used for fleece sweaters blankets etc. rPE and rPP can for example become pipes, buckets or containers for nonfood products.
LOW	Main component consists of laminated materials that are not compatible (cf. Appendix A)	Sub-components contain incompatible plastic types, metal, paper etc. Sub-components are not separated in use.	Cover and labels are incompatible with the main components and cannot be removed. There is a great deal of ink printing on the packaging.	The packaging cannot be emptied of residues after normal use. (e.g. toothpaste tube).	Mixed plastic can for example be used for concrete filling, RDF and plastic to diesel.

FIGURE 12.1 Design guide (All The Way To Paris).

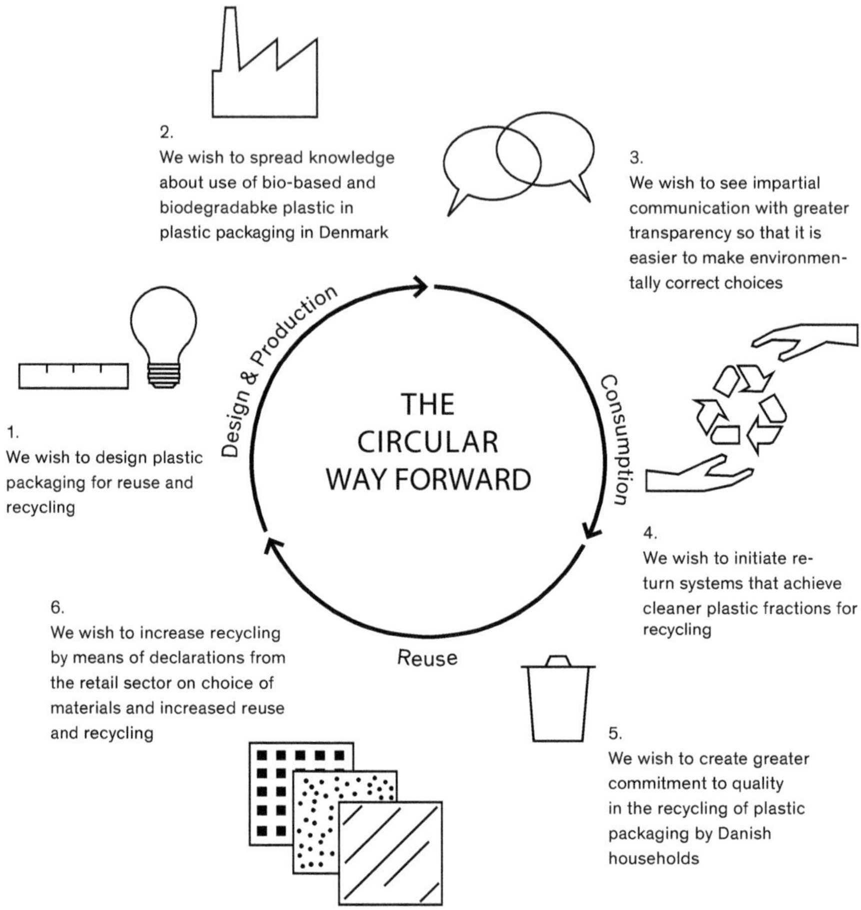

FIGURE 12.2 Plastic vision (All The Way To Paris).

> **Question:** Consider your day; how much plastic waste have you created?

References

Freinkel, S. (2011). *A Toxic Love Story*. Mariner Books.

Knapton, S. (2017). Our Seas Have Become a Plastic Graveyard – But Can Technology Turn the Tide? *The Telegraph*. https://www.telegraph.co.uk/science/2017/02/11/seas-have-become-plastic-graveyard-can-technology-turn-tide/

Parker, L. (2017). A Whopping 91% of Plastic Isn't Recycled. *National Geography & UN News*.

The Economist (2018). Only 9% of the world's plastic is recycled. https://www.economist.com/international/2018/03/03/the-known-unknowns-of-plastic-pollution
The European Union (2018). Plastics in a circular economy. https://ec.europa.eu/info/research-and-innovation/research-area/environment/circular-economy/plastics-circular-economy_en
United Nations (2022). Historic day in the campaign to beat plastic pollution: Nations commit to develop a legally binding agreement. https://www.unep.org/news-and-stories/press-release/historic-day-campaign-beat-plastic-pollution-nations-commit-develop

13

BUILDING THE CIRCULAR WAY

In the next 40 years, the total building mass will double worldwide. The UN estimates that 230 billion square metres of building stock will be added by 2060 (UNEP, 2017) to meet the growing population's demand, increasing middle class and urbanisation. At the same time, we know that the construction industry relies on finite resources, which are becoming increasingly scarce because the rate at which we consume far exceeds nature's ability to regenerate resources. Thus, how we design and create both buildings and cities at large is extremely important. Therefore, this chapter will be dedicated to buildings, the next chapter to cities and the chapter after that to mobility systems. While in university, I had no idea that I would not long after be part of the construction sector and be used to putting on safety shoes and visiting building sites. Neither did I imagine that I would find it interesting to read reports on how to enable the reuse and recycling of bricks, concrete, wood, etc., and I certainly did not imagine that I would be part of the scientific projects behind those reports. Nevertheless looking back, it is what I have been doing a great deal of! And I am delighted that I have because there is truly so much to do and so much that needs to be done. Building and construction are responsible for 39% of global CO_2 emissions (World Green Business Council, 2019). So while change is difficult, it is not impossible and exceptionally advantageous if successful.

The world is calling for change, and the industry is getting ready for it. Demand is growing not just for more but for better buildings on a global scale. In the European Union (EU), one key driver is the new green taxonomy providing regulatory requirements for the financial sector to disclose their portfolio's environmental footprint, including the buildings they either build or own.

DOI: 10.4324/9781003261018-13

In that sense, while the fact that buildings have to such a degree, become a financial asset class, which has so far had substantial negative consequences for the building sector's environmental performance – it now presents an opportunity to accelerate the transition and improve the built environment. Because the investors need it. So commercial interest is growing at a rapid pace. Even the smaller developers are starting to see that not building with more alignment with our planetary boundaries imposes an increased risk of the buildings business case or, in their terminology, their asset risk becoming a stranded asset they will, at best, have to sell at a reduced price or risk not being able to sell at all.

Given the building industry's immense impact on the environment, it will play a crucial role not just in improvement in the building sector but in the success of societal decoupling of value from CO_2 emissions, delivering on the goals set in the new European Green Deal (EGD). EGD strives for the decoupling of economic growth from resource use and total climate-neutrality through net-zero emissions by 2050 and a reduction of at least 55% by 2030 (The European Commission, 2019). So what seems clear is that there is a need to develop methods and systems in which we, simply put, can get a lot more out of a lot less.

Luckily, the circular economy is gaining momentum in the built environment – and for good reason. Because if done right, we might overcome the challenge of ensuring housing and infrastructure for our growing population. This ensures a balanced climate and healthy environment for people to prosper and thrive, preserving embodied carbon and minimising resource scarcity to stay within our planetary boundaries. Hence, building The Circular Way is an essential tool to lower our emissions considerably but without compromising on the necessary improvement for our global population because if we are to achieve societal improvement for the first time by providing running water and a roof over their heads to the growing middle class eliminating poverty, we must work to not only make the built environment less of a problem but also set the ambition high – so high – that the built environment becomes part of the solution.

To achieve that, we must work towards improving individual materials and buildings as well as working to improve and question the sector as a whole, that is, as a system as already explored in Chapter 3 on systems design, because as Kenneth Frampton so rightfully writes in his preface to *Modern Architecture: A critical history*:

> Herein lies the paradox confronting the architecture of our time, for while techno-science in the form of digitally-driven environmental and structural engineering takes the art of building to an entire new level of cultural sophistication, this seemingly positive potential tends to be vitiated by our

lack of any overarching vision beyond the perpetuation of a consumerist waste economy upon which our continual accumulation of maldistributed wealth depends.

Frampton (1980)

In that sense, we must be mindful that the circular economy becomes a friend rather than foe for improving the built environment and moving us towards creating value for people while staying within our planetary boundaries because, as already shared in Chapter 4, too little absolute effects of circularity in the built environment has happened as of yet.

Case 13.1 Presumption of possibility: Upcycle Studios

Over the last decade, the circular transition in the construction sector has developed rapidly. We've seen examples of material innovations, selective demolition plans, circular pilot projects and some of the first commercial housing projects carried out based on circular building principles. The benefits of the transition are manifold, covering everything from cost savings in the construction budget, significant reductions of emissions in the building and operation phases, and fewer sick days to more qualitative value creations such as conservation of architectural identity and history as well as added brand value and unique aesthetics. One of those first examples is Lendager's Upcycle Studios, which I thus had the privilege of being part of.

Located in the Ørestad South district of Copenhagen, Upcycle Studios, designed by Lendager and built for Nordic Real Estate Partner (NREP), is a block of 22 townhouses based on the circular economy principles – reflected in the project's high degree of flexibility and in the materials used to build it. They

FIGURE 13.1 Lendager's Upcycle Studios (Rasmus Hjortshøj, Coast, Lendager).

were finished in 2018 and are now leased to families at a medium price. Just the week before writing this, I had the pleasure of visiting one of the houses between tenants and seeing how the community was thriving and how well the building was reused. Recycled materials were functioning three years after the first tenants moved in.

As our cities are expanding and the majority of the world population are now living an urban life – we find ourselves standing at a crossroads. On the one hand, we will need more housing and office spaces than ever before. On the other hand, we must accept that we cannot just build more in the way we have been used to without also significantly increasing our negative footprint on our climate. And that calls for a change. Luckily, several trends and solutions are emerging and paving the way for new building methods to solve our global challenges without compromising on the rising demands for buildings in our cities or the urgent need to mitigate climate change. So we might have to check our needs and desires to ensure that what we get is what we need. That's how the idea of Upcycle Studios came to be: Building the house of tomorrow with the waste of today. At the same time, Lendager designed a flexible building that utilises the square metres better.

To start with, each home in Upcycle Studios – divided into three floors – can be used as combined housing and workspace for creative freelancers, self-employed entrepreneurs and medium-sized families with various daily rhythms, routines and interests (Lysgaard Vind & Lendager, 2018). The freedom to divide the apartment into separate spaces and areas allows the owner to rent out different parts of the house permanently or for a shorter period of time. This ensures the best possible use of the homes at all hours of the day and in different phases of life. And as touched upon throughout this book, it is about re-imagining and moving away from the unfortunate increasing trend of the larger, the better and the vast amount of unused square metres for most of the day.

The concept simultaneously tackles three other significant issues: Resource scarcity, inconceivable waste accumulation and climate change. To lay the foundation of Upcycle Studios, the project recycled 1400 tonnes of waste concrete from the Copenhagen Metro expansion.

This was enough to substitute 20% of the new concrete eliminating a waste challenge and reducing the emission of CO_2 at the same time (Lysgaard Vind & Lendager, 2018). Using this aggregate from old, crushed concrete saves 12–15% CO_2 per tonne. This might not be the most impressive reduction, but the massive scale of concrete we use today could add up to a global saving of 2 billion tonnes of CO_2 annually – 12 times the Danish yearly CO_2 emissions. And that is just the beginning. As the recycling of concrete improves, more reductions can come, but as previously mentioned when it comes to concrete buildings we need to use the methodology of the 4Rs – The Circular Way and activate not just *Recycling* but work to *Reduce* the total amount of concrete both in regards to how many concrete buildings we put up but also in regards to how much of the material ends up being wasted during construction. We must consider adopting *Reuse* because when we reuse we do not have to use new cement to bind the material together with great CO_2 reduction benefits to be had and a lot of the concrete that is demolished today could easily be reused either at the same use-value or a slightly lower use, and lastly we need to look at *Replace* both in regards to replacing concrete with wood or maybe even mycelium structures or other biobased materials and bioengineered solutions in the future. When we do need to use concrete, we need to work to replace the cement as a binder. Cement alone makes up 7% of total global CO_2 emissions (Scientific American, 2018).

And there is good reason to use the 4Rs – The Circular Way to improve our concrete usage. Apart from water, concrete is the most commonly used material globally. This has been true for a long time, and global trends suggest it will remain so in the eminent future. Just look at China, where it only took three years (2011–2013) to use more concrete than the US throughout the 20th century (Forbes, 2014). And the environmental footprint of concrete could easily become worse if we continue doing business – and buildings – as usual. Because as you might recall, it is estimated that our built square metres globally will double by 2060. That means globally; we will build an equivalent to the entire New York City every month for the next 40 years (Architecture 2030, 2021).

Another example of how circular economy was applied in Upcycle Studios is old window glass – taken from abandoned buildings in northern Denmark. Seventy per cent of all windows in the new dwellings – as the name of the building indicates – are upcycled as well, upcycled because the glass was reused through the design and could live up to the new and higher energy efficiency requirements than they had been in their first use phase. If you wonder what impact that makes, the upcycled glass saves more than 50% CO_2 compared to new glass (Pedersen & Lendager, 2020).

On top of that, all floors, wall coverings and façades on Upcycle Studios are produced by off-cut wood waste from the exclusive Danish wood manufacturer Dinesen. Besides the ability to reuse an obviously valuable resource, doing so also eliminates all use of chemicals in otherwise needed paints, sealants, silicone, lime and wallpaper. In addition, they are keeping all materials natural and healthy for a sustainable indoor climate.

In total, Upcycle Studios, Lendagers commercially scaled circular residential project, is proof that by building on the principles of circular design, it is possible to lower emissions and reduce the use of virgin materials – all without compromising on aesthetics, price or quality – building the world of tomorrow with the waste of today. It was not easy – but as the 22 families now living in Upcycle Studios will tell you, it was doable.

It started with the idea that waste could be turned into a resource and the endless repetition of the two questions: Why shouldn't it be possible? How can we do it?

This is why I called this case chapter presumption of possibility. Because I genuinely believe that one of the key strengths at Lendager and regenerative designers at large is always believing something is doable until we have been proved otherwise. We always have a "presumption of possibility." And so we keep going and, more often than not, find a way forward and design a new type of product and value chain with the right partners to succeed.

However, although it is technically feasible to achieve high-quality and cost-efficient results – the demand for circular building materials is still too low. Several vital barriers are yet to be overcome to reap the benefits of circular economy (CE) on a larger scale in the construction sector. Actors in the built environment are still not convinced to work with CE principles due to a lack of knowledge regarding availability, quality, prices, responsibilities, methods for taking down and circulating, and, last but not least, regulations. In other words, for CE in the built environment to move from niche to mainstream, processes need to be standardised and agreed upon across the whole sector, ensuring more stable supply chains, closing the knowledge gap, decreasing the risk and making it easier to receive permissions for applying circular building materials in new projects. So while innovations are needed to achieve the necessary impact, we must also scale the existing innovations and make them readily available.

Interview with Mikkel Bulow-Lehnsby

> You never change things by fighting the existing reality. To change something, build a new model that makes the old model obsolete.
>
> *Buckminster Fuller (1969)*

A quote from the inspirational book *Operating Manual for Spaceship Earth* by R. Buckminster Fuller and, to me, a good representation of what Mikkel Bulow Lehnsby and NREP try to do – that is, to change things by creating solutions that are better than the existing alternative. To set the bar high and have the ambition to use sustainability as a positive, creative constraint that enables better solutions for both people, the planet and business. Thus, the quote reflects on the impact of positive approaches to creating change. Rather than focussing on criticising the existing norms, NREP provides alternative solutions and strategies in the built environment that make the existing solutions obsolete. Instead it is crucial to highlight that it is possible to create both environmentally and economically viable models if we dare to challenge the norm. With the same ambition that Buckminster Fuller's thought leadership set forth back in the 1960s, only these projects are not merely theoretically proven to be feasible. Instead, NREP manages to realise the projects at scale to physically demonstrate the new design model, as is the case with Upcycle Studios and in the next chapter with the Resource Rows.

In the following conversation, Mikkel shares his reflections and thoughts on the importance and opportunity of taking responsibility for the future. Through his observations, he sheds light on the impact of design not just on buildings and products but also on a societal level. The fact that Mikkel, being the visionary doer and highly skilled problem solver that he is, has set his mind on solving the climate crisis gives me hope.

D: If you could design your ideal world, what three words would you use to describe it?

M: That would be regenerative, liveable and caring.

First, regenerative signifies moving towards a natural, circular system in balance. Everything is connected, and we design systems built on circular flows that naturally eliminate waste. I am motivated by seeing how we are currently wasting massive amounts of resources, and I see it for what it is: A dire problem in need of solving. So, circularity is not the goal but a tool for creating a natural and beautiful flow where we regain respect for our resources and habitat.

The second word is liveable, and a core ambition for me is to create liveable cities. Globally, we have too many cities that seem more like concrete jungles than liveable cities. So, we must rethink our cities and instead use an approach inspired by mother Earth to design cities that nurture humanity, and the city creates the frame for us to develop holistically, which leads me to the third word: Caring. Because in addition to designing regenerative systems and liveable cities, we must always remember the social element and the importance of us as humans. 'Caring' requires human involvement and incorporates empathy and sociality in all of our solutions.

D: What motivates you to want to change the world for the better?

M: Quite simply, my primary motivation is to solve problems and help set people free.

D: And how does this relate to your decision to focus on solving the climate crisis?

M: The climate crisis is a massive problem with purpose and urgency. So, in that sense, to me, choosing to work on fixing the climate crisis is an easy choice. As humans, we all love using our skills to do good, right?

And due to the problem's scope and urgency, we need to fix it fast. This makes it very meaningful to take part, as there is a need for everyone to take responsibility and participate in creating solutions and reducing the complexity of the crisis.

D: By reducing the complexity of the problem, it hopefully becomes more actionable. What do you believe is the most important problem to act on in terms of solving the climate crisis?

M: The core problem is that we need to move away from the shareholder approach and back to the stakeholder's approach and find a tangible measurement unit for stakeholder value that is as simple as measuring the profitability for shareholders.

We have gotten to where we are now, first. due to lack of knowledge and ability to comprehend the severity of the problem. Still, fundamentally, I believe the problem is that companies stopped optimising for better problem-solving and started optimising for financial gains. Originally companies were created to solve problems, and the financial industry was designed to help companies do that. However, somewhere along the way, we put the cart before the horse and then companies started servicing the financial industry rather than the other way around, leading to short-term thinking and a lack of long-term structural problem-solving.

Unfortunately, I see the same tendency within our political system: Short-term thinking leads to populism and decreasing value of merits. Because long-term reforms aren't always popular amongst the public, many politicians are now more likely to be short-sighted to please the voters before the next election. The political system shouldn't be a popularity contest. Instead, there is an urgent need to take responsibility and make the necessary choices. So, the two systems that are key to shaping our world are led by short-termism rather than science-based long-term problem-solving. Which, if you think about it, is obviously a significant problem?

D: Super important point. We must look at the underlying changes in our incentive structure in society to solve the climate crisis.

M: Yes, because we have created societal systems that are no longer organised for long-term thinking – which isn't viable if we want to create a sustainable future for the next generations. So, we need to work to tweak and once again design our systems for long-term thinking and valuing science and merit.

D: You mentioned needing a simple unit to measure the stakeholder value generated. Something I find counterintuitive is our tendency to measure the positive environmental impacts in negative terms. We measure our reduction of carbon emissions and strive to avoid positive feedback loops within our planetary boundaries. At the same time, our desire to grow and evolve has driven innovation and solutions so far. So do we need to find simple ways to measure our impact positively to incentivise us to move in the right direction?

M: Yes, and that is why creating a regenerative society and a regenerative economy is so important. Sacrifice won't get us there; we need to find the positive elements to replace what we must leave behind. Luckily, I see a growing tendency towards that, especially within business, where many are waking up to the business opportunity of solving the climate crisis. So, a tangible positive measurement form could be "return on emissions."

D: Going back to your point of the cart before the horse regarding the structure of business and the financial system. Can we get there within our current societal system, or do we need to change that first?

M: We would get there quicker if we moved the cart back where it belonged and remembered the original purpose of business, but I know we can also do a lot within our current system. In NREP, our ambition is to be carbon neutral in 2028. So, we are working on how to make buildings not just less harmful but part of the solution for society, for instance, working to measure how much we have increased biodiversity and how much we have reduced carbon emissions. We do it because we see it as a commercial opportunity, and we continuously try to create positive change within the system by being the business case that shows that even within the current financial logic solving the climate crisis makes sense commercially. So, what I see is that in the current shareholder modus operandi, it still makes sense because the solutions that are best at solving the problems become the best business. However, I think the short-term lens of the shareholder's modus operandi has gotten us to where we are today, where we have let the problem become much too big before we really started working to solve it.

D: What actions are you most proud of, and what do you still want to do?

M: First, I am very proud of the work with Lendager and realising Upcycle Studios and the Resource Rows, where we managed to do what no one believed was possible. I think the projects' key value have been inspiring the industry towards sustainable innovation and highlighting the commercial viability.

But it has also made me realise that we need to change the mainstream building industry at large. And the way we at NREP can be part of creating that change is by demanding new processes and setting precise requirements for the building's environmental performance, as well as continuing to imagine new ways in which buildings can positively help create liveable cities and a regenerative society.

Therefore, our approach is to push the system from the top and create demand by requiring that the projects become CO_2 net zero by 2028.

When we started communicating our ambition to our partners in the value chain, they began to push back and explain how difficult it was. And they are correct; it is difficult, however, we need new solutions to achieve net zero. So, at the same time, we invest in the companies and technologies creating the necessary solutions so that we can point towards those solutions and empower our partners to deliver net-zero buildings. So, by doing a top-down approach pushing the value chain and demanding sustainable solutions, it is not about removing responsibility from us but instead about utilising our power in the best way possible. One thing I look forward to working more on is strategically integrating our philanthropic giving. At NREP, we give 10% of our profits to philanthropic purposes, which we have traditionally used to support a wide variety of projects, but we are now starting to use strategically as venture philanthropy to support the innovative solutions not yet commercially viable as investments. Thus, we are working across all our activities to empower change on all levels.

D: When thinking of how we best design our systems to make sure that we as people and the planet are friends rather than foes for the long term – could one say that you are essentially trying to leverage the capitalistic system to create change?

M: Yes, exactly. We are demanding and investing in solutions to empower rather than thinking that we must do everything ourselves, which also represents a shift in my mindset. Some years back, I used to think we needed to invent everything ourselves and own the value chain. Now we need an open-source approach because we will only be able to succeed in changing the industry if we unite and work together. So, our goal is to take clear leadership in the industry and try to inspire people and companies by sharing our findings and knowledge widely and essentially believing that transitioning the built environment isn't a zero-sum game. The more successful we can make others, the better it will be for everyone, including ourselves. And there is no way we will make it in time if we do not work together because no one can create the needed change alone. This is also what our new venture fund 2150 is all about; driving change across the global industry by backing the companies making the solutions and curating a space for all built environment actors to find solutions. Because as I see it, Denmark and the Danish society would be a perfect pilot for global sustainability at large and should be the test bed for sustainable buildings. We have both the opportunity and experience for it.

D: What pops into your mind when thinking of Danish design?

M: First, I think of the Danish architect Arne Jacobsen. Second, if I were to describe Danish design, I would use the three words: Simplicity, useability and aesthetics. The city of Copenhagen is an excellent example of how old and new designs intertwine, utilising qualities of both traditional and contemporary material trends and balancing aesthetics and functionality. Like what can be said of Danish design in general, cohesiveness is visible in both our architecture and design heritage.

Another important point for me is that I do not see aesthetics as absolute. It is always a result of the changing times and context; Danish design balances that very well. In that sense, aesthetics and sustainability are not antagonists but rather prerequisites for each other: Aesthetic architecture and design are valued by generations, and not going out of style creates implicit sustainability. But perhaps what makes us value it the most is the simple fact that we can see that someone really made an effort.

D: Yes, I see some key learnings from the Danish Design Heritage as the value of taking the time to care and continuously ask questions.

M: Yes, absolutely. My education has been centred around economic theory, utilisation and utility. But as I have become older, I have gained an appreciation of aesthetics and design created with care and passion. Good design isn't rushed to make the highest short-term profit. "Good" design takes the time to care and puts both functionality and aesthetics in focus, which will ultimately lead to long-lasting sustainable approaches that nurture us.

D: Something that has continued to come up in my research is the Danish societal model and how it has enabled people to acquire quality products such as furniture. Can we use those experiences on a global scale?

M: To me, the stakeholder model is very much inspired by the Nordics and works very well with the Danish societal model. It is almost irrational that in the shareholder modus operandi, we have accepted that all gains through increased productivity, etc., go to the shareholders. So why not create a more significant societal coherence by having a third go to the shareholders, a third to customers via lower prices and a third to society through a carbon tax? I think this type of model came almost naturally 60 or so years ago because the ecosystems for our business were smaller, and our dependence on each other was more tangible.

D: As citizens and consumers, are we sufficiently mindful of the situation?

M: First, I see that consumers are starting to change their behaviour. Users and consumers are becoming more aware of how their choices affect the planet. This leads to new demands in the market that will eventually force companies to act and adjust. However, one barrier for both people and companies is that many are willing (and want to) change but don't know how because the problem is so complex. Luckily the increasing attention in media and other sources means knowledge is increasing, which is crucial to changing people's perceptions and enabling them to act. Behavioural science is also essential, as it can be part of changing consumer habits and demand. Architects and designers have a crucial responsibility in driving citizens' behaviour towards actions benefitting both people and the planet. Furthermore, technology can help uncover the possibilities we need to take advantage of.

D: Change is happening, but at the same time, it seems there is still a lot of money to be made in the traditional and more harmful way?

M: Yes, but that is changing, and it is happening at a rapid speed. Again, people want change, but it is difficult to understand what to do. We need to get better at letting science help us find the way to ensure we choose the right solution. The solutions that are not just easy to communicate, but those that deliver the necessary effect. In the built environment, that includes getting better at transforming rather than demolishing existing buildings, reducing emissions from concrete and steel and increasing biodiversity.

D: What gives you hope?

M: People's creativity and problem-solving abilities often impress me. One of our biggest problems is our tendency to get stuck in old habits. However, an incredible trait of ours is our ability to adapt. One positive takeaway from COVID-19 is that the pandemic has proven how our society, and we as individuals, can adapt and solve complex and emerging problems quickly. Everything can be changed in a split second; therefore, we must be willing to adjust rather than sticking to old habits and norms that our social structure and world have outgrown. One of the most significant traits is our human ability to imagine. We need to be able to dream it, to create it.

D: Seeing that impossible barriers are most likely social constructions that can be changed?

M: Yes, exactly. Ultimately, whatever we can imagine – we can create. So a lot depends on our ability to imagine.

Mikkel Bulow-Lehnsby is a Danish serial entrepreneur and investor. He is the co-founder of NREP, a leading Northern European real estate investment house. Since 2023 NREP is a part of Urban Partners that exist to power the progress of cities and citizens to help solve the most pressing urban problems. NREP was founded in 2005 and Mikkel Bulow-Lehnsby was the CEO until 2018, when he became the Chairman. Mikkel is also the Chairman of The Danish Green Building Council, a board member of the Museum for the United Nations, and co-founder and partner at the venture fund 2150.

NREP strategy: Net Zero by 2028

NREP pledges to decarbonise their real estate portfolio fully by 2028. They aim to become Net Zero without offsets years ahead of IPCC's target date of 2050. With this and several other initiatives, NREP hopes to push other actors in the industry towards a scalable, sustainable built environment (Nordic Real Estate Partners, 2022).

For more on Net Zero targets, see the UN's expert group on Net Zero targets and their 2022 report: "Integrity Matters: Net Zero commitments by Businesses, Financial Institutions, Cities and Regions" (UN's expert group on Net Zero targets, 2022).

Moving from niche to mainstream

Luxurious, high-quality, handcrafted design, built to last and made to be made again – created using scrap from your local landfill. It doesn't exactly sound like your traditional premium building, does it? Yet, in the not-too-distant future, it might be just that. If you had asked anyone ten years ago to build a commercial housing project from waste materials, most people would have thought you were delusional and told you to wake up from whatever dream state you were in. Today – a decade later – we have tested and demonstrated that through innovation and good craftsmanship, one man's trash can become another woman's treasure and thus turned into new resources, on par with conventional building products, without compromising on price, quality or aesthetics. We have also proven that reusing and recycling building materials in new projects significantly reduces carbon footprints.

So convincing building industry practitioners to construct with circular materials should not be a hurdle; it should be the norm. And that's slowly what is beginning to happen. For example, most developers and contractors are not afraid of using recycled bricks in new projects today, which would have been a significant barrier just five years ago. Yet we still see scepticism throughout the sector when we suggest designing buildings with reused concrete and windows, as we still do not have a well-established framework. So how do we make sure that recycling and reuse of old building materials are not just a few stand-alone and feel-good stories; but will become a mainstream method of ensuring we get the most value out of the existing building masses of today? In short, we need scalability and availability.

The circulation of building materials is no different from any other pioneering project: It takes time and involves risks, challenges and uncertainty. Because there is still a knowledge gap and missing data on what, when, where and how much potential reusable and recyclable material exists. This creates a need for more streamlined approaches to how we source and market circular building materials. Once these enabling technologies are well-implemented into the building process, the circulation of materials will more easily scale-up, maximising value while minimising waste.

However, we must act quickly to continue seizing the opportunities to utilise the existing building stock as the building materials of tomorrow. So we must continue to create positive case studies, identify existing barriers and actively contribute to creating future regulations in which the circular flow of building materials is enabled to maximum potential. Finally, we need to dare to take risks and responsibility in collaboration with the rest of the value chain because the potential and dire need for a circular build industry are there.

Luckily, I have had the opportunity to work with pioneering public, institutional and private developers who have dared to take the first steps towards a more sustainable building environment. Despite challenges along the way the projects have brought social, material and environmental value to all involved. With this in mind at Lendager The Circular Way we asked ourselves: How do we help circular building materials move from niche to mainstream? So to find out where circular building materials have the most potential to move from niche to mainstream as part of the EU funded research project Circular Construction in Regenerative Cities CIRCuIT (EU, 2021) we spoke to four clients and leading building developers in the Nordic Region about their experience with CE in the building sector, and how they believe we can push for change. So this chapter is literally about building The Circular Way, meaning that here I share four practical experiences and insights that the team at Lendager The Circular Way have gathered through conversations with some of the pioneering developers we have been fortunate enough to partner with. Developers that have tried constructing buildings with reused and recycled materials. I genuinely wanted to celebrate those who dare to try. Sure, we still have a long way to go, and we must work really hard and quickly to become more sustainable in society in general and in the built environment in particular. That means, we really need less talk and more tangible actions and results. And that we must remember to celebrate both the big and small steps in the right direction. What we need now is practitioners to drive the transformation. In other words: It is time for people and organisations with vision and courage to go out and try, test, fail, try again and – in the end – succeed. Whether it be in the private or the public sector, a truly sustainable future for all is only possible when we dare to go against the existing norms and in the succeeding sections you will hear first-hand from four of the pioneering developers who have had the courage and foresight to build The Circular Way share their key findings regarding both opportunity and barriers.

Practical experience 1: PensionDanmark

> For us at PensionDanmark, building with reused materials is equally motivated by two factors. The reduction in carbon emissions, and the value you get from keeping the identity and aesthetics of the used materials.
>
> *Mikkel Melamies Project Development Manager, PensionDanmark*

PensionDanmark is a large Danish pension fund that invests in real estate with a core focus on sustainability. In 2023 PensionDenmark expects to open the doors to Tælasten, a sustainable neighbourhood in the city of Aarhus, Denmark. Trælasten will be located at the former lumberyard site where the old warehouses, timber merchants and office buildings are still intact. This project serves as a stepping stone for PensionDenmark's sustainable journey. Lendager TCW provided consultancy which resulted in the detailed material mapping of the site. The material mapping quantified the material, environmental and economic resource value available, while also qualifying and describing innovation potentials. This study was supplemented by an idea catalogue to showcase existing circular solutions and spark creativity for new innovations to be used in the development of the project. Combined the deliveries created a clear goal, or rather a design dogma to be utilised by all project partners involved in the revitalisation of the area, in which the material mapping and idea catalogue serve as a qualified decision support tool, to enable the recirculation of old materials into new buildings.

An interview with Mikkel Melamies

Why do you work with CE in your building projects?

For us at PensionDanmark, building with reused materials is equally motivated by two factors. The reduction in carbon emissions, and the value you get from keeping the identity and aesthetics of the used materials.

We are not like the average pension fund investor. When we do projects, we tend to get very involved in the process. For example, we have our own in-house architects. For us, liveability is key. Which is often connected to a strong identity. The identity we get and preserve in the architecture when we build with used materials is a big advantage, in addition to it being an advantage from a sustainability viewpoint.

What do you see as the main barriers to developing circular building projects?

First of all, the barriers are always a result of how you approach a project. One barrier is the availability of used materials. To my knowledge, there is no way to ensure this. If you want to build a house from used bricks – a single supplier most likely won't have enough materials alone, and then it becomes a big puzzle to get the remaining bricks needed to cover the demand.

One thing is the availability itself. Second is the knowledge of availability. Not knowing what, where and when materials are available is also a big barrier.

Third, we experience a barrier when trying to convince the architects to design with and the contractors to build with used materials. The latter is probably the hardest to convince because they are more directly involved with the risk assessment. Dealing with used materials requires a lot of preliminary investigation going forward for the implementation in a new project.

Are there any barriers related to economy when building with circular materials?

Well, the economy will be the first concern the contractor is going to use as an excuse for not using recycled materials. "It's going to be too expensive," they would say. Or, "Who's going to take the responsibility?" In fact, it is not only the contractor who has a concern with responsibility. As the investor and developer, we are also taking a risk. As such, the system does not really work in favour of using recycled materials today.

Second, the price of recycled materials seems to increase. The first time we used recycled bricks, back in 2014, the price was about 500 DKK (approximately €0.8) per piece. The last time we used recycled bricks, the price was up to 700–800 DKK (approximately €1). When the prices fluctuate because of an unstable supply or availability, we need to analyse the situation every time we start up a new project.

Often, there is money to be saved by building with recycled materials, but we cannot be sure before we have analysed the market.

How do you think we can overcome the current barriers of working with circularity in the building sector?

Someone needs to be responsible for actually collecting the data we need; where and when the materials are available, and in what quantity and quality they come. It could be a supplier or an agency doing this. Either in the private or public sector or even through one of our unions or trading associations. We should of course keep in mind that the demolishers are the ones who have access to all the buildings and materials we need.

I don't know of anyone who doesn't think the demand for sustainable solutions is going to be higher tomorrow than it is today, the smart thing would be to invest accordingly.

Have you found it difficult to live up to the demand for sustainability due to the current barriers?

Yes. If the availability of materials at a certain demolition site doesn't meet the total demand for a new project, and we don't know how to get more [materials], we end up saying "there is just not enough materials here". If we only have half of the materials we need, and we do not have the knowledge of where to source the rest, we would probably have to discard the whole idea of using recycled materials.

Are there any materials or applications you are particularly focussed on?

For the sake of the environment, being able to directly reuse some of the heavy polluters like concrete and glass would be good.

How have you succeeded with implementing CE in your projects so far?

We had you guys [Lendager TCW] do a resource mapping on which materials were available on-site and in which quantities. Based on that, your designers came up with a set of design dogmas for circularity and a catalogue of ideas on how to incorporate these materials in practice. These were then given to the architects on the new project.

Summary of key findings

Potentials

- Reduced carbon emissions in our buildings
- Preservation of architectural and geographical identity in the areas we build
- Cost savings in our building projects (if done correctly)

Barriers

- The availability of reused materials is too uncertain
- The fluctuating market for reused materials is making the project's economy difficult to predict
- The unknown price and risks make it hard to convince contractors to build with recycled materials

Needs

- Better data on the availability, quality and quantity of used materials
- Bigger focus on circulating the heavy polluting materials such as concrete and glass

- Public–private partnerships to coordinate availability and create a stable supply of materials

Practical experience 2: NREP

> The story of the building shouldn't be underestimated. It is difficult to underline exactly what it is, because we still don't know it yet. Some recycled materials have a neutral value, but others give buildings a unique aesthetic value. Even more, in some cases, when using upcycled materials, we can get access to higher quality for a fraction of the price.
>
> *Gustaf Lilliehöök Partner & Head of Business Development, NREP*

NREP is a Nordic real estate developer, investor and operator who has a strategic focus on pioneering sustainability solutions. NREP and Lendager Group have had a close collaboration in the creation of two award-winning projects: the Resource Rows and Upcycle Studios. Both projects were designed by Lendager ARC and with material innovations delivered by Lendager UP. Lendager TCW played a key role as the project manager of a demonstration and development project funded by the Danish Environmental Protection Agency (MUDP), of which results were directly applied in both case projects. These projects have led to further analysis of the environmental and economic impacts (LCA and LCC) showcasing the achievements of the synergistic work carried out by Lendager Group as a whole. These showed that the Resource Rows and the Upcycle Studios would perform with emissions of 6.64 kg and 8.08 kg CO_2-eq/m2/year both below the voluntary sustainability standard published this year. Together, a rowhouse from each project has achieved a reduction of 85 tonnes of CO_2-equivalents compared to the benchmark and saved 1377 tonnes of waste.

An interview with Gustaf Lilliehöök

Why do you work with CE in your building projects?

It fits in as one of the many levers that we need to work with at NREP. We need to improve our CO_2 footprint and need to contribute to decreasing the impact of the industry as a whole. Real estate is a laggard industry that is not used to change, so while we are trying to contribute to change, it's not easy.

It's all about striking the right balance. Making it competitive and attractive for developers to work with recycled materials, but also making sure it has an environmental impact when doing so. What do we do if it has a material impact, but is not cost-competitive? And vice versa. We need to move the needle on what can be achieved when recycling materials. Impact, economy and identity are all values we are influencing. We need to work with all the levers to make it attractive because if we fail to do so it will never be adopted by the broader industry and thus never have real impact.

What other value drivers do you see?

There's the value from a future landlord and owners' perspective. The story of the building shouldn't be underestimated. It is difficult to underline exactly what it is because we still don't know it yet. Some recycled materials have a neutral value, but others give buildings a unique aesthetic value. Even more, in some cases, when using upcycled materials, we can get access to higher quality for a fraction of the price. These materials have all had a previous life, and that's coming through in the new architecture our users are getting exposed to. This is both in terms of quality and history. New materials struggle to deliver that.

Another driver is the economic side to it, but we are not quite there yet. So why are we doing it? In order to make an impact and move the industry, we need to take on responsibility. But at the moment, that comes at a cost. However, we do see it has a direct value for us as a company. Doing something extra and changing the course of the industry is engaging and motivating our staff. That's an important value for us, as the developer.

What do you see as the main barriers to developing circular building projects?

There are three aspects to this: A product angle, a procurement angle and a regulatory angle. The first two are mostly opportunities, whereas the last one is mostly a barrier. In terms of production; it is a barrier that many upcycled materials and products simply haven't been invented yet. Of course, this is an opportunity too. This comes down to being willing to do this before it is proven viable.

When it comes to procurement, the lack of access to upcycled materials with predictability in terms of volume, quality, purity and timing constitutes a very important barrier. Currently, the procurement processes are significantly longer compared to conventional processes.

Last are the regulatory barriers, concerning the risk assessments of using recycled materials and getting the right permits to use them. For many of the recycled materials, you can get them more or less in a cost-neutral way; so regulations are definitely a bigger barrier than cost.

What products and or services would you most like to see offered?

Material banks for a predictable procurement of upcycled or recycled materials would be a service I'd like to see. Today we have many materials in the manufacturing process that most would see as waste, but that could be valuable input streams. But we don't have a central marketplace for these materials if we are to recycle them. Specifications are not identified properly, and that makes it harder to recycle otherwise perfectly fine materials.

How do you think we can overcome the current barriers of working with circularity in the building sector?

Continuing on the topic of material banks, if it was efficient and predictable to procure upcycled materials, it would probably be in much higher demand. Predictability of the volumes and specifications is key. What, when and where – to get clarity on these questions today is a very manual and labour-intensive process for any project that seeks to use upcycled materials.

The procurement would be much more competitive if there was a common ground to do so. Struggling to deliver these materials is true across the board. The lack of a cohesive structure introduces risk and that has an effect on the quality and quantity. If you're faced with it being super hard to deliver these materials, it's a very fundamental barrier. At the end of the day, it is about making a supporting system that makes it possible for these waste management companies to provide the service. They should be in charge and make these banks. The demolition should be regulated in a way where they are adding to the banks instead of filling up landfill or roadfill.

Both for procurement to become easier and for the use of upcycled materials in buildings to become easier, improvement of the regulatory framework is an important enabler. The regulatory environment today is not very supportive. Clearly, there are some regulatory concerns that need to be addressed. But we can't just sit and wait for the regulations to change. We need to push forward to take those first steps with projects that pioneer solutions that will make subsequent steps easier for future projects. And hopefully, that eventually prompts a change of regulations and hopefully, some solutions eventually get adopted by the broader industry, and with that scale achieve real impact on the challenges that we are seeking to address.

Summary of key findings

Potentials

- Reduced CO_2 footprint and negative impact of the industry as a whole
- Recycled materials can add a unique aesthetic and history to a building that new materials can't
- Pushing sustainable boundaries can motivate staff and increase the morale in a company

Barriers

- Many innovations for how to technically succeed with reusing materials are yet to be invented
- Lack of predictable access to materials constitutes a barrier and slows down the building process

- Difficulty in getting the right building permits to recirculate materials in new builds

Initiatives to accelerate the transformation

- A (digital) system to predict the availability and accessibility of materials for circulation
- The development of materials banks would secure and stabilise the procurement process
- Demolition processes should be adapted so that materials are put in the bank, not landfills

Practical experience 3: Mustad Eiendom

> We were able to re-assess the transformation of one of our existing buildings after we had the materials and embedded CO_2 in the building mass analysed. In the end, we decided to demolish much less of the building than initially planned, making sure to keep as much of the existing, carbon-intensive structure as possible through refurbishment.
>
> *Olav Line Chief Executive Officer, Mustad Eiendom*

Mustad Eiendom is a Norwegian developer and building operator with a long term and sustainable focus on developing the area of Lilleaker and Lysaker located outside Oslo, Norway. Mustad has been operating manufacturing companies in the area for almost 150 years and is now transforming it into a sustainable neighbourhood. Mustad and Lendager The Circular Way started their collaboration in 2018 when Lendager facilitated the development of a shared vision among project partners for the development of the sustainable neighbourhoods in Lilleakerbyen and Lysaker. This was embodied in a vision paper defining a clear vision and concrete steps of how to achieve it. Through a rough and detailed mapping of the area, Lendager TCW identified and quantified potentials for recirculation and reuse of the construction on environmental, material and economic parameters of Lilleakerbyen. This was done to envision a sustainable new path for the neighbourhood while cherishing the historic area. Lendager TCW later brought the exhibition WASTELAND to one of the old warehouses in Lilleakerbyen to display Mustad's sustainable ambitions for the area. The exhibition displays a variety of different upcycle solutions and it was brought to Lilleakerbyen with the aim to bridge sustainability and the rest of the industry by hosting presentations, industry conferences and informative networking events to make Lilleakerbyen a beacon for circular construction and start the circular transformation of the Norwegian building sector. Thereby, highlighting the role of the construction industry in the transition to a circular economy and facilitating the development of new ways of collaborating across the value chain to lead the way.

An interview with Olav Line

Why do you work with CE in your building project?

Until we started our collaboration, we did not work with implementing CE at all. We were like most other developers, and had little interest in it because we thought it meant more work and additional costs. But as we started working on our first sustainability report and strategy, we found out our industry has one of the biggest footprints, and that we as a whole have been taking too little account of the environmental impact of our work. On the other hand, we also realised that not only do we (the construction industry) have the financial muscles to make an impact, but we also work within a field where our competencies and influences can really make a difference.

How have you worked with CE principles in your projects so far?

Now that we have an overview of the material potential and value of our existing building mass here in Lilleakerbyen, we can use that knowledge when we start new projects in the projection phase and make sure we start the process based on circular building methods. But I also believe that in order to succeed, we must take one to two steps at a time.

We will not reform ourselves or the whole industry through one project. But we believe that we must do something. For example, we were able to re-assess the transformation of one of our existing buildings, after we had the materials and embedded CO_2 in the building mass analysed. In the end, we decided to demolish much less of the building than initially planned, making sure to keep as much of the existing, carbon-intensive structure as possible through refurbishment.

What is the value of implementing CE in the built environment? I see three main arguments for the CE. First, our whole industry is behaving like all our resources are infinite and inexhaustible. And for that reason alone, we are really in need of change. If everyone waited for someone else to do something, nothing would ever be done. That's what motivates us to be frontrunners; to pave the way for the rest of the industry.

Second, we strongly expect the authorities to start requiring us to document how much we can circulate in our building projects, and how well we can take care of our existing building masses.

Third, we also believe that when doing this now, going first, it will become profitable for us. But of course, in order for this to happen, we must not only teach ourselves how to do this but also make sure our partners and the whole industry are catching up. If we can achieve this, we believe there is a huge potential.

What do you see as the main barriers to developing circular building projects?

Ten years ago, 'energy renovations' was a big hurdle for our industry to get started with. Back then, the authorities in Norway kickstarted a large program where developers would receive subsidies for energy renovations. We think that if the government were to start similar incentive programmes and initiatives for CE in the built environment, it would make a great difference for the society. This would speed up the process and transition.

Second, we still see how easy it is for our industry to continue business as usual. That's why I believe authorities should create requirements for developers when they apply for building permits. For example, in order to get permission to build, applying circular building methods in the project would be a legal requirement. And honestly, I expect this will happen within not too long.

Third, I think we need to widen the efforts; making sure that it is not just the most visionary and front-running actors in the industry that changes, but also mainstream companies start working with CE. In the end, what holds us back is the difficulty in finding someone willing to participate, that is a contractor that is willing and able to think circularly: One that understands that the materials are already here and that we can selectively demolish and reuse the materials on-site or locally.

Furthermore, very few contractors have the required knowledge or business model that allows for reprocessing and upcycling our building materials. Already, before even attempting a circular project most actors think it is too complicated and too far outside our traditional practices. There is a growing movement of companies doing this (circular building projects). But we are extremely dependent on their continued growth, interest and ambitions within this agenda.

How do you think we can overcome the current barriers of working with circularity in the building sector?

Directive on construction quality, and a CE certification scheme: Those two areas are both designed to only operate with new products. This means that if we were to carefully take down and recycle one of our own materials, the system for certification is horribly troublesome. This system or bureaucracy of today is difficult to overcome and should be changed to ease the transition for the whole industry.

Have you found it difficult to live up to the demand for sustainability due to the current barriers?

I do not know if it says something about Norway as a whole, but so far, we haven't experienced that our tenants have put up any specific demands for more sustainable solutions. So, in a way, what we see is that the demand is lacking behind. Nevertheless, we still think we must push this agenda forward and we expect the demand to change over the coming years. That one day it is non-negotiable; those tenants will absolutely refuse rent from us if we cannot document sustainable and circular practices. So, in that way we are carefully following where the demand is moving towards. Especially when we are working over such long time spans, we must future-proof our projects and foresee that perhaps in ten years from now, what we see as something special and challenging will have become a matter of course. And then we must acknowledge the big difference in our generations. Many adults and the elderly are not as peremptory as the young generation is. The young generation will without doubt be driving this transformation in a more uncompromising manner.

What products and/or services would you most like to see offered?

On the service side, we really want to see more contractors willing to work with upcycling and materials: To see our waste as resources. Here, we especially need to focus on reusing and recycling concrete, which still is a very widespread and preferred material in our industry, but unfortunately very complicated to circulate. This also means that the architects and engineers need to start thinking differently. That not everything has to be demolished and built from scratch with new materials. So, in a way, we both need new thinking in the advisory and executive phases of the value chain.

But we are experiencing a growing market and it is easier to create enthusiasm in the business. The architects work with BIM – and we encourage our advisors to work with BIM – thus if we could convert the material mappings with this system it would be fantastic. I think it would be a milestone if we could succeed in cataloguing and integrating our resource mappings with BIM.

Summary of key findings

Potentials

- With its financial muscles and competencies, the construction industry can be a driver for sustainable development
- Early adoption of CE principles can put you in the forefront of future regulations and requirements to operate in the built environment
- Expectations of CE investments to come out profitably in the long run

Barriers

- It's too easy for actors in our industry to continue doing business as usual
- There are not enough "doers" in the industry willing and capable of thinking circular
- Construction directives and the CE certification are not designed to operate with reused materials

- Needs state or municipal initiated incentive programmes focussing on pilot and innovations projects
- Authorities must require more of developers, advisors and contractors when granting building permissions
- Resource mappings and CE potentials should be integrated with the BIM system

Practical experience 4: Gladsaxe Municipality

> There are lots of advantages when building greener. We actually see a decrease in sick days amongst the personnel in our Eco-labelled buildings. The numbers are about 1.5% lower than what we normally see, which of course is having a positive impact economically as well as in terms of health and working environment.
>
> *Helen Glindvad Kristensen Arkitekt MAA, Gladsaxe Municipality*

Gladsaxe is the first municipality in the Nordic countries to incorporate the UN Sustainable Development Goals in their official development strategy. In 2022, they plan to open the doors to Svanen (The Swan), the first circular kindergarten in Denmark. In this project building materials from the existing school, the building will be circulated and incorporated into the new facility on-site. This project is an ongoing collaborative effort between the following partners: Gladsaxe Municipality, Lendager Group, Tscherning and Niras. It is through early communication and close collaboration that this project is able to be the first of its kind. Svanen provided an investigative ground for developing new construction industry processes. Typically, in the construction industry, architects provide a design brief that stipulates material choice. In this project, the building material stock dictated the design brief developed by Lendager ARC. In addition to facilitating the tendering process, Lendager TCW assisted the municipality to discover what inherent value they already had in their possession through a resource mapping of the old school. This led to a study of material innovation potentials with the purpose of identifying the opportunities for selective demolition. Materials were pre-qualified by the following criteria: available amount, construction performance, contamination levels, economic value, carbon equivalents and waste reduction. Today the ongoing selective demolition process is well underway and the materials are stored on the premises in the circular construction site. Materials such as structural timber, roofing tiles, bricks and steel cladding will be used 1:1 in the new kindergarten. In other cases, materials such as windows will be reused as a thermal barrier in a greenhouse.

An interview with Helen Glindvad Kristensen

Why do you work with CE in your building projects?

To try out new things with material recycling, to work with our CO_2 reduction and to reduce the use of virgin materials. In addition to that, we have also been working with CE in relation to the Nordic Swan Ecolabel (Svanemærkningen), since it is important to be aware of any environmentally harmful substances in the materials when working with kindergartens. There are lots of advantages when building greener. We actually see a decrease in sick days amongst the personnel in our Eco-labelled buildings. The numbers are about 1.5% lower than what we normally see, which of course is having a positive impact economically as well as in terms of health and working environment.

Because we have a large number of properties, we also have a big responsibility. As a public building developer, it is important for us to take the lead in the sustainable development. Of course, we ask ourselves whether it is possible to reuse and recycle materials for the same price. By reusing many resources in the new kindergarten directly from the demolition of the old school, we were able to deduct the price it would have normally cost us to dispose of the waste. So, when looking at it from a bigger perspective, using old materials from a demolition in another project does make sense, and gives an economic incentive. Yet, saving money is not really the essence of why we work with CE in our projects.

For us, it is more a question of being able to create value on both an economic and human scale: Being able to create better conditions for our citizens and employees as a municipality. We are fully aware that circulating materials are more costly in terms of hours and manpower spent throughout the process; from the initial planning and advising to the demolition and construction of the new building. But at the end of the day, it is a conscious choice to invest a bit more in the total construction costs, knowing that it will pay for itself on several fronts; creating more local jobs while reducing our waste, emissions, chemicals and use of virgin materials.

What do you see as the main barriers of developing circular building projects?

The responsibility of the recycled materials is a big barrier. And as long as we don't have set fees on CO_2 emissions, this will continue being a challenge. Guaranteeing the durability of the recycled materials, while also keeping our expenses on maintenance and operation at a responsible level is another challenge we face. The question of durability is especially tricky. Take roof tiles for example: They look good and they have a lifespan of at least

30–50 years more. But they have already been on the existing roof for 80 years. Who is going to be responsible for ensuring the quality and lifespan? If they only last on the new building for ten years, it might have been a better investment to buy new ones from the beginning. This spirals into our first challenge: Who will take responsibility for the assembly and mounting of the recycled materials? When using old products, there is no manufacturer who provides instructions for how to treat and assemble them. This creates a huge uncertainty and affects the guarantee and durability.

As the developer, we can take the responsibility, but as a contractor or craftsman, you cannot be fully depreciated of responsibility, should something happen to the recycled materials that aren't related to the fact that they are, as such, recycled. This has to be taken into account when writing the tender. There has to be nuances to which kind of guarantee and responsibility you are to take care of. This is why contractors are often reluctant to use recycled materials, and prefer much more, materials that come with clear instructions and guarantees from the producer.

Finally, there are some materials that are especially hard to handle because of strict regulations in place. Windows are a good example. Here, you can save a lot on CO_2 emissions and raw materials by reusing them, but we see a lot of regulations standing in the way. If categorised as "waste" it is not allowed to contain any harmful materials. But if categorised as a new product, there is yet another threshold. The processing over this with authorities makes it (recirculation of materials) difficult. PCB is always a question. Are we allowed to have lead in the paint? How about galvanised panels for the façade? For the façade panels, if we are allowed to use them again, they are going to be defined as a temporary extension of the landfill. The galvanisation is still strong, so why categorise it as waste?

How do you think we can overcome the current barriers of working with circularity in the building sector?

The Svanen project is a pilot project, and we know that we haven't yet built with recycled materials in this scale before. Therefore, we know we have to use more resources and time to make it happen. Also, we have a strategy in the municipality where we are working with the UN Sustainable Development Goals, which is another way we frame our goal to work with sustainability in the built environment. Projects using old building materials need a longer and more controlled process. You need to make way for extra consulting, knowledge, time and costs in the budget. And these factors should be considered as part of the pros and cons for the overall benefits of the project. I also think we need to be better at ensuring the quality of recycled materials by making the right tests beforehand; how durable are they, and what is their remaining lifespan?

Are there any materials or applications you are particularly focussed on?

We are seeing a lot of experiments with interior building finishes. For example, Lino mixed with cacao shells to increase the durability, experiments with casting new plastic shells of ocean plastic waste. All of these things can help challenge the assumptions on products made from recycled or alternative materials. Using recycled materials can have its charm, but you also need to know that it will last in both durability and aesthetics. Bricks are easy; we get the most beautiful facades from reused bricks, and the old bricks are often also stronger than new ones. When you are working with the type of buildings that I do – institutions, schools, kindergartens and half public houses – the right choice of materials is extra important. Schools and kindergartens are tough environments, and we need to make sure that we have nice, good and most of all durable materials when building these. If a material already looks old and worn out after 5–10 years, it shouldn't be used in these types of buildings. It is our responsibility to create the best and most robust building with a good indoor climate for citizens, users and staff. In the end, we are using the citizens' money and we have a great responsibility for doing so in their best interests.

Summary of key findings

Potentials

- Lowered the sick days of our users and employees when building sustainably
- The money saved in waste disposals fees is better spent on upcycling material resources
- Recycling materials in building projects can help reach overall strategic sustainability goals on a state or municipal level.

Barriers

- There is a responsibility vacuum – who will guarantee the durability and quality of reused materials?
- Contractors are reluctant to use recycled materials due to lack of instructions and guarantees
- Unclear regulations and definitions of waste complicate the recirculation of materials in new builds
- Needs better testing methods of old materials to forecast their durability and lifespan
- Standardised instructions for how to carefully demolish and assembly reused materials

- The responsibilities between actors involved in demolition and reuse of materials have to be better outlined in future tenders

New European Bauhaus and the new taxonomy for sustainable finance

The New European Bauhaus launched in 2020 is an environmental, economic and cultural project initiative instigated by the European Commission aiming to combine three core elements: Beautiful, Sustainable and Together to look towards culture and design to future-proof both Europe and the planet. Aligned with Alexander Von Humbolt's work and notion of consilience as already touched upon, the goal is to create a platform for experiments and knowledge sharing to bridge the gap between science, arts and culture. As Ursula Von der Leyen, president of the European Commission, puts it, the Bauhaus project revolves around "concrete actions against climate change" or, in other words, converting the sustainability agenda into tangible solutions. Specifically, the initiative is looking for solutions that are:

- Enriching, inspired by art and culture, responding to needs beyond functionality
- Sustainable, in harmony with nature, the environment and our planet
- Inclusive, encouraging dialogue across cultures, disciplines, genders and ages

Financially, the European Commission has already dedicated €85 million through several of its subsidiaries, which for example, will enable the development of a "think and do" tank to realise the large ambitions of the project in accordance with the 2019 European Green Deal's 2050 goals. Furthermore, the Bauhaus is seen as the first vital push towards a more circular European economy, where the Union acts as an innovative first mover and stops its unsustainable degradation of nature and raw materials. Regarding project management and modelling, the plan is built with valuable knowledge from the unprecedentedly large and rapidly negotiated €750 billion EU COVID recovery plan, hoping to replicate both the ability to attract capital and the relative political efficiency (at least for an EU process). The Bauhaus aims to develop several strong public-private partnerships, such as Europeana, an online European culture platform whose General Director describes the project as "resonating strongly with the community" and additionally supporting the digitalisation agenda as a positive externality. The New European Bauhaus was created to shape a more humane and sustainable future in Europe by radically rethinking our current approaches and ways of thinking.

Denmark is a core player in the project. The Danish proposal focussing on how art, architecture and design can and must make the green transformation a cultural movement and the irresistible choice was selected as one of three pilot projects in May 2022.

EU taxonomy for sustainable finance

The EU taxonomy launched in 2020 is a European economic activity classification system that contributes to achieving climate and environmental goals. The EU taxonomy is a critical element of the EU Action Plan for Sustainable Finance, and its primary goal is to enable and accelerate the transition towards green investments. By classifying sustainable activities, it will become easier for both the financial market and companies in the EU to find sustainable investment opportunities.

The Taxonomy is built on six environmental objectives: (1) Climate change mitigation, (2) Climate change adaptation, (3) The sustainable use and protection of water and marine resources (Frampton, 1980), The transition to a circular economy, (5) Pollution prevention and control and (6) The protection and restoration of biodiversity and ecosystems. For economic activities to be considered environmentally friendly, it requires a substantial contribution to climate change mitigation within at least one of the environmental objectives and additionally avoiding significant harm to the other objectives.

> **Question:** What does your dream home look like? How many square metres do you live on? Are you sharing anything with others? If so, what, and with whom?

References

Architecture 2030 (2021). Why the Building Sector. https://architecture2030.org/why-the-building-sector/

EU (2021). Circular Construction in Regenerative Cities (CIRCuIT). https://cordis.europa.eu/project/id/821201

EU (2021). New European Bauhaus. https://europa.eu/new-european-bauhaus/index_en

EU (2022). EU Taxonomy for Sustainable Activities. https://finance.ec.europa.eu/sustainable-finance/tools-and-standards/eu-taxonomy-sustainable-activities_en

Forbes (2014). China Used More Concrete in 3 Years than the U.S. Used in the Entire 20th Century. https://www.forbes.com/sites/niallmccarthy/2014/12/05/china-used-more-concrete-in-3-years-than-the-u-s-used-in-the-entire-20th-century-infographic/

Frampton, K. (1980). *Modern Architecture: A Critical History*. Thames and Hudson.

Fuller, B. (1969). *Operating Manual for Spaceship Earth*. Lars Muller Publishers.

Lysgaard Vind, D., & Lendager, A. (2018). *A Changemakers Guide to the Future*. Copenhagen.

Nordic Real Estate Partners (2022). Net Zero 2028. https://nrep.com/netzero/

Pedersen, E., & Lendager, A. (2020). *Solutions*. Arkitektens Forlag.

Scientific American (2018). Cement Producers Are Developing a Plan to Reduce CO_2 Emissions. https://www.scientificamerican.com/article/cement-producers-are-developing-a-plan-to-reduce-co2-emissions/

The European Commission (2019). A European Green Deal Striving to be the First Climate-Neutral Continent. https://ec.europa.eu/info/strategy/priorities-2019-2024/european-green-deal_en

UN's expert group on Net Zero targets (2022). Integrity Matters: Net Zero Commitments by Businesses, Financial Institutions, Cities and Region. https://www.un.org/en/climatechange/high-level-expert-group

UNEP (2017). As Buildings and Construction Sector Grows, Time Running Out to Cut Energy Use and Meet Paris Climate Goals. https://www.unep.org/news-and-stories/press-release/buildings-and-construction-sector-grows-time-running-out-cut-energy

World Green Business Council (2019). Bringing Embodied Carbon Upfront. https://www.worldgbc.org/news-media/WorldGBC-embodied-carbon-report-published

14

DESIGNING OUR CITIES THE DANISH WAY

Having an infection in your little toe can cause a fever in your entire body. The reason? Your body is composed of trillions of interconnected parts, and what goes on in one part can influence your overall physical and mental well-being. Similarly, what we put into our cities matters to the general well-being of our society. An example is the supply of coal power to cater to an increasing demand for energy, resulting in polluting the air of countless cities. As a result, citizens' health is threatened, and air pollution caused by human activities is killing millions of people every year

Hence, as seemingly harmless as our modern functions of the city may seem, they are not without consequences. Burning fossil fuels leads to rising temperatures and climate change. Our actions affect the planet, affecting our ability to thrive. Air pollution leads to lung and heart diseases. Changes in water patterns can cause both floods and droughts. Production and consumption lead to infinite amounts of waste and pollution and the contamination of oceans, soil and air. Claiming and transforming nature to create dense human settlements not only eliminates existing food sources, communities and renewable natural materials, but also rapidly annihilates Earth's natural ecosystems that have been balancing the inputs and outputs of natural resources for millions of years by naturally capturing and storing the carbon. Therefore, we must fundamentally change how we plan, build and manage cities. We must reset the urban metabolism and its flows and reinvent a system in which cities and their inhabitants do not have to thrive at the expense of, but in harmony with, nature. This is where the notion of designing The Circular Way comes in handy.

DOI: 10.4324/9781003261018-14

Urban Metabolism can be a challenging concept, so allow me to explain. By seeing the city as a living organism, we can investigate how the different parts of the city's body are connected and how vital they are for the proper function of the whole. Therefore, we must pay attention to what we feed the "body" to ensure it is healthy and can regenerate its cells. A so-called regenerative city. Because our cities, like our bodies, have a metabolism. But unfortunately, we are not being thoughtful about how we nourish them. This is the reason urbanisation has such adverse effects on our climate. But it does not have to be that way. Urbanisation and the built environment could play crucial roles in creating a regenerative world rather than being a main contributors to the problem. Because to move toward creating value within the planetary boundaries, we need to rise above the individual building and interact with cities and society at large to change the rules of the game and set a new vision. We can start by seeing the city as a living organism, much like how Alexander von Humboldt (Kellner, 2023) rejected the notion of nature as a machine and introduced a new understanding of Earth as one great living organism – an organism connected through ecosystems influencing and determining one another's existence. And while nature is not a machine, machines are part of our cities. Having entered the Anthropocene epoch, man and machine are forever connected. We must ensure that the connectedness benefits nature and society.

Similarly, we should consider the built environment and cities as parts of a larger living organism. The benefit is that when we start seeing the bigger picture and begin connecting the dots – the citizens, the materials, the buildings, the districts, the cities, the nations, the regions **synergies will arise so that individual problems can become part of a collective solution**. With reference to the design principle of connectedness in the Manifesto for design in the Anthropocene in Chapter 7, it is essential to understand that if buildings and cities are to seize the potential and drive the transformation to mitigate climate change, they must have a greater purpose than themselves alone. To succeed in creating a sustainable society, we must also create social cohesion. And not just any social cohesion – but one that adds value to both the strong and the weak – ensuring it's the highest common denominator that sets the standards. It is part of a regenerative society in which resources are not shared in a zero-sum game but are valued and circulated for all to prosper.

A science of cities

It is all too often forgotten that the whole point of a city is to bring people together, to facilitate interaction, and thereby to create ideas and wealth. To enhance innovative thinking and encourage entrepreneurship and cultural activity by taking advantage of the extraordinary opportunities that the diversity of a great city offers.

West (2017)

To inform this transformation, I build on the theories and ideas of Geoffrey West, the British theoretical physicist (West, 2017), who developed a scientific model of cities, mapping the flows of inputs and outputs, and used the findings to diminish the negative carbon footprint systematically. Indeed, there is no reason not to. But it is one thing to be mindful of a city's resource flow and its effects. It is another to ensure that we utilise the resources to their full extent and at their highest value. In my opinion, the chief function of the city is to create a synergetic flow of resources and to ensure that they work towards a prosperous future for all. **In other words: Cities can help create regenerative and restorative societies.**

The notion of urban metabolism is nothing new – we've known about it for centuries. It just never occurred to us to connect this accumulated massive information to our planning of cities and urban areas. I genuinely believe that the scenario of a thriving city giving back more than it takes is not a utopian fantasy but a well-documented and feasible development of our world's urban spaces – whether in Copenhagen, Beijing, Nairobi or New York.

Today, 54% of the world's population lives in urban areas, accounting for 85% of the global GDP generation, according to a report on Circular Cities from The Ellen Macarthur Foundation (The Ellen Macarthur Foundation, 2019). In the era of late modernity, cities have thus become the epicentre of problems and opportunities for future prosperity and health of our planet and our growing population. According to the Circular Cities report, cities are the dominant "aggregators of materials and nutrients, accounting for 75% of natural resource consumption, 50% of global waste production, and 60–80% of greenhouse gas emissions".

So, what should we do to prevent massive environmental damage further? Simply break up the cities and move towards a decentralised urban planning approach. Surely there are other ways forward, and here is why: *the city does not scale linearly*. When we scale cities, we use less and get more. Sounds odd? Let's take a closer look at the facts and arguments. We will examine this aspect in detail as I want to give you the entire picture.

Geoffrey West presents empirical examples highlighting the existence of solid regularities in the data structures, suggesting that cities quantitatively scale with size. *A Science of Cities*, as he calls it. What he found is that we experience a 25% discount per citizen on necessary inputs such as energy, water and raw materials with the doubling of the city's size (West, 2017). West has been collecting and analysing historical data on the development and growth of cities for most of his career. However, he begins from a very different starting point than most, as learning from nature, he starts by asking:

"Could there conceivably be a few simple rules that all organisms obey, indeed all complex systems, from plants and animals to cities and companies?" (West, 2017).

West explains this as a result of the 'metabolism of the city, understood as the biological process of energy transformation and waste management in the cells of living organisms. And it gets even better. When we scale cities, not only do we get a 25% discount on input – we also evoke a 15% increase in the output of cities, including an upsurge in patents and innovations much needed to drive the necessary improvement towards a regenerative society. He also finds this systematic behaviour a global phenomenon, similar to all cities where data was obtained (West, 2017).

Of course, that does not mean that cities are the only solution for structural living. Digitalisation might have made it more accessible to deliver the same output at a distance due to our ability to be hyper-connected with relevant communities regardless of our physical whereabouts, as seen during the COVID-19 lockdowns. The need and benefits of being connected to nature in or outside a city and the importance of the local community must be remembered.

However, cities are a crucial part of our modern way of living, and for a city to be regenerative, it needs to give back more than it takes. It is, therefore, a crucial factor that a city does not simply turn inwards – focussing solely on the well-being of the citizens within its geographical perimeter. Instead, it should seize the increased power that urbanisation and geopolitics give the city. Simply put, the city now has part of the responsibility for our global well-being, and much as we explored in the previous chapter on buildings, the city must give back more than it takes. So it is necessary to ensure that the benefits created within the city benefit not only the city itself but its surroundings and global citizens. Luckily, we are seeing more and more city officials stepping up the game and taking responsibility for creating better solutions, moving us closer to staying within our planetary boundaries while creating value for people.

As West further discovered via his empirical data collection, cities share similarities with other living organisms. Their mode of operation can be called 'urban metabolism,' a notion known from our bodies. Still, its use on a societal level goes back to the 19th century when Karl Marx and Fredrich Engels made the first references to actual metabolism (Bellamy Foster, 1999) when discussing the relation between physical labour, natural resources and industrialisation. While West discovered that cities share similarities with other living organisms, one radical difference stands out. Cities rarely die. In fact, they can continue to thrive for centuries and millennia. This is also one significant difference between cities and corporations, which, unlike cities, have a relatively short lifespan and scale differently. Cities have the privilege of running on a less top-down controlled framework and are divided by autonomous, diverse, multi-dimensional entities and subcultures. West thinks this results in the cities' outstanding resilience, open-ended growth and superlinear scaling (West, 2017).

But are cities' future longevity always assured? Even though people generally take root in urban areas to a greater extent, the concept of urban depopulation, where cities are shrinking, has been a well-known phenomenon since World War II. In an era of continuous Industry 4.0, automation, digitalisation and web 3.0 – where jobs are moving from resource extraction and manufacturing to the service sectors – some cities are struggling to avoid becoming obsolete ghost towns. We've seen it everywhere, from US cities such as Detroit, Flint and New Orleans to the Northeastern city in China, Yichun, where more than 100,000 people left the city between 2005 to 2015 due to excessive resource depletion in the area (Yang, 2019).

These two simultaneous trends of rapid urbanisation and urban depopulation call for an increased emphasis on the need for urban development strategies to make our cities more agile, liveable and forward-moving. We cannot rely only on the cities' seemingly innate ability to scale inputs and outputs alone. **What matters is what we scale, not just the rate at which we do it.** Yes, we want growth, but it must be the right kind. It has to be a means to provide value for people, particularly sharing prosperity with those currently living in poverty. And this is where we humans and our ability to design become essential. We guide the path, creating innovations and designs that enable transformation. And our importance only increases as our global population grows. As a start, we need to open both eyes and see the hidden resources and possibilities hitherto unimaginable for most of us. Imagine what we could do with the abandoned industrial complexes, the old shipyards, the laid-off infrastructures and many empty houses. What if we found a way to reactivate these leftovers that could help us lay the foundation for new communities?

In some areas with urban depopulation, local entrepreneurs are now trying to replace fossil fuel jobs with jobs in the renewable energy sector by re-educating its workers and setting up locally funded solar and wind-power projects with considerable success. This is just one example of how we can kickstart the development of new, regenerative societies by decoupling future economic growth from the excessive use of virgin materials – which has been an inevitable precondition for development. It is time to explore what we believe is a replicable methodology of West's notion of urban metabolism – grounded in the principles of the circular economy.

Interview with Helle Søholt

> Nothing in the world is more simple and more cheap than making cities that provide better for people.
>
> *Gehl (2013)*

A quote by Jan Gehl, who with Helle Søholt founded Gehl – with Helle at the steering wheel ensuring that the pioneering thoughts on city design and prosperity are continuously developed and turned into tangible solutions and realised projects. All are highlighting the importance of good design and working with cities and companies worldwide to do just that: Design good cities and communities that provide better for people in synergy with nature. So I am delighted Helle agreed to participate here because, to me, the work of Helle and Gehl, as the global leaders of urban human-centred design, represents a vital part of the future for Danish Design in the context of global sustainability. They are already working globally, exporting tangible solutions and values of Danish Design to improve global sustainability.

In this interview, Helle shares her experiences and insights, including the importance of having a holistic approach and continuously developing solutions based on the specific context. She also reminds us of the importance of collaboration and societal coherence and the role of designers and architects to facilitate it and take responsibility for the individual product and the process.

D: If you could design your ideal world, what three words would you use to describe it?

H: The first word I would use is green. I'm dreaming of a green world where we use less energy and recycle more and where nature is much more prevalent in our lives than today. Rethinking our way of living by designing our cities focussed on improving people and nature's ability to thrive and increase well-being by using our physical environment to encourage citizens to exercise, increase movement and encourage interaction with nature and each other in community. Doing that should help improve our global citizens' physical and psychological well-being, secure greater biodiversity and benefit the individual city and society.

The second word is inclusive. In Gehl Architects, a key part of our methodology is to understand human needs and behavioural psychology both from a theoretical point of view and that of a practitioner. Thus, always looking at and analysing the specific context in which we work. Through our extensive work collecting data and analysing communities, we often come across systemic discriminatory practices that exist in our society and exclude certain groups from participating. It exists everywhere, but especially when working on a global scale, you get exposed to systemic discriminatory elements based on race, gender and age, to name a few. So, improving inclusion is one of the most important things we must do.

Communities and even countries are often quick to reject discriminatory practices because they can be challenging to spot with the inattentive eye. Some might even be unaware of the unjust systems they have created. But the lack of attention to the problem can lead to increasingly unfair systems and a decrease in overall societal coherence. So, we need to be more aware of how social structures and systems affect citizens, their well-being and the opportunity to impact their local community and global society positively.

The last word(s) I would use is innovation and the ability to adapt. In our current societal design, we have created systems that keep us locked in structures that we can't break out of and prohibit us from working across silos and instead, having defined institutions and organisations that have removed our possibility and maybe even decreased our ability to change.

However, the COVID-19 outbreak has taught us that we need to experiment. Both humans, companies, and the public sector have had to adapt and create quick fixes and longer-term solutions. It has forced us to rethink our approaches, ways of communication and much more. So, despite being a terrible situation, I hope we can learn from this experience and improve our ability to adapt and innovate together because we have experienced the power of innovation and the willingness to change. We have had to change routines that we naturally felt comfortable with and revisit some of our fundamental values. Sometimes it requires a crisis to make humans see the need and gain the ability to change.

D: Agreed, a key takeaway from the COVID-19 pandemic is that we are more capable of change than we might think. So, if the critical issue prohibiting adaptability and change for the better is our mindset and our inherent choice of sticking to "business as usual," – what are the important problems to solve or solutions to create?

H: First, a good start is to ensure people have the right surroundings to encourage innovation and adaptability, not least because it is a basic human need to be able to breathe fresh air, move around and be in community with others – something that has been forgotten in the design of too many global cities today. So, to improve innovation and adaptability, we must look towards designing cities that make people thrive. A great place to start is our public spaces. Irrationally and unfortunately, as things are now, we tend to put a much higher value on the private spaces utilised by few and lesser value on the common public areas used by the many. It points to a systemic flaw, but nonetheless, it is something we can work to fix short term. With simple design solutions, we can improve public spaces and increase the biodiversity and desirability of the surrounding areas. We are making them more valuable to individuals and the city through increased coherency. Another important gain is that it ensures public spaces that we are nurtured by. However, once the new solutions are realised, we must continuously remember to take care of our public spaces – remembering that they, like our individual homes, are ours to both enjoy and protect. Fortunately, Denmark has a positive movement towards more strategic city planning that considers the importance of public areas. New areas mixing nature with the ability to move are popping up because the municipalities have realised how important it is and have, thus, started prioritising and investing in it.

But they are not the only ones that have realised the benefits because as it improves the well-being of citizens as well as enhances the overall desirability and thus the value of the area, another emerging positive trend in Denmark is public–private partnerships between developers and building owners and the municipalities to improve and innovate our public spaces to increase community impact. I hope that trend will continue to grow and expand outside of Denmark. In general, an important point when designing better cities for the future is the importance of transferring and sharing knowledge. Denmark is quite good at designing cities and creating public–private partnerships, something that we should use to innovate and improve existing solutions in Denmark but also share globally – treating liveable cities as the system's design that it is – and thus something that can be shared and exported globally.

Another key tool is what you are working on: Circular economy, and we must utilise circularity much more. First, (again) design of our cities and buildings is vital because if designed for circularity, synergy arises, and circularity can create better and more sustainable housing by using better materials, optimising our square metres and ensuring the building use potential is fulfilled by designing and utilising it for several purposes. Second, how we physically design our cities and buildings can help facilitate the circular economy, for instance, by making waste sorting more convenient and improving the accessibility and value of sharing or reselling our otherwise individual products.

D: What pops into your mind when thinking of Danish design?

H: Firstly, to me, Danish design is about humanism. The human-centred design focusses on aesthetics in combination with ergonomics and functionality and often has an inherent value of inclusion, coherence and community. In many ways, the design brings people together.

Second, Danish design represents simplicity and natural materials of high quality rather than perishable. Due to the simplicity of the design and the quality of the materials, the products become timeless. There is a strong tradition for products from the heritage of Danish design passing through generations. Third, I would use the word pragmatic because we have an excellent tradition for and ability to find each other and create solutions together. Through this, functionality also becomes aesthetically beautiful. Finally, a key reason for our ability to collaborate is the fact that we are a small nation. At the same time, we have a relatively high level of equality in our society, increasing our level of coherence.

However, I am more interested in the values Danish design represents than the mere fact that it is "Danish" and branded as such. Instead, I think it is about taking the learnings and values and transforming them into a given context. For instance, the Danish design model proposes a way of design focussing on durability and inclusion, which I think is remarkable. However, this isn't a statement about Danish design being the best; instead, it reflects on the design philosophy that the individual designs are built upon. And what is a good solution in one context might not be an answer for others. So, to truly live up to the promise and philosophy of Danish design, it is essential to focus on the local conditions and remember that design is about humans. At Gehl, we believe that humans globally have everyday needs and that regardless of culture, everyone needs comfort, security, community, a hospitable climate and more to function and live. To make these conditions as good as possible, one must understand the local cultural context, historical events and tradition.

D: Understanding the specific context and remembering that design is about humans is a great point. Can you give an example of how you have used that insight in a particular project?

H: Yes, a project that comes to mind in collaboration with Danish pharmaceutical company Novo Nordisk asking us to find both cause and solution to the rise in urban diabetes, specifically analysing three cities in the United States. When researching and mapping the poorest neighbourhoods, you instantly become aware of the food selection that the citizens have access to, particularly the lack of fresh and healthy food. Even in hyper-modern western cities, there are poor areas with no supermarkets or proper public transportation, so the only food accessible to buy is fast food or food from food trucks or corner stores. When mapping, you need to be aware of what resources are available and what is lacking from a holistic point of view; in this case, we found that another issue is that even if a supermarket was available, one might not even be able to afford the food in the supermarkets or even be able to transport themselves that far. Identifying this problem allows us to find innovative solutions that work in the practical context: Can we grow food locally, set up private–public partnerships and attract new supermarket investors? It's just a few of the examples of potential solutions to the problem of rising urban diabetes.

Most importantly, we must start to rethink the approaches and design of cities to ensure quality and healthy food for everyone. The lack of attention will become dangerous for people's health and simultaneously result in increased financial costs for society due to increased health complications. Food is a basic human need that everyone is entitled to. It should be easy and cheap to make the "right" choice and to choose healthy options. For example, in Copenhagen, using a bike as a transportation tool is way easier than a car due to the lack of parking spaces and busy roads. This incentivises the citizens to incorporate exercise into their daily lives by choosing the easiest and most healthy option: Biking.

In the same way, we should use Copenhagen's design for bikes as inspiration to create easy and healthy food choices, not because the solution should necessarily be to create bike lanes for people to bike to the grocery store – but because following the philosophy of biking in Copenhagen the ambition for our solution should be that the healthy choice is the most convenient. The dream is that we create structures where our actions benefit ourselves and each other. And it is not just about our health choosing the "right"; sustainable options should be the easy choice, and as architects and designers, we have a key responsibility to create these options for the citizens, thereby improving both the individual's quality of life and the condition of our world.

D: What motivates you to want to change the world for the better? And what do you still want to do?

H: I'm motivated by the drive to make the world a better place. When looking back at my childhood, professional career, and my life in general, I have always been privileged enough to have a feeling of freedom and prosperity, which I think everyone is entitled to experience. Additionally, my career has given me insight into some of our global problems that are too large to ignore, so I can't help wanting to participate in the change.

To me, being an architect and, thus designer is essentially about solving problems. Design thinking is a methodology for problem-solving, thoroughly accessing the problem but focussing on finding solutions through ongoing iterations and continuously improving the solution design. In general, collaboration and working together across disciplines is a shortcoming. So, I hope to continue to use design to increase cross-sector collaborations, and we should encourage dialogue and partnerships between actors with a focus on design as a process. In continuation of this, there has become a large gap between architecture and the role of facilitators. We must keep challenging the norms and structures we have created through design as a process. We must keep evolving by designing, testing and evaluating what we do to improve it. Thereby, making design tradition an iterative work process that keeps changing and reflects our current social structure. Making it less about creating icons or the latest fashion and more about collaboration and contributing to positive change.

Helle Lis Søholt is a Danish architect and Founding Partner and CEO of Gehl. She founded Gehl with Professor Jan Gehl in 2000. The company has become well-known for its work within urban design and urban development, specialising in making cities more liveable and sustainable around the world. Through their work, Gehl has gained international attention. Helle Lis Søholt sits on the board of Design Museum Denmark, Planetarium and Urania Foundation and is the chairwoman of Bloxhub, the Nordic Hub for Sustainable Urbanization.

Case 14.1 The future of Copenhagen and the Resource Rows

From abandoned buildings to thriving communities: Imagine a city defined by its abundance rather than its scarcity of resources. A city with a thriving, healthy population known for its world-class regenerative innovations, low socio-economic inequality, high sense of community and unshakeable feeling of trust among its citizens. Delicious sustainable food is found on every street corner, and the air quality is the best among world capitals. Similarly, biodiversity, industry and the business community are all thriving in the 86.39 square kilometres that make up the city of Copenhagen. It has often been called the happiest place on Earth, but that's not the point. The point is that it has become the world's first regenerative, carbon-positive city. Does this urban centre sound like a utopia? Let us quickly tell you it is not. With a bit of help, it can be real. How do I know that? Because I live in this city. Or, perhaps not

FIGURE 14.1 Upcycled wall elements form a piece of the puzzle of the Resource Rows (Rasmus Hjortshøj, Coast, Lendager).

entirely. But every day, little by little, we work to ensure that Copenhagen – our city – will become the city we dream about.

Then you might ask: Can other larger cities copy Copenhagen's model? Definitely. Especially when we look at a long string of global megatrends and leap-frogging technological progress. Moreover, even though Copenhagen still has a long way to go before it finds genuinely sustainable practices to reduce waste production and CO_2 equivalent emissions, I dare to believe. One of the things that makes me hopeful is the Resource Rows, a residential project created by Lendager for NREP in one of Copenhagen's new urban developments called Ørestad. The inhabitants live in a community of attractive, modern buildings. While buildings are traditionally made of materials imported from afar, that is not the case here. Instead, the buildings are primarily made of local resources, typically considered useless waste. However, due to a circular design phase where locally available waste "materials" was seen as a positive, creative constraint, with a fair amount of audacity, and a lot of skilled local workers, it was possible to reactivate this so-called waste by transforming it into high-quality and valuable building materials.

Due to the circular design and skilled local workers, the inherent value of what was otherwise discarded as waste was reactivated and transformed into high-quality and valuable building materials without compromising on price, quality or aesthetics. As a result, fewer new materials were needed, and CO_2 emissions during construction and embedded in the materials were reduced. One example is the wood reused for both facades and interiors. The public transportation system expands throughout Copenhagen, making metropolitan travel even more efficient. In making the new subway tunnels, 900 tonnes of larch wood was used to transport concrete elements. Once at its destination, the wood was no longer needed. It went from being high-quality material to end-of-use waste, which the Metro company typically would have had to pay to get rid of. Luckily, Lendager got hold of 300 tonnes of the wood before it was thrown out. So now, instead of being burned and down-cycled in a waste-to-heat process, the wood was used to build beautiful facades, terraces, floors and balconies at the Resource Community, serving middle-class families of Copenhagen at a median price point. For all the wood used outdoors, we apply an old Japanese technique (Yakisugi) of charring the surface with fire to impregnate it – making it fireproof and resistant to fungus and insects (and fire, too) entirely without using any chemicals. Thus, instead of being burned in a waste-to-heat process, which is not part of a circular economy, the wood was used to build beautiful facades, terraces, floors and balconies at the Resource Community, serving middle-class families in Copenhagen at a median price point (Lendager & Lysgaard Vind, 2018).

Another essential material in making the Resource Rows come true was re-using bricks from old, abandoned buildings. Deindustrialisation and urbanisation are two immense forces leaving a lot of old factories, warehouses and homes behind. Raising the question: How do we even out this transition from industry to services, from land to city, without losing valuable materials? What if we could bring our houses, or part of our houses, with us when we moved?

Once upon a time, it was the norm to recycle old bricks. But since the 1960s, we started using cement rather than lime mortar, making it so strong that the bricks are now breaking before the mortar does when trying to take them apart. Therefore, Lendager came up with a way to cut out brick walls as whole modules rather than trying to use the individual bricks one by one. While at the same time designing for circularity, making the brick modules applicable as an aesthetical facade element. Hence, instead of demolishing the buildings in the traditional way, a method was created to cut out the brick wall in large elements and re-install them as facades in a patchwork of various brick colours.

Specifically for the Resource Rows, Lendager was able to re-use the bricks from part of the old iconic headquarters of the Danish brewery Carlsberg and other abandoned houses and factories in Denmark. Instead of simply crushing the old brick walls and using them for roadfill, we bring the value and history of the used materials into a new community.

That was the idea of the Resource Rows from the beginning: To take something from the building industry with a perceived low value and prove it to be a treasured resource for a large group of people. Not just providing housing but creating a healthy community based on core Danish values of sharing, helping one another and enjoying life together.

Speaking of community and connectedness to each other, you might wonder how the process of upcycling waste through the principles of a circular economy can be worth more than just making the built environment more environmentally sustainable? Besides mitigating climate change, the upcycled materials – if used correctly – can also be a valuable resource to secure connectedness. That was the case with the recycled bricks, where one added benefit of the bricks was that we brought older parts of the city and Denmark into a new urban area, thus connecting it to the cultural heritage of Copenhagen.

But that is not all. The roof area on top of the Resource Rows was utilised to provide outdoor space and greenhouses – made from upcycled window glass. Here, residents can connect with the outdoors and each other, and grow their own produce, not least providing an opportunity to be part of something; a community. To connect the two sides of the roof, an old industrial footbridge was reused and run over the courtyard, giving the residents a chance to visit each other and see the whole community from above.

Now, keep in mind that we did all this without compromising on either the price, quality or aesthetics of the building. Instead, at a cost-neutral price compared to any other benchmark buildings, we were able to challenge the issues of the built environment, food, water and energy – while also creating local jobs in the making. This is just one example driven by passion and a refusal to give up or give in. Imagine the possibilities if we combined global efforts and started working together across industries to accelerate and scale the journey towards regenerative buildings, communities and cities in harmony with nature. We can do it.

Question: Name three things you appreciate the most about your favourite city. How is it possible to scale those things?

References

Bellamy Foster, J. (1999). Marx's theory of metabolic rift: Classical foundations for environmental sociology, *American Journal of Sociology*, *105*(2), 366–405.

Gehl, J. (2013). Exhibition "Changing Mindsets" – Jan Gehl's Life of Work, Interview. https://www.dki.lv/exhibition-changing-mindsets-jan-gehls-life-work/

Kellner, C.L. (2023). Alexander von Humboldt. Britannica [online]. https://www.britannica.com/biography/Alexander-von-Humboldt

Lysgaard Vind, D., & Lendager, A. (2018). *A Changemakers Guide to the Future*. Lendager Group.

The Ellen Macarthur Foundation (2019). Circular Cities: Thriving, Liveable, Resilient. https://ellenmacarthurfoundation.org/topics/cities/overview

West, G. (2017). *Scale: The Universal Laws of Growth, Innovation, Sustainability, and the Pace of Life in Organisms, Cities, Economies, and Companies*. Penguin Press.

Yang, Z. (2019). *Sustainability of Urban Development with Population Decline in Different Policy Scenarios: A Case Study of Northeast China*. Chinese Academy of Sciences, Beijing.

15

COPENHAGENIZE

Designing regenerative mobility

> To the moon and back – twice – or 33 times around the world.
> That's how much the citizens of Copenhagen bike in total... every day!
>
> *(Astrup, 2016)*

We can call Copenhagen's mobility system a regenerative moonshot, a moonshot being: "an idea so big, so bold, as to be impossible until it is not," as coined by John F. Kennedy.

In fact, due to support from a broad coalition of politicians, public officials and, not least, architects and designers, Copenhageners are using bikes more than cars, and the city has become globally renowned for its pro-cycling attitude. Not only do these physical upgrades make a big difference in everyday life of Copenhagen's citizens, but the strategic political investment in making the city the world's biking capital has also yielded significant benefits. This is a tangible example of the potential benefits of reducing fossil fuel dependency and moving towards creating value for people while staying within the planetary boundaries.

First, bike riding has had a measurable effect on the environment, helping the city save 90,000 tonnes of CO_2 emissions annually (Cycling Embassy of Denmark, 2015). The plan to continuously increase bike traffic is a big part of Copenhagen's ambition to become the world's first carbon-neutral city. Besides these obvious CO_2-reduction results, supporting a city of pedalling habitants has helped the city reap significant health benefits regarding air quality and individual health at the advantage of public healthcare companies and citizens at large. Proving the thesis of the 4Rs – The Circular Way that Replace, is vital to driving improvement and allowing us to create value for people while staying within our planetary boundaries. In this case, replacing

DOI: 10.4324/9781003261018-15

cars with bicycles and thus reducing the amount of both vehicles needed and the gasoline used.

When my fellow Copenhageners and I jump on our bikes instead of into cars to go to work, school, yoga or the supermarket, it helps to create a more sustainable, lovable and liveable urban area with lower noise levels, as well as lowering the mortality rate by almost 40% (Murnane, 2017). A study in Denmark shows that if we Danes increase our biking by 10% – we can save 267,000 sick days a year and generate an extra $160 billion for society each year. In fact, for every kilometre a bicycle rider pedals, society gains the equivalent of 18¢, whereas every kilometre an automobile driver travels results in a loss of 17¢ (Schiller, 2015). And in the Capital Region of Denmark, which has a population of 1.8 million people, the biking culture already prevents at least a million days of sick leave every year – contributing positively to the bottom lines of the public and the private sector (Cycling Embassy of Denmark, 2018).

Furthermore, Copenhagen's bike strategy of decoupling transportation from CO_2 emissions has been indispensable in the successful branding of Copenhagen as a modern, health-conscious city that people want to live in and visit, attracting talent and investments. In a recent analysis of tourism in Denmark conducted by Wonderful Copenhagen, 52% of the respondents reported that biking was one of their three main reasons for choosing Copenhagen as a destination (Cycling Embassy of Denmark, 2018).

The efforts to encourage bicycle riding have made the municipality of Copenhagen a global case study for city planners and policy-makers. Every year (at least pre-COVID-19), some 60 international delegations visit the city to gain know-how and inspiration from its successful theory of change that, among other things, led to the fact that 660,000 citizens of Copenhagen own bikes – 6.6 times more than the total number of cars – and over the last 20 years bike traffic has increased by 68%, accounting for 45% of all trips to work or school. More than a fourth of all families with children own a cargo bike (Cathcart-Keays, 2016). And don't be mistaken – biking in Copenhagen is far from a low-class phenomenon. People earning more than half a million DKK ($80.000) a year bike 29% more than those who earn half (Cycling Embassy of Denmark, 2018). Even our royal crown prince Frederik can occasionally be seen biking his kids around town in a cargo bike.

An international design magazine suggested that visitors to Copenhagen take a walk on the Knippelsbro Bridge in central Copenhagen when it rains and note the number of people on bicycles in defiance of the weather conditions as a tourist attraction. The city has 179 wet days per year, but rain or shine, wind, fog or snow, 31,620 cyclists cross the bridge daily, simply because it is the easiest and most efficient transport modality. Indeed, for many years, the bike traffic on Knippelsbro bridge was even more hectic – up to 40,000 crossings every day (Cycling Embassy of Denmark, 2018) – but as more bike-and-pedestrian designated bridges have appeared around the city, the system is rebalancing the traffic load as people migrate to quicker routes.

Over the years, the Copenhagen municipality has prioritised the construction of bike paths over roads and parking areas since 2005; for example, it has spent one billion DKK ($160 million) expanding the cycling infrastructure with new bridges, tracks and renovations aimed at "softer" transport modes (Cycling Embassy of Denmark, 2018). One of these being The Bicycle Snake, as will be explored as a case later in this chapter.

This megatrend – often called Copenhagenization – caters to the rising need from the increase in global population growth and the rise of the global middle class while simultaneously fighting climate change, pollution, obesity and time-consuming traffic congestion. Indeed, a report from 2011 concluded that if all EU countries adopted a cycling pattern similar to Copenhagen's, greenhouse gas emissions from all transportation could be reduced by up to 26% (Walker, 2011).

An opportunity that deserves to be taken seriously. Thus, I am pleased to share the work and insight from two of our leading Danish mobility players: Architectural studio Dissing and Weitling and Design Studio Biomega. The first work within architecture to build the necessary infrastructure is in Copenhagen, now scaling it globally. The second is from an industrial design perspective, ensuring we have the necessary products (bikes) to make the transformation desirable and drive demand for global regenerative mobility.

Case 15.1 Dissing+Weitling bridge design

FIGURE 15.1 Photos of the Xiamen Skyway (Ma Weiwei, Dissing+Weitling).

Whenever I bike to the two Lendager developments Upcycle Studios and the Resource Rows, I, like so many other Copenhageners, use The Bicycle Snake by the Danish architectural firm Dissing+Weitling connecting the two sides of Copenhagen and enabling quick and convenient transport by bike – highlighting what great design can do to improve convenience in our everyday lives. So naturally, I wanted to feature their work locally in Denmark as well as internationally here and very happy that they agreed. As the case highlights Dissing+Weitling as a design studio is very much part of the future of Danish design but have also played a key role in the Danish Design

Heritage in particular as collaborators and professional "heirs" to Arne Jacobsen. Their work as such included finishing Arne Jacobsens work with the iconic Danish National Bank.

> Architecture must be a catalyst for everyday joy! Dissing+Weitling has extensive knowledge and passion for urban adjustment, bridge works, strategic landscape and city design, and we use our insights to ensure that the quality of environment enhances the urban realm and create inviting spaces for everyday use. What we want and what we bring to the world is extraordinary everyday spaces. We believe that inspiring people to change behaviour and modify their personal transportation habits can have a huge positive impact on our climate.
>
> *Tine Holmboe, Managing Director, Dissing+Weitling*, 2023

Dissing+Weitling has developed a strong reputation for designing buildings and bridges with people in mind. The firm's DNA is dating back to Danish Architect Arne Jacobsen's legendary work and studio, and since 1971 it carries on a unique heritage in both mind and work when exporting integrated design solutions all over the world – to this date the firm has been involved in more than 400 bridge and site development projects in 60 different countries across six continents. Irrespective of the type of construction, where it is in the world, or its scale, the firm strives to make a positive difference for the people who use the infrastructure it creates. Cycling through a city should be fun, working in an office should be comfortable and waiting for a train should feel safe. Dissing+Weitling believes that architecture should be a catalyst for good experiences as it moves people through space and across distance.

Launched as a part of the Danish architectural firm's green mobility projects in China, the Xiamen Bicycle Skyway (2017) is the world's longest aerial bicycle lane and China's first elevated cycle path. It is inspired by Copenhagen's world-famous bike lane, the Bicycle Snake (2016), and is an example of Danish design 'export', demonstrating how customised solutions can not only meet transit needs, but also inspire and facilitate greater cycling uptake.

While the scale and pace of the two bicycle bridges, the Bicycle Snake in Copenhagen and Xiamen Bicycle Skyway in Xiamen, are worlds apart, the goal is the same: a desire for green transport solutions and well-being in urban life. Chinese metropoles are struggling with air pollution and traffic congestion, developing its local transportation systems at a breathtaking pace – looking for inspirational examples of clever urban planning with – optimally – positive side effects. It was the massive international attention of the Bicycle Snake, which led to Chinese delegations travelling to Copenhagen to see the bridge first-hand

– and later, led to Dissing+Weitling working on urban revitalisation and mobility solutions in Xiamen among other cities.

Copenhagen is among the front-runners in demonstrating how urban 'liveability' can be done. The ambitious *City of Copenhagen's Bicycle Strategy 2011–2025* has resulted in more pedestrian and bicycle bridges, providing vulnerable road users with safe, healthy and direct mobility solutions. The goal for the bike city Copenhagen is part of the vision of Copenhagen as an environmental capital – the city being carbon-neutral by 2025 – and at the same time the political strategy and the (architectural) results have become the source of great interest for journalists, researchers, politicians and urban planners from every corner of the world. The realisation of Dissing+Weitling's Bicycle Snake stems from this city strategy and is today a symbol of Copenhagen's praised urban qualities.

The Bicycle Snake as a role model

The Bicycle Snake is a slim structure, an elevated 230-metre two-way bike lane at first-floor level that wriggles its way over the quay and the harbour, seamlessly connecting The Quay Bridge across the inner harbour with a major roadway some 5 metres above the quay. The bridge enriches the area around a shopping centre, which was characterised by being an 'uninviting' area, with conflicting interest between cyclists and pedestrians. Instead of just being a connection between two places, the idea was to create something the city and its people could benefit from.

The aim was never to build something extravagant or iconic – something functional and beautiful, yes absolutely – but to a great extent the aim was to add value to the city and its people.

All in all, one can say that urban planning in Copenhagen and the vision of the architects demonstrate that it is never enough for new initiatives to be 'just' functional – there is another tradition that's equally important: that of Danish design thinking. Whether it is a beautifully curved, meandering Bicycle Snake on its straight white pillars in the waters, a stylish harbour bath, or a welcoming urban space, the importance of making a difference for the people using the design shines through. This is the idea of Scandinavian well-being and welfare.

Xiamen Bicycle Skyway

In Xiamen, the 8-kilometre long, elevated bicycle pathway, Xiamen Bicycle Skyway, was built along a busy traffic road that integrates pedestrian bridges, ramps, roundabouts, bicycle parking, bicycle service pavilions and other points of interest. It covers the city's five major residential areas and three business centres and there are 11 entries on the path, which connect with 11 bus stations and two subway stations.

In both the Bicycle Snake and Xiamen Bicycle Skyway, Dissing+Weitling had – of course – to focus on architectural aspects, but also on the local constraints and the act of riding a bicycle to create more than a crossing. In Copenhagen, Dissing+Weitling saw a potential in unfolding the ramp, stretching it out and curved it. Across the water, in between the buildings and down close to the Quay Bridge. Hereby not only making it more joyful to ride on, with less steep gradients and better curvature, but also making it an element that could pull together an area with a multitude of incoherent buildings and meeting the needs of different road users. In Xiamen, the bicycle path was connected to a whole system of staircases, bridges, buses and elevators. It helped solve a pragmatic transport-related problem, while at the same time an answer to the increasing traffic congestion and pollution. It is a step towards a greener and more liveable city while accommodating the needs of the many. What seems to be an underlying Danish principle in these projects is the understanding of infrastructure being public space and therefore belonging to all of us – it is where we meet and interact, and it is an important part of what tie communities together and creates coherence between us as individuals. When treated with attention and respect, and from a people-centric viewpoint, designing public infrastructure and the public spaces in connection with it can have a great impact on many people's lives. Architecture has the power to revitalise run-down areas, to make life more fun and to make it safer. A well-designed solution can reinvigorate local infrastructure and possess an architectural value, making people proud of it for as long as it stands.

Xiamen Bicycle Skyway won the Danish Design Award 2019, in the category Liveable Cities. The solution was recognised as 'having a positive effect on the city environment and ecology.'. The Danish Design Award Jury 2019 said: 'Bringing new life to an otherwise dead part of the city and integrating different forms of traffic, the Skyway solves a very complex challenge. The Skyway involves Danish architects reviving a part of Chinese daily life – cycling culture – in a new context. The design quality is impressive for a project on this scale, and the Skyway is overall a great example of how Danish design DNA can be adapted into a different local fabric.'

Designing urban mobility by Jens Martin Skibsted

Jens Martin Skibsted is one of the most skilled designers I know when it comes to designing urban transportation and mobility but also is one of the most enlightened thinkers when it comes to the importance of design in general and the principles behind, which is why I am thrilled that he has agreed to write this essay to share both his philosophy and tactile design through his company Biomega that has created designer electric bicycles as well as city bikes.

FIGURE 15.2 Biomega bike (Biomega).

Designing urban mobility, an essay by Jens Martin Skibsted

Usually, the urban mobility perspective is infrastructure – roads, rails, data, finance, etc. In Biomega, we view our transportation challenges from a user and an industrial design perspective. You might ask: Would there be bike lanes without bikes?

When it comes to the objects that help you, the user goes from a to b within cities. There is very little consensus on how to do it sustainably. However, all rule out cars: They kill more people per year than corona did per year at its peak. Mostly from direct air pollution, secondarily from the effects of global warming, lifestyle diseases and traffic accidents. Their replacement – electric and intelligent cars will kill fewer, but they are still very ineffective regarding space efficiency and safety. If we make them driverless, they can clog up cities even more regardless of efficiency gains, as the average ridership can go below one person per car.

When it comes to bikes, experts agree that they are desirable in cities. They are equitable by being cheap, often the fastest means of transport in dense city centres, healthy as they are active and extremely space efficient; – and by far the most energy-efficient machine ever made by humans – beyond transportation. Much more so than walking and electric scooters. While bikes don't work well in spread-out cities, electric bikes partly solve this. If you had to pinpoint one object disrupting urban mobility right now, it wouldn't be drones or EVs (electric vehicles) but electric bikes. They far outsell electric cars. And while electric cars are all over the media as significant disruptors of urban mobility. These stories seem to consign to oblivion that electric cars take up as much space as their combustion counterparts and, arguably, take up even more of our time than guzzler cars – and that, in terms of sheer numbers, the real game changer is the electric bicycle.

That is why I founded Biomega in 1998 to make bicycles capable of competing with cars in cities and was the first manufacturer to redefine how bicycles were perceived and valued. The idea is that cities are improved with any and every car that bikes displace out of cities. That dream is what drives Biomega in the creation of its urban-landscape-changing bikes. The goal is to create a paradigm shift in how society imagines transportation. To compete directly with cars by designing bikes that are so beautiful that they imbue our cities with new meaning, making us healthier, happier and more connected than a car ever could.

And if you need more reason for choosing the bicycle, consider your benefits regarding time management and well-being. Choosing to bike might be one of the actions an individual can do short-term that best combines our planetary well-being with our individual well-being.

Time is the single most precious thing we humans have. It's the one thing money can't buy. The quality of our time depends mainly on personal choices. Yet, many of us lack what one could call "time hygiene." Hygiene is understood as a set of practices conducive to maintaining a certain quality of health. Likewise, we could think of *time hygiene* as practices conducive to quality of time: An optimal time balance, preventing stress and promoting happiness through conscious choices.

Our everyday choices affect how much time we have for our preferences. Our daily commuting habits take up a lot of this time. Most people seem unaware that bicycles are roughly as fast as cars in cities and that during rush hours, they are much faster than cars – in Europe, on average, 40% faster. Comparing electric vehicles and electric bicycles doesn't change the equation in favour of cars. On the contrary, electric bicycles are even faster than bikes without assistance. And they are far quicker than electric cars when we add to the actual travel time the amount of time that we spend working to afford our vehicle.

So, *time hygiene* is about finding more time for ourselves: To think; to do what we like. Leisure activities such as contemplation strolls or bike rides boost our overall health, well-being and creativity. In this sense, *time hygiene* embraces effectiveness as a way to work better – and not just more.

All the discussion about urban mobility comes back to the fact that the car-centric model has failed. It is impractical for the developing world to follow a similar model. Even if we accept the health implications of pollution and the impact on global warming, from a simple space management perspective, mobility will eventually collapse in cities prioritising the automobile. My point is that we need simple narratives to create change. The present narratives represent old interests and do not reflect the space management perspective that actually drives much of the locomotion in cities. The battle of the three-wheelers and the public versus private self-driving busses is where we should redirect our storytelling efforts.

In Biomega, our design philosophy, as explored here, drives our ability to create a new narrative for urban transportation – one that sets you, the user, in the centre of mobility design to ensure we continuously create and improve holistic solutions creating optimal value for the individual user and society.

A new philosophy of design

Biomega's philosophy is optimising technology, ethics and aesthetics: New Tech, New Ethics, New Aesthetics. Simply put, bikes and those who ride them can transform the world into a more beautiful place and blend dreams for the future whilst meeting the needs of the present. Ideally, it only takes one look and one ride to understand the difference a well-designed bike can make as a bike the rider and the design become one.

Tech

High-tech is a strange concept. "High" often seems simply to mean that there's a lot of tech; frankly, who gives a damn about how much tech there is in a certain product? It's about the quality of it, not the quantity. We operate with two tech concepts in our bike design work: Mega- and Meta-tech. Mega-tech is when the fascination with a certain technology becomes the driving force of the bike design, and innovation arises from a clash between form and function and this technology; Meta-tech is where technology becomes instrumental to the bike design and subsequently can cause paradigms to break in the application of technologies.

Ethics

The common perception of ethics is a static imperative: You should do x, y and z. Through our work with total quality management, it has become apparent to Biomega that ethical good can be viewed as a simple quality that can be improved through process control rather than trying to achieve an absolute and static state at once. Ethics can be as simple as making it better and better.

Aesthetics

Biomega's history of style and value has a Danish Heritage. However, Danish design has often become its own pastiche: Exaggerated, lifeless minimalism. This was not what the Danish Masters intended. Biomega has looked for a cheerful strain of Danish design and breathed new life into this tradition. This style was anchored in furniture, then interior Danish design. Biomega is moving this interior Danish design aesthetic to the outdoors – or if you prefer, Biomega envisages the entire urban landscape as an interior.

Question: What is your ideal mode of transportation and why?

References

Astrup, S. (2016). Det cykler for København. Politiken. https://politiken.dk/indland/kobenhavn/art5649047/Det-cykler-for-K%C3%B8benhavn

Cathcart-Keays, A. (2016). Two-wheel Takeover: Bikes Outnumber Cars for the First Time in Copenhagen. *The Guardian*. https://www.theguardian.com/cities/2016/nov/30/cycling-revolution-bikes-outnumber-cars-first-time-copenhagen-denmark

Cycling Embassy of Denmark (2015). Our Daily Bike Rides Benefit the Climate Immensely. https://stateofgreen.com/en/news/our-daily-bike-rides-benefit-the-climate-immensely/

Cycling Embassy of Denmark (2018). Facts about Cycling in Denmark. https://cycling-solutions.info/satisfied-cycle-tourists-facts-and-figures-about-cycling-tourism-in-denmark/

Murnane, K. (2017). New Research Indicates Cycling to Work Has Extraordinary Health Benefits. *Forbes*. https://www.forbes.com/sites/kevinmurnane/2017/04/25/new-research-indicates-cycling-to-work-has-extraordinary-health-benefits/?sh=2b231b9f3e62

Schiller, B. (2015). How Copenhagen Became a Cycling Paradise by Considering the Full Cost of Cars. *Fast Company*. https://www.fastcompany.com/3046345/how-copenhagen-became-a-cycling-paradise-by-considering-the-full-cost-of-cars

Walker, P. (2011). Cycle Like the Danes to Cut Carbon Emissions, Says Study. *The Guardian*. https://www.theguardian.com/environment/2011/dec/12/cycle-like-danes-cut-emissions

16

TRUST THE FUTURE – IF WE DO THE WORK TO CREATE IT

As humans, we have the power to destroy our home: Earth – or at least the power to destroy our ability to live and thrive on planet Earth. However, if we have the power to destroy, we must also have the opportunity to reclaim and utilise that power. Therefore, it is our choice to let the dire facts numb us or to reclaim that power as a positive source. I believe in the second. That if we work hard for it, we can regain control and use our powers to build a better world within the planetary boundaries.

> We are currently living it. We are all its authors and still writing.
>
> *Wallace-Wells (2020)*

American author David Wallace-Wells writes in his scarily enlightening and surprisingly beautiful book *The Uninhabitable Earth: Life After Warming* about the dire state of our planet and how we are headed towards a world not possible for our civilisation to inhabit. Our only chance is to acknowledge our part, claim our power and write the story of a prosperous future rather than the end of civilisation. In other words, through our thoughts, actions and systems, we are writing our own story because what we do affects our planet, which affects our ability to thrive on the planet we call home. So, what history will we collectively write for ourselves? And what role will you play – the hero, villain or bystander?

I hope it will be the story of human ingenuity. The story of how we turned our grand troubles into opportunities and fixed our system so that we can once again provide value for people while staying within our planetary boundaries. To achieve our goal, **we must stubbornly hope in the power of**

DOI: 10.4324/9781003261018-16

the imagination. We must believe in ourselves and that we can bring back optimism as a stellar force for the larger good, empowering us to act and design to harness global superpowers from the arts, tech, biz and nature. Reaching across professions to take the best from each so that we can truly design solutions that cater to global demand without compromising mother Earth.

So, there is still a beacon of hope and cracks of light shining through. We need to grow that hope and those cracks in the current system and let a new and prosperous future for all shine through. It will not be easy, and we need to ensure that the sustainability agenda does not become simply about doing less or, even worse, more of the same. Instead, we need to design to ensure the planetary boundaries become positive, creative constraints. We need to cultivate that because it has been the opposite for a long time, so designers, businesses and society have largely forgotten the opportunity design holds and the unique ability to work within constraints and barriers that improve the final design. For some reason, we have not used the planetary boundaries as barriers to heighten the ambition of the overall design but instead expected it to be at the expense of the overall design. Therefore, it is time to reclaim that power and reach for the stars and move from despair to repair and ultimately to a reimagined world.

While design is about creating products and systems, it is also about mindset: The power to question the existing and thus the ability to reimagine. How can we cater to our inherent desire to create and grow without the negative consequences? **It comes down to our grand challenge of redefining success in the Anthropocene.** Considering the fact that our actions have consequences in the Anthropocene, we can no longer measure success without considering those actions. Should we admire those who create unnecessary products because they make a lot of money that can be spent on symbols of excess? Or will that become a thing of the past? Instead realising that enough is enough – and billionaires don't have to be the new millionaires. In fact, the prevalence of billionaires may indicate a fundamental flaw in the design of our societal system. So, what does success look like in the Anthropocene? We don't fully know yet, but what matters is that we make it about people and the planet again: That we create value for people while staying within our planetary boundaries. Again, the Danish Design Heritage provides a valuable lesson that a design's success should be measured in its use rather than exchange value and when in doubt you can always look to the guiding star of rather or not it creates value for people while staying within the planetary boundaries, just as the manifesto for design in the Anthropocene provides tangible inspiration as well. So, the best medium to long-term bet for our global population as well as your business is to create the solutions necessary and leave those quick high-margin returns of low-quality consumer goods behind. Take part in writing our prosperous future.

First, it is a matter of opening our eyes to new opportunities and start questioning all that we take for granted in the status quo. If we don't, there is a massive risk of redoing our past failures anew. Fortunately, design can help us question the status quo and stay with the trouble while doing so. As such, design provides the ability to solve problems in unknown times. How? By combining the arts with the practicalities of the natural world through cross-pollination of expertise allowing for the necessary diversity and enabling Enlightened Action.

Let your imagination run wild

Our desires and the power to imagine are the driving force behind our ability to shape a better future, better than the one we must leave behind. While **we know the problems, we need design to help us create the solutions**. It starts with the power of imagination, beautifully described by Olga Tokarczuk, Nobel Prize-winner in literature:

> In Doctor Faustus, Thomas Mann wrote about a composer who devised a new form of absolute music capable of changing human thinking. But Mann did not describe what this music would depend on; he merely created the imaginary idea of how it might sound. Perhaps that is what the role of artist relies on – giving a foretaste of something that could exist and thus causing it to be imaginable. And being imagined in the first stage of existence.
>
> *Tokarczuk (2019)*

Yet in a world focused on speed and enchanted with technology, we continuously tend to forget and underestimate the importance of that imaginary idea of what the world we move towards might sound, smell, feel and look like. Hence, we must practice to ensure we possess the ability to let our imagination run wild; otherwise we will continue to do incremental change without really moving towards value creation. We must dare to imagine that however tricky times are now and will be in the imminent future, there is an opportunity for long-term change for the better. We need to help each other overcome short-term difficulties and come together and unite towards a regenerative future. We should help each other cultivate the power to imagine and thus ACT to shape a world that is not yet ours. Or as economist and creator of the Donut economics, Kate Raworth (2017), says: "The most powerful tool in economics is not money, nor even algebra. It is a pencil." Because with a pencil, you can redraw the world.

In other words, we desperately need design to help question the status quo and all the things we collectively take for granted as natural truths. Things are often based on choices and thus could be different. And who knows, perhaps different in such a way that we as humans were nudged or incentivised to nurture our long-term individual and collective interest rather than our short-term interests? Because it has become painfully evident that we humans have the power to destroy. Now I believe it is worth a try to do our best to reclaim that power and design our society, businesses and products in such a way that our individual short- and long-term interests, as well as our collective and individual interests, are aligned and do not contradict. Unfortunately, there are too many such instances today – largely so due to the societal systems we designed. So, we need to cultivate the other side of us; asking the question of how might we design to incentivise the part of us that longs for connectedness, that caters to our actual interests and can break free of what Danish design icon Poul Henningsen saw as our minds being entrapped by mass production as described in Chapter 2.

That does not necessarily mean rejecting capitalism entirely; rather it implies the need to reclaim growth as a tool rather than an end itself. Capitalism is not the purpose but, again, a tool to a thriving society. This perspective encourages us not only to replace the existing system but to critically question the fundamentals. Should the solution to a fossil fuel-driven SUV always be an electric SUV? No, that's moving from despair to repair and optimising within the existing structures, not truly reimagining a new and improved world. Instead, our focus should be on creating value for the user and society, not exchange value for the financial systems needed for continued consumption. Less becomes more and the emphasis shifts from quantity to quality, just like in the Danish Design Heritage.

As professor Donna Haraway describes in her book *Staying with The Trouble*:

> It matters what matters we use to think other matters with; it matters what stories we tell to tell other stories with; it matters what knots knot knots, what thoughts think thoughts, what descriptions describe descriptions, what ties tie ties. It matters what stories make worlds, what worlds make stories. or "It matters what ideas we use to think other ideas." or It matters what thoughts think thoughts. It matters what knowledges know knowledges. It matters what relations relate relations. It matters what worlds world worlds. It matters what stories tell stories.
>
> *Haraway (2016)*

Design in the antropocene

=

Despair → Repair → Reimagine

FIGURE 16.1 Design in the Anthropocene (Kathrine Hagemann Snabe, The Circular Way).

Most importantly, **it is about believing that our greatest accomplishments aren't behind us**. By harnessing our artistic potential and combining it with the incredible opportunity given by nature, creativity and technology, we have the power to shape a better future. The vision aligns with the new scientific paradigm of the Anthropocene based on the understanding that our actions have consequences. While overcoming our dependence on fossil fuel may have been seen as a barrier to development in the old scientific paradigm, in the new, it becomes a positive, creative constraint. This constraint enables us to expand the solution space and create true value for people while staying within the planetary boundaries. So as Jim Hagemann Snabe, a Dane and pioneer in global business and sustainability, in his foreword to this book writes, we are at a crossroads of light and darkness – I believe our only hope is to systematically empower our humanity and have faith in our collective ingenuity. So that we ensure our great minds get to work on solving our greatest problems – So I choose to be a stubborn optimist and hope you will join me. Because, believe me – the world needs you! As Vaclav Smil so accurately describes it, part of our troubles today is that:

> The proverbial best minds do not go into soil science and do not try their hand at making better cement; instead they are attracted to dealing with disembodied information, now just streams of electrons in myriads of microdevices. From lawyers and economists to code writers and money managers, their disproportionality high rewards are for work completely removed from the material realities of life on earth.
>
> *Smil (2022)*

Being a stubborn optimist

I believe that if we learn to "stay with the trouble," as Donna Haraway calls it, then however bad things are – that also provides an opportunity for purpose, for connectedness with both our nature and society. So much like the Danish Design Heritage and society at large was built on the synergy between serving a social purpose and an ambitious vision, making the final product and business better – I believe similarly that is the opportunity we have today. To turn the current despair into actions that repair and, most importantly, reimagine our society and engagement with our planet. Therefore, the choice to care is ours and is a big one. It is an opportunity to write our part in history and a choice of which side we are, either on the side of those who acted or not?

I mean, when you think about it, the time we live in is quite crazy. We are in the midst of the scientific revolution of what are and what are not facts regarding climate change, particularly the needed solutions. At the same time, the only constant is change, and we are still determining exactly where in our opportunity space we will go. The only thing we know is that the coming years will be wild and unforeseeable. Hence, our best bet is to be smart about it and take matters into our own hands:

"We cannot predict the future, but we can invent it," as Dennis Gabor (1963), Nobel Prize winner in physics, elegantly expressed in 1963, a quote that has since been rephrased by many. Among them, Peter Diamandis, co-founder of the Silicon Valley institution Singularity University, puts it as, "The best way to predict the future is to create it yourself" (Diamandis, 2010). Last and not least, regenerative design icon Buckminster Fuller relating to the theme of this book said: "The best way to predict the future is to design it" (Fuller, 1969).

We, that is, you and I, have been given the historic responsibility to set things right. We have the unfathomably great opportunity to be alive at the most decisive time in the history of humanity. The time has come for us to tell this story, and change the ending. Together, we can still avoid the worst consequences. We can still prevent catastrophe and start healing the wounds we have inflicted. Together, we can do the seemingly impossible. But make no mistake moving from our fossil fuel dependency will be difficult and no one else will do it for us.

Yes, things are dire, and we need to act swiftly, but I still choose to be stubbornly optimistic. It is an active choice and, in my subjective opinion, a powerful one to make. A choice that we must encourage rather than look at as naive. Because we have to keep going, science can't tell us that we can't fix things (if we hurry). History, however, tells us that change has always come when it seemed impossible because people dared to believe against the odds. Just think of Martin Luther King's "I have a dream" or Nelson Mandela's saying, "It always seems impossible until it is done" – if they could do it, who are we to believe that we can't? Change is happening as we speak, and we need to act now to mitigate it. But from despair comes opportunity both within improved innovation and technology and very much regarding demand and new regulatory requirements. And, as already touched upon in some of the interviews, there is gold to be struck for those that find and enable the solutions that make business and climate prerequisites rather than opposites as demand is especially high for business-to-business (b2b) solutions and in general need is much higher than supply for solutions that can create value for people while staying within our planetary boundaries. Don't worry; you still have an opportunity to develop good business because more than ever we need you to create the solutions we as a global society need and creating prosperity for people while staying within our planetary boundaries is the greatest business opportunity ever had.

More than anything, we have the choice to act, to make sure that this truly becomes the time for action and that this decade becomes the decade we finally turn things around and start making business and climate prerequisites rather than opposites. We can change things for the better and create new ways of operating by challenging what we blindly consider the norm. Because while things are indeed troublesome – and every day new data confirm this in new and discouraging ways. Collectively, we need to put our minds to work: Keep working towards a greener planet, mitigating climate change and enabling prosperity for all. We need to view the glass as half full rather than half empty and be an apocaloptimist, which means – quoting the Urban Dictionary – "to know that it's all going to shit, but still think it will turn out OK" (oblivion3, 2012).

An ability probably needed more now than ever, but also a concept not new to human behaviour and thinking. To F. Scott Fitzgerald, the notion behind apocaloptimism is the very essence of human intelligence, which he so brilliantly explained back in 1936 in his collection of short stories titled *The Crack-Up* (albeit he of course was not yet talking of climate change):

> The test of first-rate intelligence is the ability to hold two opposite ideas in the mind at the same time, and still retain the ability to function. One should for example be able to see that things are hopeless and yet be determined to make them otherwise.
>
> *Fitzgerald (1936)*

So, I encourage you to be conscious of your possibilities and choices. Will you care? Will you challenge the status quo? Will you act? Will you be a stubborn optimist in the midst of our troubles? The results will guide your life and determine the contribution you will make to your profession, society and legacy. The good news is that you are already well on your way. Reflecting on the possibility of doing things differently – opening your eyes, reading this – are all conscious choices.

So continue to be conscious of the choices you make. Don't decide anything just because it reflects the norm or the traditional way. Don't accept that things have to be just how they are and have always been. Realise that you have the ability and responsibility to design and create your desired future. It all comes down to the choices you make.

This might sound daunting and scary. But it does not have to be. It comes down to your ability to listen to your gut feeling. Remember that you will make the wrong choice from time to time. That is okay because it is part of being human. What matters is how you handle your mistakes. So that you learn from it, correct what you can and get back to work. **Frankly, what you should be worried about is not making enough mistakes.** And, sure, there will be lots of hard work and bumps on the road, but the feeling of having acted and made purposeful choices will drive you on your journey, feeding you with passion, energy and love for the great opportunities in front of you.

And remember Denmark and the Danish Design Heritage is by no means perfect but it does provide a real-life example of how value creation can be aligned between people, planet and business. Highlighting via decades of experience within product, business model and systems design that a social purpose can heighten the final design. Thus, it provides a road map for how to design in the Anthropocene, considering the planetary boundaries as positive creative constraints that improves the solution, but that does not mean you should simply copy paste the Danish solutions. Instead you should be inspired by the philosophy and look to solve the solve societal problems relevant to your context by viewing the planetary boundaries as positive creative constraints, focus on use rather than exchange value and take the time to care.

Hence, I hope that every morning you will take on the responsibility of looking at yourself in the mirror and make the conscious choice to find solutions that can regenerate nature, collect water, clean the oceans, clean the air, harvest clean energy, eliminate food waste and convert waste to resources. Give people a roof over their heads, access to energy and so many other things, all providing value for people while staying within our planetary boundaries or at least moving us in the right direction. Finally, I want to leave you with this: Believe in yourself. Believe in your dream. But look for the nutrients that you need to grow. Just like a city, you are a metabolism yourself. So, believe in yourself but also have an open mind. Stand for the things you believe in, even when it is hard. Do the work, ask the questions, make the choices and great things will follow.

We are all at the beginning of our journey from despair to repair and ultimately towards reimagining and creating value for people while staying within the planetary boundaries. So, my best advice is to make sure you have both eyes wide open that you stay curious and ready to question your previous beliefs and see opportunities in a new light – combining skills, materials and schools of thought with an original point of view – a blank canvas of possibility.

> To me, hope is not something that is given to you, it is something you have to earn, to create. It cannot be gained passively, through standing by and waiting for someone else to do something ... Given the right circumstances, there are no limits to what we can do. We are capable of the most incredible things – the ability to change our minds, to invent, to forgive.
>
> *Thunberg (2022)*

FIGURE 16.2 Easel: The vision (Kathrine Hagemann Snabe, The Circular Way).

Question: Hopefully this book inspired you to act; so what three things are you going to do first?

References

Diamandis, P. (2010). The Best Way to Predict the Future Is to Create It Yourself. https://www.singularityweblog.com/peter-diamandis-on-the-best-way-to-predict-the-future

Fitzgerald, F. S. (1936). *The Crack-up*. New Directions Publishing Corp.

Fuller, B. (1969). *Operating Manual for Spaceship Earth*. Lars Müller Publishers.

Gabor, D. (1963). *Inventing the Future*. Secker & Warburg.

Haraway, D. J. (2016). *Staying with the Trouble: Making Kin in the Chthulucene*. Duke University Press.

oblivion3 (2012). Apocaloptimist. https://www.urbandictionary.com/define.php?term=Apocaloptimist

Raworth, K. (2017). *Doughnut Economics: Seven Ways to Think Like a 21st-Century Economist*. Random House.

Smil, V. (2022). *How the World Really Works: A Scientist's Guide to Our Past, Present and Future*. Penguin Books Ltd.

Thunberg, G. (2022). *The Climate Book*. Penguin Books Ltd.

Tokarczuk, O. (2019). Olga Tokarczuk Nobel Lecture: The Tender Narrator. https://www.nobelprize.org/prizes/literature/2018/tokarczuk/lecture/

Wallace-Wells, D. (2020). *The Uninhabitable Earth: Life After Warming*. Tim Duggan Books.

INDEX

Note: *Italic* page numbers refer to figures.

For Product Safety Concerns and Information please contact our EU representative GPSR@taylorandfrancis.com
Taylor & Francis Verlag GmbH, Kaufingerstraße 24, 80331 München, Germany

www.ingramcontent.com/pod-product-compliance
Ingram Content Group UK Ltd.
Pitfield, Milton Keynes, MK11 3LW, UK
UKHW022021180926
475701UK00005B/956

* 9 7 8 1 0 3 2 1 9 8 2 0 0 *